Emma Rowe's ambitious and insightful book masterfully explores and charts the new conceptions of public education as embedded in, or aligned with, the logic of markets. She pulls off an amazing feat of integrating global patterns with on-the-ground evidence, highlighting both the intellectual and social roots of this world-wide movement. The result is a remarkable analysis of the winners (and losers) in a new competitive and contested landscape of "public" schooling.
—Christopher Lubienski, Professor of Education Policy, Indiana University, USA

Middle-class School Choice in Urban Spaces brilliantly conveys the extent to which public education across the globe has become a site of struggle and contestation. We gain a rich and vivid sense of the contradictions and tensions that arise for the middle classes as they strive to juggle commitments to the public with private interests. At the centre of the book is a carefully considered and nuanced ethnography of middle class educational campaigning which provides a powerful springboard for a wide ranging and convincing analysis of class work within education that has worldwide significance.
—Diane Reay, Professor of Education, University of Cambridge, UK

Rowe presents an incisive and original account of how class and race traverse the dynamic political terrain of contemporary school reform. The monograph subjects policy and social movements across the globe to a sophisticated analysis, drawing expertly on rich institutional and ethnographic sources. An extremely useful contribution to public education scholarship.
—Joel Windle, Adjunct Senior Researcher, Monash University, Australia.

This theoretically rich ethnography provides an important global perspective to studies of school choice and the marketization of education.
—Maia Cucchiara, Associate Professor of Urban Education Policy, Temple University, USA

Middle-class School Choice in Urban Spaces

Middle-class School Choice in Urban Spaces examines government-funded public schools from a range of perspectives and scholarship in order to examine the historical, political and economic conditions of public schooling within a globalized, post-welfare context. In this book, Rowe argues that post-welfare policy conditions are detrimental to government-funded public schools, as they engender consistent pressure in rearticulating the public school in alignment with the market, produce tensions in serving the more historical conceptualizations of public schooling, and are preoccupied by contemporary profit-driven concerns.

Chapters focus on public schooling from different global perspectives, with examples from Chile and the US, to examine how various social movements encapsulate ideologies around public schooling. Rowe also draws upon a rich, five-year ethnographic study of campaigns lobbying the Victorian State Government in Australia for a brand-new, local-specific public school. Critical attention is paid to the public school as a means to achieve empowerment and overcome discrimination, and both local and global lenses are used to identify how parents choose the public school, the values they attach to it, and the strategies they use to obtain it. Also considered, however, are how quality gaps, distances and differences between public schools threaten to undermine the democracy of education as a means for individuals to be socially mobile and escape poverty.

This book makes an important contribution to our understanding of global social movements and activism around public education. As such, it will be of key interest to researchers, academics and postgraduate students in the field of education, specifically those working on school choice, class and identity, as well as educational geography.

Emma E. Rowe is is a lecturer in the School of Education at Deakin University, Australia.

Routledge Research in Education Policy and Politics

For a full list of titles in this series, please visit www.routledge.com

The Routledge Research in Education Policy and Politics series aims to enhance our understanding of key challenges and facilitate on-going academic debate within the influential and growing field of Education Policy and Politics.

Books in the series include:

Modernising School Governance
Corporate planning and expert handling in state education
Andrew Wilkins

UNESCO Without Borders
Educational campaigns for international understanding
Edited by Aigul Kulnazarova and Christian Ydesen

Education and Political Subjectivities in Neoliberal Times and Places
Emergences of norms and possibilities
Edited by Eva Reimers and Lena Martinsson

Local Citizenship in the Global Arena
Educating for community participation and change
Sally Findlow

Using Shakespeare's Plays to Explore Education Policy Today
Neoliberalism through the lens of Renaissance humanism
Sophie Ward

Middle-class School Choice in Urban Spaces
The economics of public schooling and globalized education reform
Emma E. Rowe

Education and the production of space
Political pedagogy, geography, and urban revolution
Derek R. Ford

Middle-class School Choice in Urban Spaces

The Economics of Public Schooling and Globalized Education Reform

Emma E. Rowe

LONDON AND NEW YORK

First published 2017
by Routledge
2 Park Square, Milton Park, Abingdon, Oxon OX14 4RN

and by Routledge
711 Third Avenue, New York, NY 10017

Routledge is an imprint of the Taylor & Francis Group, an informa business

© 2017 Emma E. Rowe

The right of Emma E. Rowe to be identified as author of this work has been asserted by her in accordance with sections 77 and 78 of the Copyright, Designs and Patents Act 1988.

All rights reserved. No part of this book may be reprinted or reproduced or utilised in any form or by any electronic, mechanical, or other means, now known or hereafter invented, including photocopying and recording, or in any information storage or retrieval system, without permission in writing from the publishers.

Trademark notice: Product or corporate names may be trademarks or registered trademarks, and are used only for identification and explanation without intent to infringe.

British Library Cataloguing in Publication Data
A catalogue record for this book is available from the British Library

Library of Congress Cataloging in Publication Data
A catalog record for this book has been requested

ISBN: 978-1-138-12041-9 (hbk)
ISBN: 978-1-315-65173-6 (ebk)

Typeset in Galliard
by Apex CoVantage, LLC

For my family –
Elisabeth, Frances and Clementine

Contents

List of figures and tables		x
Acknowledgements		xiii
1	The derivatives and dissolution of public schooling in the global landscape	1
2	Social movements for public education	18
3	Campaigning for choice	38
4	Glocalization and evocations of whiteness in the local education market	66
5	Private versus public schools	84
6	White flight and repopulating the urban public high school	114
7	Rebranding and marketing the urban public school	136
8	After neoliberalism: Social democracy within the corporate economy	156
Appendix: Methodology and data sets		170
Index		191

Figures and tables

Figures

2.1	Protestors demand the government to improve education quality. A protest rally in Santiago, Chile.	21
3.1	A map of the parental campaign groups as denoted by the inner-ring neighbourhood in which it is located, and proximity of surrounding high schools.	39
3.2	Secondary school enrolment divided by sector and state/territory in Australia (2015): includes all states and territories in Australia. Full-time secondary school students only.	43
3.3	Economic profile of the Lawson neighbourhood and gentrification, from 2001–2006.	44
3.4	'New School for Lawson' is located in the neighbourhood of Lawson. This map shows the proximity of surrounding high schools.	46
3.5	The Smith High Campaign is located in the neighbourhood of Smith. This map shows the proximity of surrounding high schools.	47
3.6	'We want a local high school', New School for Lawson event (2012). This image is an adaptation of the original photograph.	48
3.7	'This village needs a high school', Smith High Campaign event (2012). This image is an adaptation of the original photograph.	50
3.8	'High School, Not High Rise' (Ballot Box ticked). Photograph by Elisabeth Devereux, in the neighbourhood of Smith (2012).	51
4.1	'New School for Lawson' is located in the neighbourhood of Lawson. This map shows the proximity of surrounding high schools.	75
5.1	Total percentage of enrolment by school sector in Australia (%): Independent, Catholic and Public (2015 figures).	85
5.2	Full-time students enrolled in secondary school by sector (includes all states and territories in Australia), 1996–2015.	86
5.3	Full-time students enrolled in secondary school by sector (includes all states and territories in Australia), 1980–2015.	88

5.4	A profile of surrounding public high schools within the data set, ranked from the lowest to highest ICSEA score. The higher ICSEA score equates to a more advantaged student cohort.	95
5.5	Public high schools and inverse levels of advantage and disadvantage according to their ICSEA score.	96
5.6	A profile of schools by ICSEA score of school and percentage of students who are from a language background other than English (LBOTE).	97
5.7	Financial profile of public high schools from sources a–j: includes private/parent sources, and government funding. It shows government funding from lowest to highest (2012–2013).	99
5.8	Financial profile of public high schools from sources a–j: includes parental/private sources, and government funding. It shows parental/private sources from lowest to highest (2012–2013).	101
5.9	Public high schools: total capital expenditure (2009–2013) and ICSEA score of school.	102
5.10	School financial profile: includes net recurrent income per student from lowest to highest (2009–2013) and capital expenditure (2009–2013).	103
7.1	The changing school enrolment zone for the public Thompson High, one year following its opening.	138
7.2	The 2016 enrolment zone for public Thompson High (the square around the school).	139

Tables

4.1	Country of birth and proportion of residents by school catchment area. The table is organized from lowest to highest as based on the proportion of Australian-born residents (2012 data).	71
A.1	Method, data sets and description.	172
A.2	A list of the interview participants and brief description.	176
A.3	Median Weekly Household Income for twelve school catchment areas, including Lawson and Smith. It is organized from lowest to highest as based on median weekly household income (2012 data).	180
A.4	Country of birth and percentage of residents by school catchment area: includes twelve catchment areas. The table is organized from lowest to highest as based on the proportion of Australian-born residents (2012 data).	181
A.5	Religion and levels of religious affiliation according to each catchment area. This is organized from lowest to highest,	

	as based on Christianity affiliation (2012 data). Christianity includes nineteen affiliation religions in the Census, and is not a strong marker of differentiation between rejected and popular schools. 'No Religion' affiliation is a stronger marker for popular public schools, and Islam affiliation is a stronger marker for rejected schools.	181
A.6	A profile of fifteen public high schools within the data set, which indicates levels of advantage and disadvantage. All data sourced from *My School* website (published by ACARA).	182
A.7	Financial profile of fifteen public high schools within the data set: Net recurrent income $ per student, from private sources and parent contributions (2012 and 2013). This is ranked from lowest to highest, according to the total sum of private sources and parent contributions (2012–2013).	183
A.8	Financial profile of fifteen public high schools: Net recurrent income (AUD$) per student, from Australian Government recurrent funding, and state/territory recurrent funding (2012 and 2013). This table is ranked from lowest to highest, according to the total sum of funding that the school received from both levels of government (2012–2013).	184
A.9	Grand total school funding and private sources: grand total received from both levels of government, and grand total received from student, parental and private sources (2012–2013). This table is ranked lowest to highest according to federal/state government funding (2012 and 2013).	185
A.10	Grand total funding and private sources: grand total received from both levels of government, and grand total received from student, parental and private sources (2012–2013). This table includes fifteen public high schools within the data set. This table is ranked lowest to highest according to parent contributions and private sources.	185

Acknowledgements

This study would not have happened without the input of the campaigners. I am very grateful for their generosity, time commitment and willingness to be involved. They allowed me to attend many meetings and events, armed with my notepad and pen.

Since I started writing this book in 2011, I have engaged intensively with collective actions and campaigns, both theoretically and empirically. In addition to the Australian-based data that is drawn upon in this book, I have met with numerous activists from the United States. In 2015 I met with community organization groups in Chicago, and heard from the following groups: the Kenwood Oakland Community Organization, Parents 4 Teachers, Illinois Raise Your Hand, More Than a Score, the Chicago Teachers Union, Enlace and Voices of Youth in Chicago Education. In 2016 I heard from Teaching for Change, Empower DC and Shirikiana Aina in Washington, DC. My thanks to these individuals and organizations for meeting with me and improving my understanding of the US context and educational reforms. The views that are written and expressed in this book are my own, and the mistakes are my own, and are not reflective of these individuals or organizations. I also thank the many anonymous activists I contacted by email and the hundreds of written blogs that are available online.

I am indebted to scholars who assisted me with this book. My sincere thanks to Mary Lou Rasmussen, Geoff Whitty, Laura Perry, Andrew Skourdoumbis, Maia Cucchiara, Emma Charlton, Julianne Moss and Luke Cuttance for the insightful and instructive feedback on earlier drafts of this manuscript. The feedback considerably helped me to improve this work. My sincere appreciation to Mary Lou Rasmussen for your strong mentorship, tutelage and friendship over the years, I'm not sure what I would do without you. My thanks to scholars Joel Windle, Helen Proctor, Jane Kenway, Radhika Gorur, Geoffrey Sherrington and Craig Campbell for the time you gave to support this study at different moments over the years, or answer my numerous questions. My sincere thanks to the artists and photographers who allowed me to reproduce their images in this book – Melinda Holme (graphic designer) and Elisabeth Devereux (photographer).

I am grateful to the leadership team at Deakin University for supporting this work. I am lucky to be a part of such a collegial, stimulating and supportive work environment, and to work alongside many inspiring scholars and friends. Thank you to my colleagues, friends and research teams. Prior to joining Deakin, I spent many years in the Faculty of Education at Monash University, who also generously supported the development of this research for several years.

I am sincerely appreciative to my partner who has very patiently endured the development of this book since 2011. Thank you for living with my obsessions, reading the manuscript and always providing me with insightful comments.

I am grateful to the following publications for permitting me to reproduce some of my published work for this book:

> Rowe, EE (Forthcoming). Politics, Religion and Morality: The symbolism of public schooling for the urban middle-class identity. *International Studies in Sociology of Education*.
>
> Rowe, E. (2016). Rethinking school choice for the urban middle class and the dilemmas of choice. *Professional Voice, 11*(1), 17–23.

This book reproduces small portions of data that has been previously published in the following:

> Rowe EE (2014). The discourse of public education: an urban campaign for a local public high school in Melbourne, Victoria. *Discourse: Studies in the Cultural Politics of Education* 35:1, 116–128.
>
> Rowe, EE (Forthcoming). Middle-class school choice in the urban: educational campaigning for a public school. In *Second International Handbook of Urban Education*, edited by William T. Pink and George W. Noblit. Springer Publications, Netherlands. [To be published April 2017].

Chapter 1

The derivatives and dissolution of public schooling in the global landscape

Public schools are historically understood as 'non-market' or located outside the purview of the market. This book explores contemporary tensions that are produced via the entanglement of public schooling within the economy. These tensions are played out via conflict points and consumption choices, the interplay between the social democratic collective and 'education-as-individual-value-accrual' (Gerrard, 2015: 855). I will set out an argument around *post-welfare policy conditions*, as essentially hostile to traditional public schools – those schools historically distinguishable from private schools. Post-welfare policy conditions engender consistent pressure in rearticulating the public school in alignment with the market, producing tensions in serving the more historical conceptualizations of public schooling, coupled with contemporary profit-driven concerns. Conflict points are visible in global social movements and social activism around public education. This book examines social movements, collective organization and parental networks, to how more affluent choosers are engaging with the public school, and the consumption and economics of public schooling.

In an era of globalized educational reform, the public school is experiencing radical, history-making transformations, although this is hardly new. The public school has consistently been at the centre of heated debates surrounding social welfare, economic reform and democracy. With the rapid global expansion of public schooling dissolution since the 1990s, corporate and nongovernment policy actors are increasingly and simultaneously visible and non-visible in critical policy reform. The public school tends to be utilized as a proxy for wider measures of social equity, social justice and access to learning and is at the centre of: fiscal debates surrounding supply and demand, economic efficiency, productivity and output; court-ordered interventions demanding schooling desegregation; and federal interventions into curriculum, funding and education policy. Herein, this book explores the government-funded public school – or the 'state' school, as it is understood in the United Kingdom[1] – from a range of various perspectives and scholarship, drawing on policy analysis and policy theory, to urban school choice studies, in order to examine the historical, political and economic conditions of public schooling within a globalized, post-welfare context.

Almost twenty years ago, Whitty et al. (1998) asked whether devolution and choice in education demonstrates a global phenomenon, amidst policy convergence across England and Wales, the United States, Sweden, New Zealand and Australia. Their questions continue to be salient today. Whilst there are key and distinct differences across these sites, there are also similarities in how policies shape, facilitate and influence consumerism and consumption of schooling, or in other words, parental choice. Government policy clearly plays a temporal and pivotal role in how parents interact with schooling. Policies intend to generate change, in that they offer 'an imagined future state of affairs' (Rizvi and Lingard, 2010: 5). The structuring of funding, and how this is delivered to schools; the role of teachers and how teachers are supported to teach; and the active dissolution of public schooling, clearly incentivize particular consumption choices.

For those parents who have the ability to choose – often referred to in the literature as 'middle-class' – school choice represents a critically significant and weighty decision, not only for economic reasons, but for social, political and cultural reasons, informing matters around identity, religion and family. The middle class tends to be defined via their income levels, educational qualifications and employment, and in the schooling market they are regarded as highly invested, savvy and long-term choosers. In countries such as England, Australia and the US, research posits that a key commonality of the middle classes is their relationship to education, which 'has become a central mechanism of white middle-class identity formation' (Reay et al., 2013: 19). The urban middle class is increasingly defined by their 'connection to schooling . . . and the distinctive ways in which middle-class parents manage children and their schooling' (Campbell et al., 2009: 18). Herein, I utilize the middle class and their relationship to education as a central analytical lens to study school choice in urban space.

My own schooling experience was a combination of private and public schooling, quite disconnected and disparate, between my primary years and my secondary years, spatially distant but also culturally distant. They were two distinct, entirely separate, schooling experiences. I grew up in a conservative Christian family and my primary school was miles away – two bus trips each morning, over an hour each way. Regent Christian Academy sat next door to the Regent Christian Church, and the two spaces were interchangeable. On our daily trips we were herded over by the teacher, clutching our Bibles in our hands, dressed in our little suits, emblazoned with Latin mottos. Regent Christian Academy was concerned with our spiritual, our religious tutelage, and our Christian upbringing; I remember a heavy focus on creationism, prayer and daily singing. In many ways it was a happy and joyful time.

At the end of year seven, my mother and father separated, under acrimonious circumstances, and we moved from the beach-side to a neighbourhood called 'Illawong',[2] from a brick home to a fibro-asbestos home that we were 'borrowing'. My new space was far inferior to the old space, and this was inferred to me in a number of ways, mostly from clues that are dispensed along the way: I heard Illawong was dangerous and Illawong High School a breeding ground for drug dealers and would-be criminals. As place, Illawong was constructed as 'notorious' through a discourse of whiteness and racism. I learnt very early on that it contained Indigenous people and poverty. The two were interconnected and undesirable according to the discourse I was privy to. I became implicated with this undesirable social landscape and social identity and this was quite a memorable engagement with social exclusion. My childhood friends were disallowed from visiting, their parents citing the danger of Illawong, and the danger of socializing with 'broken' families.

Illawong High was like a completely different world, so completely separated from Regent Christian Academy. Some of the teachers walked out of the lessons, during classes; a group of white kids took it upon themselves to spit on me, every day if they could; an Indigenous girl befriended me, but I thought we were too different. A girl who looked like a boy came to the school, and everyone whispered and pointed.

As a school, Illawong High reminded me of a prison – violent, pointless and dilapidated. There was a strong sense of survival contained within those high barbed-wire fences and trying to escape was futile. Violent fist and knife fights broke out regularly. The facilities were non-existent, the grounds and classrooms seriously neglected. If it was back to basics, then the basics were missing – no heaters or cooling, cold in winter, stinking hot in summer; the chairs fell apart when you sat on them, so you would be forced to sit on the floor during the lesson, the other kids spitting paper spit-balls at your head. I remember the science classes with two or three Bunsen burners; our recreational equipment was the one solitary (and broken) basketball ring on gravel.

The neglected state of the school, the impression of 'locking them up and throwing away the key' constructed a sense of futility and meaninglessness. For the people that filled that space, we were 'the underclass, the excluded, the marginal' (Rose, 1996: 345). A lack of individualistic hard work or ability (meritocracy) is routinely attributed to the gross failures within schools 'like these' – those that are filled with poverty. However, in my view, occupation in spaces of poverty and marginalization constructs an internalized sense of failure and meaningless. Poverty and social stigma undermines a sense of agency.

Academically speaking, I was a high achiever, and incredibly introverted and shy. I hated being bullied and started to evade school as much as possible. I dropped out of high school at the age of fifteen. It wasn't about my results. For over a year, I worked as an 'office junior' in the basement of an insurance company. I detested the time working there: the six-dollars-an-hour pay cheque, fetching cupcakes for my boss, filing useless pieces of paper – the never-ending filing, the cold calls. Eventually I returned to school and completed my university entrance examinations (college entrance) over the course of two years. Admittedly, there is a personal sense of frustration when it comes to my own education. I often feel it was a grandly deficient education. As an adult, I am a highly strategic and invested school chooser – overly anxious for my children, both to be schooled in the local and public primary school.

I disclose this personal narrative to point to the cultural distances reproduced via schools, the spatial contrasts and boundaries, alongside personalized experiences of class and displacement. In taking up this research around public schooling within the globalized context, I acknowledge that my own positioning is idiosyncratic and at times, contradictory; but so too, it is pragmatic and measured. In this chapter, I introduce the central scope of the book by tracing the historical narrative of privatization and globalized school choice policies to the more contemporary landscape of public school 'derivatives'.

Free to choose

School choice, 'like neoliberal policy itself, is a remarkably consistent phenomenon across nations' (Doherty et al., 2013: 127). The central scope of school choice is typically characterized by the privatization of government-owned schools and the devolution of centralized ownership, which encourages parents to take up 'choice' – or in other words, to be rational and effective consumers. Across many national contexts, including England and Wales, the US, Australia, Chile, Sweden and New Zealand, school choice became a forefront and important policy issue for governments in the early 1980s, resulting in widespread educational reforms in the 1990s (Whitty et al., 1998). The seeds were planted far earlier though, and the political and economic changes that were brought about as a consequence of World War Two lay the contextual groundwork for the major reformation of education in years to come (Furlong and Phillips, 2002). As the workforce dramatically transformed, alongside 'the shifting of economic policies from the Keynesian welfare model to the neoliberal post-welfare state' (Hursh, 2005: 3), the role of education changed too, as the system experienced a significant growth of students completing secondary schooling.[3]

It was not only the growth of secondary students that was shifting, but also changing ideologies around consumerism, religion and democracy. In the 1960s in Australia, school choice was introduced within parliament as a parental, civil right (Marginson, 1997). From the US, leading economist Milton Friedman, from the University of Chicago, argued for greater parental choice and school vouchers, to transform the failing public school (Friedman, 1955, 1962). Friedman advocated for choice as a democratic right and fundamental libertarian freedom, and his work captures this transforming ideological landscape, putting forth the importance of the consumer in educational governance, as opposed to schooling institutions left to government control and ownership. This signals the historical beginnings of quasi-markets, but also a rethinking of democracy and freedom along consumerist lines (see Apple, 2006). Friedman's suggestions, however, received very little attention during this time of radical social change in the US, a time in which public schools transformed under racial desegregation, via the landmark 1954 *Brown v. Board of Education* case (Wells, 2008).

It was later in the 1980s that 'free to choose' became a popular mantra across both sides of the political fence – a mantra popularized by best-selling book and ten-part televised mini-series with Milton and Rose Friedman (1980), featuring movie stars (Arnold Schwarzenegger) and politicians (Ronald Reagan).[4] The Friedmans dedicate an entire chapter of the book to ask 'what's wrong with our schools?', again advocating for the devolution of public schooling and school vouchers.[5] Even though Milton Friedman's suggestions made little impact in the US until many years later, these propositions were resonant in the Thatcher government in England and Wales[6] with several pieces of legislation designed to promote competition between state secondary schools (e.g., the 1980 Education Act, 1986 Education Act, the 1988 Education Reform Act and 1992 Education (Schools) Act) (see, Whitty and Edwards, 1998; Hursh, 2005; Whitty, 2008). Government and media rhetoric echoed Friedman's declared crises within public schools, and schools were compelled to publish the results of standardized tests and be subjected to regular inspections by 'private inspection teams' (Whitty et al., 1998: 44). In a complex and almost contrary outcome of autonomy and devolution, schools came under far more intense scrutiny by the state.

Whilst policies like these were evident in the 1980s in Chile, England and Wales, it was during the 1990s that significant education reform occurred in many countries, including Canada, New Zealand, Sweden, the US and Australia. Evidently, educational policy reform is consistently replicated in a variety of locations. The 1990s saw the rise of charter schools and numerous versions of the charter school, voucher systems or 'virtual voucher systems' and the introduction of league tables. This is effectively the development of 'quasi-markets' within education: a competitive and devolved education system premised on market theory, operating independently and autonomously from bureaucratic control, more efficient and productive and therefore less costly to the government, but also less costly to the consumer, and more innovative and simply, better. This would theoretically be achieved through the establishment of a clean market with minimum regulations. Decentralization should ideally offer a more satisfied experience for parents and students. Whilst certain regulations were removed that inhibited choice and competition, regulations and standardization grew in other areas. The introduction of league tables and high-stakes testing, which increasingly became correlated with enrolment levels and therefore school funding levels (particularly in Australia), and also the implementation of compulsory national school curriculums, or school inspection teams, complicates the notion of school autonomy (Whitty et al., 1998). As autonomy and deregulation allegedly increased, so did the level of surveillance, high-stakes testing and the threat of school closure, particularly for the public sector.

In the US, school vouchers were first introduced in Milwaukee in 1990, as part of the 'parental choice program' (Witte, 1998). The voucher would enable lower-income parents to choose a private school, with several 'equalizing' factors built into the voucher system – students who were more disadvantaged would receive a higher-value voucher; schools had to accept the voucher as full payment of tuition fees (Moe, 2001). Vouchers were contentious as they were seen to be moving public money to private schools, with evidence suggesting that school vouchers did little to support the poorest members of society (Paquette, 2005). In 2001, the *No Child Left Behind Act* was introduced, legislation that was similar to England's *Education Reform Act* of 1988, pushing forward many of the policy shifts evident in the 1990s by promoting public-private partnerships, charter schools and the publication of league tables. There would be 'consequences for failure' (U.S. Department of Education Office of the Secretary, 2001).

At the same time, Australia adopted policies that were increasingly competitively based and meritocratic. Since the advent of mass-compulsory schools in Australia in the late 1800s, the states have been primarily responsible for the administration and governance of schools, with the federal government only involved in allocating 'top-up' subsidies to private schools.[7] State-federal relations became increasingly convoluted and complex, following a number of conservative reforms by the federal government in the 1990s. Federal policies enlarged their scope and involvement in schooling, in a number of ways (Lamb, 2007). One such example is the controversial removal of the *New Schools Policy* in 1996, abolished by the federal government to encourage direct competition between private and public schools, and later in 2001, the extension and broadening of recurrent funding for private schools, referred to as the socio-economic status (SES) funding model. During this time, the number of private schools proliferated and scholars argued that the flawed SES model lacked transparency, coherency and fairness (Vickers, 2005). Even though these measures were introduced by a conservative government, similar policies continued to be replicated throughout successive governments. In 2010, Australia introduced their own version of competitive league tables with the publication of the *My School* website, value-added league tables that rank schools according to their standardized test scores (see, Rowe and Windle, 2012).

The backdrop of these educational reforms within the global market was a relatively loud and vocal campaign regarding the 'crisis of public education' (Chubb and Moe, 1990). Allegedly, reforms are necessary on the basis of a (very serious and dramatic) crisis in the public sector and so-called 'white flight' from the public sector, constructed as failing via a racialized lens. For the critics, the public school is grossly underperforming and economically inefficient, with a large proportion of public school students who cannot reach basic minimum standards in reading or mathematics.

So too, the curriculum of the public school routinely comes under attack. It is pro-gay, pro-feminist and unapologetic about its leftist 'propaganda'. In Australia there have been long-term and contentious debates over whether Indigenous 'perspectives' should be included within the history curriculum, and whether students should learn about the Stolen Generation – Indigenous children forcibly stolen from their families and homes – or whether the curriculum should focus on the 'discovery' of Australia by British settlers (Windle, 2015: 37). In the US, the surge of home-schooling is attributed to the 'Godless-ness' of the public school (Apple, 2006). Whether it be debates over the inclusion of religious instruction, curriculum or funding, the public school is anything but neutral – it evokes battles, debates and class wars across religious, cultural and political lines. The crisis regarding public schooling may be authentic, but it may also be 'manufactured' (Berliner and Biddle, 1995). After all, 'only a crisis – actual or perceived – can produce real change' (Friedman, 1962: xiv). I now turn to briefly capture the central benefits and risks of choice as put forth by the literature.

The benefits and risks of choice

There are several key arguments surrounding the benefits of choice. The first, and arguably the most influential, is that choice policies – greater competition and marketization in schooling – decreases governmental spending and improves economic productivity and efficiency (supported by Hoxby, 2003a, 2003b). The second claim is that choice produces greater competition, and therefore results in higher academic outcomes, innovation and less disruptive student behaviour (supported by Wöessmann et al., 2007). Choice advocates have long since argued that devolution will improve educational equity for the most disadvantaged (Friedman and Friedman, 1980; Chubb and Moe, 1990). Devolution of public schooling poses the question: if schools are exposed to market forces, including competition and consumerist principles, will they better serve the citizen-consumer?

The Organisation for Economic Co-Operation and Development (OECD) identifies that 'a number of potentially negative, even vicious, equity problems' are associated with a system that is demand-driven (2006: 139). The primary risk of school choice is the notion of equity, or the relationship between socioeconomic status (SES) and educational achievement. Equity in education is constituted by full participation, inclusion and access to quality education regardless of gender, race, social, economic or cultural background (OECD, 2012a). In recent years global policy statements have argued that an equitable education system equates to a higher-performing education system (OECD, 2012b), and choice programs need to be regulated in order to negate equity risks (Field et al., 2007; OECD, 2012a). Although, I recognize there is an inherent tension in drawing on OECD scholarship to explicate the importance of educational equity. The publication of the Programme of International Student Assessment (PISA) plays a highly influential role in fuelling globalized standardized testing culture and choice reforms.

In returning to the intellectual origins of choice, there are concerns in Friedman's (1962, 1980) influential arguments. If we compare schooling services and provision to consumer products (for example, the manufacturing and selling of cars, which Friedman does in *Free to Choose*), we need to step back and reassess the purpose of schooling. For advocates of choice, it is the achievement of minimum standards in mathematics and literacy, but are there social and cultural outcomes of schooling? Indeed, this was the founding vision of US crusader Horace Mann, in his vision of common schooling. Are schools critical instruments and structures for enhancing social equity, civil participation and harmony?

Further, Friedman is reconciled with the acceptance of 'lesser' schools or gaps in school quality. Indeed, in a market vision, there are success stories and failures – the superior and the inferior. The acceptance of lesser schools is not questioned in Friedman's analysis, and rather the onus is placed onto the individual to avoid the lesser school. However, this is an assumption that can be scrutinized. Research indicates that between-school variance differs from country to country, and certain countries are more effective in minimizing the gaps and differences between schools (OECD, 2004). Depending on which country you live in, the school you attend will have significant effects on the outcomes which you achieve, regardless of your individual socio-economic status. Finland, for example, maintains minimal differences in individual academic outcomes that are related to between-school variance. In a country such as Australia,

> the socio-economic profile of the *school* matters substantially in terms of academic achievement . . . Our descriptive analyses show that increases in school SES are consistently associated with increases in students' academic performance, and that this relationship holds regardless of individual students' SES.
> (Perry and McConney, 2010: 72, my emphasis).

It is clear that school choice policies exacerbate segregation along various economic, cultural and social lines within and between school sectors. The relationship between school choice policies and segregation is well established across OECD countries (e.g., Weiher and Tedin, 2002; Lubienski, 2005; Paquette, 2005; Hsieh and Urquiola, 2006; Gulosino and Dentremont, 2011; Elacqua, 2012; OECD, 2012a; Roda and Wells, 2013). In Australia, the majority of students representing the highest bracket of social advantage, on the basis of parental income, level of home resources and geographical location, are clustered within the Independent (private) school sector. I explore this in further detail in Chapter Five. School choice produces racial segregation, in that parents from various cultural and ethnic backgrounds will choose schools that reflect their own racial background (Ho, 2011; Roda and Wells, 2013). What are we missing by segregating ourselves? Are particular schools driving failure, whereas others are leveraging academic success?

The marketization of schools and the market agenda is by no means hidden, and critiques have been well established within educational research for many years now (Kenway, 1990; Seddon and Angus, 2000; Whitty and Power, 2000; Lubienski, 2001; Reid, 2002; Ball, 2007; Ball and Youdell, 2008). The privatization of the public and post-welfare policy conditions influence and position the individual to consume in distinct ways when it comes to schooling. Nevertheless, this argument requires a caveat. Arguing for post-welfare policy conditions is problematic, considering that certain OECD countries are moving further into comprehensive welfare systems and furthermore that government subsidies for education continue to grow and strengthen, rather than decline. Thus, the construct of post-welfare policy conditions is essentially messy, given the heterogeneous varieties of government-funded 'public' schools. Contemporary privatization has eroded the 'traditional dividing line between public and private' (Ball, 2007: 24). Indeed, as Picower (2013) argues:

> It is no longer considered radical to say that market forces are transforming public education as we know it. A few years ago in the United States, only in the circles of academia and the far left was the demise of the 'public' in the public school system at the hands of politicians, the elite, and Wall Street investors being criticized. Now such commentary has become relatively mainstream.
>
> (44)

The decline of traditional dividing lines is strikingly played out in the advent of numerous derivatives of the traditional public or common school.

Public school derivatives

In Chile, private voucher schools were first introduced under the Pinochet government in 1980 (McEwan, 2001; Elacqua, 2012). In the US, charter schools were initiated in the early 1990s, a sector that has since tripled in size (the following chapter explores charter schools and how these schools articulate with the market, in greater depth). Independent public schools were first evident in Australia in the 1990s, legislated in the state of Victoria, and many years later, legislated through federal government, aiming to make one-fourth of all public schools autonomous (Australian Government Department of Education, 2014). Many other 'charter-like' schools are evident within the global landscape, such as self-managing schools and partnership schools in New Zealand, mini-schools in Canada, free schools in England, and the *friskolor* in Sweden (Arreman and Holm, 2011). The common feature of each of these schools is its location *outside* of the traditional public school, staunchly autonomous and privately managed, even though it is taxpayer-funded.

The charter school in the US has possibly been the most successful, in terms of its growth, consumer demand and strong funding support from successive governments.[8] The US has a relatively small private system, considering the proportion of students who attend private elementary and secondary schools (10%), with a percentage below the OECD average (15%). However, this figure is further obfuscated by public school derivatives. For the 90% of students who attend public schools, this figure includes 7% who attend 'public' charter schools, a percentage that annually increases. A charter school is publically funded but privately managed, and gains accreditation by specifically stating their educational purpose within a charter (Wells et al., 1999). Charter schools are contentious for a number of reasons; the majority of charter schools are not unionized (88%) and are not required to hire registered teachers. They receive similar levels of funding in comparison to public schools, although they maintain questionable levels of accessibility and participation (Lubienski, 2001).[9] Ravitch (2011), who was a long-time supporter of charter schools and school choice but later changed her stance on the basis of evidence, is troubled by the accessibility and inclusivity of certain charter schools. From her analysis, the well-funded and highly regarded 'Knowledge Is Power Program' (KIPP) public charter schools record a very high turnover of staff and, over a four-year period, low retention of students (60%). This is possibly due to the stringent demands placed on students and staff. The students must complete the 'Commitment to Excellence Form' before enrolling:

Student's Commitment
I fully commit to KIPP in the following ways:

- I will arrive at KIPP every day by 7:25 am (Monday – Friday) or board a KIPP bus at the correct time.
- I will remain at KIPP until 5:00 pm (Monday – Thursday) and 4:00 pm on Friday.
- I will come to KIPP on appropriate Saturdays at 9:15 am and remain until 1:05 pm.
- I will attend KIPP during summer school.
- Failure to adhere to these commitments can cause me to lose various KIPP privileges and can lead to returning to my home school.[10]

However, it is not easy to enrol in the KIPP schools and enrolment is granted to hopeful students and parents via a lottery. Hence, these schools only take in highly motivated students, many who leave less than four years later (Miron et al., 2011). Their high academic results reflect only the students who are retained.

In other countries, school systems that resemble the charter school model are also emerging (or have long since emerged). Self-managing schools were a feature of New Zealand and Australian education reform in the early 1990s (Lubienski et al., 2013), and I return to discuss self-managing schools in Chapter Three, with a particular focus on the state of Victoria. New Zealand introduced partnership schools in 2015, which bear many similarities with the US charter school, such as their ability to adopt specialisms, hire non-registered teachers, or negotiate their own teacher salaries, curriculum and school days (The Government of New Zealand Ministry of Education, 2015). They are not allowed to charge additional enrolment fees. At the time of writing, partnership schools are a very small proportion of New Zealand schools.

Similarities can be drawn with the mini-school in Vancouver, Canada. Even though mini-schools are officially part of the public school system, they retain selective entry procedures and are distinguished through a unique curriculum and a more intensive academic focus (Yoon, 2011). Mini-schools are considered to be the 'upgraded alternative to the standard, comprehensive secondary school . . . yet, what has become an important characterization of these schools has been its emphasis on and adaptations of the term "community"' (Yoon, 2011: 255).

For-profit and non-profit charter schools are currently on the policy agenda in Australia, advocated by the Centre for Independent Studies (a think tank funded by private corporations to promote 'free enterprise' and 'limited government'). The Centre argues that for-profit and non-profit charter schools can boost productivity and academic results for disadvantaged students (Jha and Buckingham, 2015). Their reports generate significant media attention, notably within a mass media monopolized by the Murdoch empire (News Ltd owns 70% of the major newspapers in Australia).

The structure of the book

In the face of widespread transformations, how is the public responding to globalized education reforms? Profitable corporate organizations clearly have a growing and decisive role within the education market (Hursh, 2015), which I explore further in Chapter Two, but are there any connections to be made with social unrest, social movements and collective agitations? I will take up these questions in the next chapter by examining social movements for public education, focusing on the Chilean Student Movement and the Occupy Movement in the US. This enables me to focus on public schooling from different global perspectives, such as Chile and the US, and examine how various social movements encapsulate ideologies around public schooling. This chapter relates the political, economic and social context around these movements, in addition to enrolment differentiations between sectors and charter school takeovers. I discuss relevant theories that surround social movements for public education, including distinctions between movements and collective actions, interventions into social class and social justice.

Chapter Three introduces the five-year ethnographic study of parental networks, campaigns and activism that forms the basis of this study. The parents in this study are pressuring the government for a brand-new public high school within their immediate neighbourhood, many drawing on sophisticated and savvy strategies to elicit the attention of policy-makers, politicians and bureaucrats. For eighteen months I participated in one of these parental groups as a participant observer, recording field notes at their meetings and events, and interviewing the parents. This chapter introduces the parent groups, each located within ten kilometres of the central business district and sharing common characteristics.

At times, school choice can operate in the sense of a 'wave', metaphorically speaking, such as the so-called 'white flight' wave in the 1960s and 1970s in the US, an increased shift from public schooling to private schooling in the 1980s onwards, and a potential 'turn-back' to public schooling by certain fractions of the middle class (Crozier et al., 2011). The chapters are loosely structured around these motifs. Chapter Four utilizes the theory of 'glocalization' (Robertson, 1995; Beck, 2002) to examine the role of the neighbourhood public school in territorializing whiteness and reconfiguring class within the urban schooling market. The local education market is equally micro and provincial within the global landscape, but so too it is generative for speaking to multiculturalism, cosmopolitanism and broader concepts of globalization. This is a pivotal starting point for contextualizing the consumption choices and institutionalized strategies of the participants.

Chapter Five is titled 'Private versus public schooling', and focuses specifically on the Australian secondary schooling sector. This chapter utilizes descriptive statistics and is more quantitative in method. I explore enrolment differences between schooling sectors, differences in funding levels and tuition costs, and significant educational policies that have driven and shaped consumer behaviour around schooling in Australia. This chapter generates statistical profiles for each public high school within the data set, drawing on comprehensive data to assess the socio-economic status of the students within each school, and funding levels, as divided between the many different sources of funding. I will demonstrate how school profiles indicate substantial gaps and segregation within the public sector, as based on financial profiles for each school, and the composition of the student cohort.

Chapters Six and Seven propose a cultural turn, although this is cautiously suggested, and draws on literature from the US and UK to explore 'white flight' and the repopulation of the urban public school by the relatively affluent consumer. I explore the potential tensions of these choices, and also the affirmatives, for achieving high-performing schools and educational equity. I consider how the public school is rebranding itself for the more desirable consumer, drawing on a range of marketing strategies to reinvent itself for the discerning buyer. A central motif in each of these chapters is the import of 'community' schooling, choice strategies and the choice work of the hyper-competitive and mobile 'citizen-consumer'.

The final chapter explores the role of social democracy within the post-neoliberal corporate economy, and the limitations of public schooling in contemporary times. I endeavour to encapsulate the driving arguments and themes within this book, focusing on the economics of school choice, market fundamentalism and the work of policy in directing consumerism around schooling. Hursh (2015) contends that the contemporary scholar needs to engage with economics in order to understand educational policy orientations and movements, a contention that underscores the driving thrust of this book. The public school is frequently positioned as central in economic, political and cultural shifts and thus, warrants further attention and analysis.

Notes

1 In the United Kingdom a public school refers to a group of fee-paying and elite private schools, and the sector that is free and government-owned is understood as the 'state' sector. However, for consistency, I utilize the term 'public' school in this book to refer to a state or government-funded school, as opposed to the 'private' school.
2 Pseudonym.

3 For example, in Australia only 22% of students completed year twelve in 1968, compared to 78% in 2010. From the 1970s onwards, participation rates grew amongst minority groups in Australia, such as Aboriginal and Torres Strait Islanders, and whilst female students were heavily under-represented in secondary education before the war, completion rates subsequently increased (Burke and Spaull, 2001; Campbell and Proctor, 2014).
4 The original series is available online, see: http://www.freetochoose.tv/ftc80.php
5 See Milton Friedman on busting the school monopoly, from: http://www.edchoice.org/who-we-are/our-founders/the-friedmans-on-school-choice/article/milton-friedman-on-busting-the-school-monopoly/ (Friedman, 1983)
6 Whilst the Thatcher government represented the United Kingdom, I refer to England and Wales here, in order to be specific.
7 This changed in the aftermath of World War Two, a time in which the Catholic sector was struggling, and the Australian federal government provided financial subsidies for private schools, in the form of new science blocks. These funds were not intended to be ongoing, but the subsidies gained the right-of-centre Liberal Party considerable support from voters (see Marginson, 1997). As a consequence, ongoing financial assistance was established for private schools by the 1970s and I discuss this further in Chapter Five.
8 However, Sweden's education reforms and the *friskolor* schools are arguably more successful in terms of their academic outcomes, in comparison to US charter schools (Lindbom, 2010).
9 These figures were informed by the following sources: (OECD, 2011; National Center for Education Statistics, 2014; National Alliance for Public Charter Schools, 2015; National Charter School Center, 2015).
10 See: http://www.kipp.org/files/dmfile/KIPP_Commitment_to_Excellence_Sample.pdf

References

Apple MW. (2006) *Educating the "Right" Way: Markets, Standards, God, and Inequality*, New York and London: Taylor & Francis Group.

Arreman IE and Holm AS. (2011) Privatisation of public education? The emergence of independent upper secondary schools in Sweden. *Journal of Education Policy* 26: 225–243.

Australian Government Department of Education. (2014) *Independent Public Schools*. Available at: https://education.gov.au/independent-public-schools.

Ball SJ. (2007) *Education PLC: Understanding Private Sector Participation in Public Sector Education*, London: Routledge.

Ball SJ and Youdell D. (2008) *Hidden Privatisation in Public Education*, Brussels: Education International.

Beck U. (2002) The cosmopolitan society and its enemies. *Theory, Culture & Society* 19: 17–44.

Berliner DC and Biddle BJ. (1995) *The Manufactured Crisis: Myths, Fraud, and the Attack on America's Public Schools*, Reading, MA: Addison-Wesley.

Burke G and Spaull A. (2001) Australian Schools: Participation and Funding 1901 to 2000. *1301.0 – Year Book Australia, 2001*, Canberra: Australian Bureau of Statistics.

Campbell C and Proctor H. (2014) *A History of Australian Schooling*, Crows Nest, NSW: Allen & Unwin.

Campbell C, Proctor H and Sherington G. (2009) *School Choice: How Parents Negotiate the School Market in Australia*, New South Wales: Allen & Unwin.

Chubb JE and Moe TM. (1990) *Politics, Markets, and America's Schools*, Washington, DC: Brookings Institution.

Crozier G, Reay D and James D. (2011) Making it work for their children: White middle-class parents and working-class schools. *International Studies in Sociology of Education* 21: 199–216.

Doherty C, Rissman B and Browning B. (2013) Educational markets in space: Gamekeeping professionals across Australian communities. *Journal of Education Policy* 28: 121–152.

Elacqua G. (2012) The impact of school choice and public policy on segregation: Evidence from Chile. *International Journal of Educational Development* 32: 444–453.

Field S, Kuczera M and Pont B. (2007) *No More Failures: Ten Steps to Equity in Education*, Paris, France: OECD.

Friedman M. (1955) The role of government in education. In: Solo RA (ed) *Economics and the Public Interest*, New Brunswick, NJNJ: Rutgers University Press, 120–150.

Friedman M. (1962) *Capitalism and Freedom*, Chicago: University of Chicago Press.

Friedman M. (1983) *Milton Friedman on Busting the School Monopoly*. Available at: http://www.edchoice.org/who-we-are/our-founders/the-friedmans-on-school-choice/article/milton-friedman-on-busting-the-school-monopoly/.

Friedman M and Friedman RD. (1980) *Free to Choose: A Personal Statement*, New York: Harcourt.

Furlong J and Phillips R. (2002) *Education, Reform and the State: Twenty Five Years of Politics, Policy and Practice*, New York & London: Routledge.

Gerrard J. (2015) Public education in neoliberal times: Memory and desire. *Journal of Education Policy* 30: 855–868.

The Government of New Zealand Ministry of Education. (2015) *Key Features of Partnership Schools*, Wellington: Kura Hourua.

Gulosino C and Dentremont C. (2011) Circles of influence: An analysis of charter school location and racial patterns at varying geographic scales. *Education Policy Analysis Archives* 19: 1–29.

Ho C. (2011) Respecting the presence of others: School micropublics and everyday multiculturalism. *Journal of Intercultural Studies* 32: 603–619.

Hoxby C. (2003a) The Economics of School Choice. *National Bureau of Economic Research*. Chicago, USA.

Hoxby C. (2003b) School choice and school productivity: Could school choice be a tide that lifts all boats? In: Hoxby C (ed) *The Economics of School Choice (National Bureau of Economic Research Conference Report)*, Chicago & London: University of Chicago Press, 287–342.

Hsieh C-T and Urquiola M. (2006) The effects of generalized school choice on achievement and stratification: Evidence from Chile's voucher program. *Journal of Public Economics* 90: 1477–1503.

Hursh DW. (2005) Neo-liberalism, markets and accountability: Transforming education and undermining democracy in the United States and England. *Policy Futures in Education* 3: 3–15.

Hursh DW. (2015) *The End of Public Schools: The Corporate Reform Agenda to Privatize Education*, New York & London: Routledge.

Jha T and Buckingham J. (2015) Free to choose charter schools: How charter and for-profit schools can boost public education. *Research Report 6*. The Centre for Independent Studies.

Kenway J. (1990) Education and the Right's discursive politics. In: Ball S (ed) *Foucault and Education*, London: Routledge, 167–206.

Lamb S. (2007) School reform and inequality in urban Australia: A case of residualizing the poor. In: Daru-Bellat S, Lamb S and Teese R (eds) *International Studies in Educational Inequality, Theory and Policy*, Dordrecht, Netherlands: Springer, 672–709.

Lindbom A. (2010) School choice in Sweden: Effects on student performance, school costs, and segregation. *Scandinavian Journal of Educational Research* 54: 615–630.

Lubienski C. (2001) Redefining "public" education: Charter schools, common schools, and the rhetoric of reform. *Teachers College Record* 103: 634–666.

Lubienski C. (2005) Public schools in marketized environments: Shifting incentives and unintended consequences of competition-based educational reforms. *American Journal of Education* 111: 464–486.

Lubienski C, Lee J and Gordon L. (2013) Self-managing schools and access for disadvantaged students: Organizational behaviour and school admissions. *New Zealand Journal of Educational Studies* 48: 82–98.

Marginson S. (1997) *Educating Australia: Government, Economy and Citizen since 1960*, Melbourne, Cambridge and New York: Cambridge University Press.

McEwan PJ. (2001) The effectiveness of public, catholic, and non-religious private schools in Chile's voucher system. *Education Economics* 9: 103–128.

Miron G, Urschel JL and Saxton N. (2011) *What Makes KIPP Work? A Study of Student Characteristics, Attrition, and School Finance*. Available at: http://www.edweek.org/media/kippstudy.pdf.

Moe TM. (2001) *Schools, Vouchers, and the American Public*, Washington, DC: Brookings Institution Press.

National Alliance for Public Charter Schools. (2015) *Get the Facts: Public Charter Schools*. Available at: http://www.publiccharters.org/get-the-facts/public-charter-schools/faqs/.

National Center for Education Statistics. (2014) *Private School Enrollment*. Available at: http://nces.ed.gov/programs/coe/indicator_cgc.asp.

National Charter School Center. (2015) *National Charter School Resource Center*. Available at: http://www.charterschoolcenter.org/what-is-a-charter-school.

OECD. (2004) *Learning for Tomorrow's World: First Results from PISA 2003*, Paris: OECD Publishing.

OECD. (2006) *Demand-Sensitive Schooling? Evidence and Issues*, Paris: OECD Publishing.

OECD. (2011) *Private Schools: Who Benefits?* Available at: http://www.oecd.org/pisa/pisaproducts/pisainfocus/48482894.pdf.

OECD. (2012a) *Equity and Quality in Education: Supporting Disadvantaged Students and Schools*, Paris: OECD Publishing.

OECD. (2012b) *Equity and Quality in Education: Supporting Disadvantaged Students and Schools: Executive Summary*, Paris: OECD Publishing.

Paquette J. (2005) Public funding for "private" education: The equity challenge of enhanced choice. *American Journal of Education* 111: 568–595.

Perry LB and McConney A. (2010) School socio-economic composition and student outcomes in Australia: Implications for education policy. *Australian Journal of Education* 54: 72–85.

Picower B. (2013) Education should be free! Occupy the DOE!: Teacher activists involved in the Occupy Wall Street movement. *Critical Studies in Education* 54: 44–56.

Ravitch D. (2011) *The Death and Life of the Great American School System: How Testing and Choice Are Undermining Education*, New York: Basic Books.

Reay D, Crozier G and James D. (2013) *White Middle-Class Identities and Urban Schooling*, London: Palgrave Macmillan.

Reid A. (2002) Public education and democracy: A changing relationship in a globalizing world. *Journal of Education Policy* 17: 571.

Rizvi F and Lingard B. (2010) *Globalizing Education Policy*, London and New York: Routledge.

Robertson R. (1995) Glocalization: Time-space and homogeneity-heterogeneity. In: Featherstone M, Lash S and Robertson R (eds) *Global Modernities*, London: Sage, 25–44.

Roda A and Wells AS. (2013) School choice policies and racial segregation: where white parents' good intentions, anxiety, and privilege collide. *American Journal of Education* 119: 261–293.

Rose N. (1996) The death of the social? Re-figuring the territory of government. *Economy and Society* 25: 327–356.

Rowe EE and Windle J. (2012) The Australian middle class and education: A small-scale study of the school choice experience as framed by 'My School' within inner city families. *Critical Studies in Education* 53: 137–151.

Seddon T and Angus LB. (2000) Beyond Nostalgia: Reshaping Australian Education. *Australian Education Review No. 44*. Camberwell, Victoria: ACER Press.

U.S. Department of Education Office of the Secretary. (2001) *No Child Left Behind*.

Vickers M. (2005) In the common good: The need for a new approach to funding Australia's schools. *Australian Journal of Education* 49: 264–277.

Weiher GR and Tedin KL. (2002) Does choice lead to racially distinctive schools? Charter schools and household preferences. *Journal of Policy Analysis & Management* 21: 79–92.

Wells AS. (2008) *Both Sides Now: The Story of School Desegregation's Graduates*, Berkeley, CA: University of California Press.

Wells AS, Lopez A, Scott J, et al. (1999) Charter schools as postmodern paradox: rethinking social stratification in an age of deregulated school choice. *Harvard Educational Review* 69: 172–205.

Whitty G. (2008) Twenty years of progress? English education policy 1988 to the present. *Educational Management Administration & Leadership* 36: 165–184.

Whitty G and Edwards T. (1998) School choice policies in England and the United States: An exploration of their origins and significance. *Comparative Education* 34: 211–227.

Whitty G and Power S. (2000) Marketization and privatization in mass education systems. *International Journal of Educational Development* 20: 93–107.

Whitty G, Power S and Halpin D. (1998) *Devolution and Choice in Education: The School, the State, and the Market*, Melbourne: Open University Press.

Windle JA. (2015) *Making Sense of School Choice: Politics, Policies, and Practice under Conditions of Cultural Diversity*, New York: Palgrave Macmillan.

Witte JF. (1998) The milwaukee voucher experiment. *Educational Evaluation and Policy Analysis* 20: 229–251.

Wöessmann L, Ludemann E, Schutz G, et al. (2007) School accountability, autonomy, choice, and the level of student achievement: International evidence from PISA 2003. *OECD Education Working Papers, OECD Publishing* 13.

Yoon E. (2011) Mini schools: The new global city communities of Vancouver. *Discourse: Studies in the Cultural Politics of Education* 32: 253–268.

Chapter 2

Social movements for public education

In 2011, referred to as the 'year of protests', it was difficult to ignore a sense of growing social unrest. From the Arab Uprising and Arab Spring, to the Chilean Winter, Occupy Wall Street and Occupy Together – described by the mainstream press as a 'globalized phenomenon' – protests, riots and civil unrest seemed to be spreading like wildfire across the globe. The protests were hot on the heels of the 2007–2008 Global Financial Crisis. Many became protestations surrounding social welfare, including public education, mobilizing shifting and pluralist concepts of public and taxpayer-funded schooling. The movements are not isolated to singular continents or contexts; however, they do share similar narratives. In Chile, students have resorted to hunger strikes, choreographed dancing and long-term occupations to protest against inaccessible and poor-quality education. There are collective resistance movements to standardized testing ('United Opt Out') or teacher strikes and rallies across the US (Lipman, 2011b, 2013); street protestations against the 'good school' bill in Italy or teacher reform policies in Greece; and the 'Save Our Schools' movement in Australia, the US and the UK. Social movements for public education are occurring on the world stage, and in fairly dramatic fashion.

In discussing the Occupy and Chilean student protests, I utilize the notion of *social movement*, as opposed to collective action. This is influenced by Anyon who argues that social movements and collective actions are theoretically separate and clarity is required, because 'it is important to note that one organization, no matter how large, does not make a movement' (195). A social movement involves 'collective conflictual relations with clearly identified opponents' (Della Porta and Diani, 2006: 20).[1]

Social movements are physically engaged with hard actions. As Grayson (2005) writes,

> Popular social movements . . . have coalesced around major contradictions in the organisation of capitalist forms of social life. Typically, these have represented the interests of the poor, the oppressed and a wide range of groups struggling for their rights and representation in rapidly developing political and economic systems. (8)

The historical anti-war crusades, gay and lesbian rights, the suffragettes movement, or the civil rights movement, are physically engaged with hard actions – such as occupations (Auyero, 2003); semi-permanent blockades; or hunger strikes that result in severe hardship, such as prison or death (Dawson and Sinwell, 2012; Tazreiter, 2010). 'Hard' social movements contain individuals who express feelings of heavy restraint and are willing to commit physical harm to their own bodies (such as sewing closed their own lips, see Tazreiter, 2010), in order to achieve levels of authorization. Most importantly, and this point must be reinforced, the majority are borne out of social, economic or cultural disadvantage or, a committed fight for social justice.

This chapter seeks to emphasize the points of conflict surrounding the public school and illuminate the conditions in which the citizen-consumer is mobilized, particularly within a post-welfare market (Peters, 2004; Mayer, 2008). The corporate-backed educational reform is sustained, ongoing and well organized, playing out in numerous shapes and sizes but with shared policy enactments. The reforms have explicitly sought to inhibit unionization, whether this is teacher unionization in schools or organized activism to the reform agenda. This clearly has significant ramifications not only for thinking about equal access and participation in education, but also for more fundamental concepts around democracy, class and social justice. I will touch on these concepts in this chapter.

Social movements potentially indicate the very raw expressions and frustrations of individuals, who feel powerless within a policy space that is increasingly dominated by unelected officials, with very little transparency and recourse for the decisions they make (Hursh, 2015). Indeed, the Occupy Movement clearly illuminates this frustration, through the repeated calls that 'we are the 99%' as opposed to the powerful 1% who dominate decision-making. As suggested by this prolonged movement, there is a shared sense that citizens are unable to affect or influence decision-making, even when policies fundamentally influence their day-to-day lives – their earning capacity and levels of debt, their right to be educated, their professions, even their historical 'right to revolt' (Olssen et al., 2004: 80). I begin by focusing on the Chilean Student Movement, emerging in 2006, before turning to consider the 'year of protests', as Occupy Wall Street surged forth, amidst the Arab Spring.

Chilean student movement

Since the return to democracy in 1990, protests surrounding accessible public education have continued to grow across Chile, and it was the well-known 'Penguin Revolution' in 2006 that sparked national momentum amongst students. Initiated and led by secondary school students, mostly fifteen to eighteen years old, the famous 'Penguin Revolution' took to the streets in 'penguin suits' (black and white costumes) to demand improved quality education (Cabalin, 2012;

Wiley, 2013). The students maintained specific requests (such as concessions for school bus travel) and engaged in long-term occupations, national strikes and protests. Many were arrested.

The movement gathered volume over the forthcoming years, particularly with the involvement of university students protesting for improved accessibility surrounding higher education, hitting a boiling point in 2011. The press dubbed the large-scale, well-organized protests during 2011 as the 'Chilean Winter' (a reference to the Arab Spring), a movement coordinated by the Confederación Nacional de Estudiantes de Chile (Chile Student Movement Union), who write:

> Education in Chile is going through an acute crisis. We have a discriminatory system that perpetuates inequality through segregation and exclusion [and] operates from the schools to universities undermining democratic coexistence. There is an urgent need to recover education as a universal social and human right . . . This right must be guaranteed . . . and be based upon a new National System of Public Education, one that is to be Free, Democratic, and of High Quality, organized and financed by the state. (Confederación Nacional de Estudiantes de Chile (CONFECH), 2011: capitalized in original) [Chile Student Movement Union].

Students express anger towards the excessive cost of education, privatization and commercialization of schooling, frequently in central, focal locations, such as outside parliamentary buildings or within the city centre (Stromquist and Sanyal, 2013). The students express their dissatisfaction in creative ways: large-scale kiss-ins (lengthy kissing between couples) to show their 'passion for education'; pot-banging demonstrations; a performance entitled 'mass suicide by education', in which students performed death; public pillow fights for ask for better education; occupations of buildings (such as schools and universities); and collective choreographed dances in the capital city, Santiago. The students gathered in the Plaza of Citizenship, dressed as zombies, to stage a mass-performance of Michael Jackson's *Thriller* (Barrionuevo, 2011; The Internationalist, 2011; Taylor, 2011; Stromquist and Sanyal, 2013). The students ran a continuous relay race around the presidential palace for '1800 consecutive hours' through day and night, to 'symbolise the 18 billion Chilean pesos necessary to finance 1 year of free higher education' (Stromquist and Sanyal, 2013: 167).

Students have turned to hunger strikes to express their dissatisfaction. It was reported in the *New York Times* that 'about three dozen high school and university students have turned to starving themselves to . . . pressure the government to reform the country's education system' (Barrionuevo, 2011). Campaigners are evidently willing to physically commit themselves to arduous or painful experiences, such as hunger strikes, in order to 'reclaim' public schooling. This speaks to the often under-theorized, yet over-utilized, concept of social justice (Gewirtz, 1998). The students project education as a critical space for social justice–making, that is, the acquisition of material and non-material resources (Gewirtz, 1998). In their protests, the students gesture towards education as a pivotal relational and institutional structure for civic participation and membership. The school is located as a potential site of social power, a space that enables or disables social participation and social cooperation (Young, 1990; Fraser, 1997).

It was during the Chilean Winter, and also the following year, that saw scores of arrests and violence within the protests. Riot police were frequently involved to combat students throwing firebombs and stones. A bus was set ablaze during one particular protest in Santiago (National Turk, 2012). On August 25, 2011, students called for a national 48-hour strike to demand free and quality public education. They marched through the streets of Santiago, and many reports claimed a turnout of over one million protestors. It culminated into bloody fighting between activists and riot police, and a sixteen-year-old boy was shot and killed by the police, according to witnesses (BBC News, 2011; The Internationalist, 2011). Despite the disagreements in how they are accounted for, protests are unmistakably dramatic, involving water cannons, tear gas and smoke bombs, artillery trucks and machine tanks (RT Network, 2013; Stromquist and Sanyal, 2013). This following image shows a student demonstration in Santiago's Downtown on October 6, 2011. Riot police kick a tear gas canister into a group of protestors (see Figure 2.1).

Figure 2.1 Protestors demand the government to improve education quality. A protest rally in Santiago, Chile.

Source: *erlucho, istock image.*

The images and reports are ubiquitous across social media and alternative sources, as evident in the references I've drawn on, but less common in mainstream media. Police accounts also show discrepancies in terms of the number of protestors reportedly involved. This is echoed by Stromquist and Sanyal (2013) who write that 'these powerful demonstrations have rarely been reported in depth by the US mainstream media' and whilst social media reports ranges of 100,000 protestors at many of the events, police reports tend to claim far lower numbers, around 20,000 participants (166).

Chile has an in-depth history of student protests, but also a powerful history in terms of economic reforms. Chile is one of the first countries to implement free-market policies so extensively, revolutionizing the country with wide-sweeping reforms in the 1970s. In *A Brief History of Neoliberalism*, Harvey (2005) refers to Chile as a 'neoliberal experiment' (15), implemented by the highest levels of the US government as an attack on the socialist and democratically elected Allende government.[2] In 1973, in a military coup, the Allende government was overthrown by General Pinochet, as Paley (2001) writes:

> On September 11, the military bombed the presidential palace with Allende inside. Billows of smoke rose toward the sky as the building burst into flames . . . The brutality of the days that followed still brings terror to those who remember them. Thousands of Chileans were detained, many of them interrogated, tortured and executed . . . the country's military was cracking down not only on persons but also on the symbols and culture of the Left.
>
> (59)

Clearly, September 11 has continued to be a fateful date in the global calendar. Under General Pinochet's rule (1973–1990), neoliberal policies were extensively implemented under the guidance of the 'Chicago Boys', a team of free-market economists from the University of Chicago, schooled by Milton Friedman. Many of the Chicago Boys were appointed to senior positions within Pinochet's government, tasked with the responsibility of a full-scale implementation of Friedman's free-market policies (Harvey, 2005). After little economic success, Friedman visited Chile in 1975 to meet with Pinochet and present fully televised lectures regarding the importance of economic reform, referred to as 'shock treatment'. This resulted in many commentators referring to Friedman as 'the intellectual architect and unofficial adviser for the team of economists now running the Chilean economy' (Letelier, 1976). Orlando Letelier, the author of this commentary, was tragically murdered by a car bomb in Washington, one month following the publication. It wasn't until decades later that Pinochet was held responsible (Klein, 2007; Franklin, 2015).

Even though Friedman revelled in the so-called 'Chilean miracle' and acknowledged that he provided the policy blueprint (Friedman, 1974, 1982), it was only later when Pinochet's human rights violations came under intense scrutiny (and he was arrested for these mass atrocities in 1998) that Friedman endeavoured to fundamentally distance himself from the regime. Friedman devotes an entire chapter to Chile in the book he later published with his wife, *Two Lucky People* (1998). Friedman claimed he was only providing scientific and 'technical' advice, the way a doctor would provide advice to a dying patient (see Friedman and Friedman, 1998; PBS, 2000; Long, 2011; Friedman, 2013). Whilst he does endeavour to distance himself, he also disputes the historical accounts surrounding Allende's death[3] and takes credit for the economists that he was able to provide Chile in the aftermath. He writes that the coup was necessary after 'extensive public unrest and protest' in Chile, and 'thanks to their training' (that the Chicago Boys provided) his students were 'almost the only economists in Chile who had not been involved with the Allende government' (Friedman and Friedman, 1998: 398). Friedman's conclusions regarding the Chilean miracle are largely contested by contemporary economists, with many citing the significant and growing gap between the rich and the poor (Kirby, 1996; Stromquist and Sanyal, 2013). Chile has one of the widest income gaps and differentiations of relative poverty, in comparison to other OECD countries (OECD, 2014).

It is important to understand this historical backdrop in order to appreciate the current contention that surrounds the education system in Chile – one that is deeply entangled within politics, economics and history. Many of the Chilean student protests purposely take place in front of the presidential palace, where Allende died. During Pinochet's rule, the schooling system was opened up to free-market reform, including deregulation, competition and privatization (Rambla et al., 2011). With the introduction of for-profit charter schools and vouchers, this period experienced a dramatic increase in the number of private schools and enrolment in private schools (Hsieh and Urquiola, 2006; Elacqua, 2012). For example, between 1981 and 1988, enrolment in private schools increased from 20% to 40% (Hsieh and Urquiola, 2006). By 2013, only 37% of the Chilean population attend public schools (otherwise known as municipal schools), with the remainder enrolled at private institutions (OECD, 2013). Chile is a largely privatized system – it is well below the OECD average (82%) of the percentage of students who attend public schools. In comparison to other OECD member countries, Chile records the second-lowest proportion of students enrolled in public schools and the lowest expenditure on school services (OECD, 2013, 2015). 'Chile records the most exacerbated segregation' within their schooling system, in comparison to other OECD countries (Rambla et al., 2011: 440).

This informs the backdrop for the student protests in Chile, a movement which is asking for 'free education' and a 'stop to profit-making in education' (Stromquist and Sanyal, 2013: 162). Arguably, the most violent and dramatic protests for public education are occurring in Chile. One Chilean campaigner claimed that reforming the public school concerns the making of history: 'The whole country is watching this movement . . . watching us with hope, with faith that we have the strength to change this education system and make history' (Barrionuevo, 2011). There are connections that can be made between the Chilean Winter and the global social unrest that surged forwards in 2011, referred to as the Occupy Movement.

#Occupy Wall Street and #occupy together

As the Chilean Winter reached a climax in 2011, in the midst of the pro-democracy Arab Spring, global social unrest continued to swell. In July 2011, anti-capitalist Canadian magazine *Adbusters* called for protestors to '#OCCUPY WALL STREET' and take back critical urban space in response to capitalist greed. It was a movement 'born on the internet' as the editors spread the call-out via their magazine, blog, website and email list (Smaligo, 2014). The magazine utilized imagery and motifs from World War Two and the conscription era to call for all citizens to occupy the financial centre: '#World Revolution: What Will You Do?'.[4] The magazine appealed for all persons, from all demographics, to 'flood into lower Manhattan on September 17th, set up tents, kitchens, peaceful barricades and occupy Wall Street' (Smaligo, 2014: 13). According to *US News*, an estimated 20,000 individuals responded to the call and flooded into Wall Street (Greene, 2011), whereas a more disapproving article from *Huffington Post*, reported that 200 protestors were sleeping in the camp each night (Eichler, 2011). A report from *CNN* captured the sentiment on the first day, September 17, with interviewed protestors stating that, 'we need an economy *by* the people and *for* the people', others citing that tax concessions and bail-outs have led to mass poverty and homelessness. One young man says, 'I'm here to humanize the market and to have true participatory democracy . . . bottom up democracy' (Pepitone, 2011). Blockades were set up to discourage more protestors from moving in.

In the weeks and months following, #Occupy Together exponentially spread across the globe to hundreds of cities, such as London, Tokyo, Berlin, Tel Aviv, Melbourne, Santiago, Johannesburg and countless others, as protestors set up semi-permanent and physical occupations in central financial districts (Rogers, 2012; Catalano, 2013; Halvorsen, 2015). Their decision to occupy financial districts, as coupled by the famous slogan of 'we are the 99%', gestures towards their major emphasis – an overriding dissatisfaction towards growing economic and social disparities, the gap between the rich and the poor, and a dissatisfactory democracy (Kellner, 2013). Protestors called for greater transparency and accountability of the corporate sector. As urban spatial practices, these social movements aim to fundamentally redesign and restructure the political and economic landscape. Whilst Occupy was criticized for its alleged lack of specific requests or demands, it maintained an ideological emphasis on restoring democratic decision-making into public spaces, rather than dominated by corporate interests, using technology to aim for more 'horizontal' democracy as opposed to 'vertical' democracy (Boler et al., 2014). When the physical occupations ended, many argued that Occupy was never constrained to 'literal, narrow occupation of particular locations' and,

> The cry to *occupy* is a call to fill up all the political space available, as the great Brazilian educator Paulo Freire once said. It's a metaphor, a quest to fill our society with equality and justice.
> (Editors of Rethinking Schools, 2012: emphasis in original)

The Occupy Education movement, also referred to as 'Occupy the Department of Education' was initiated alongside Occupy in 2011, to protest against what they perceived as educational injustices (Picower, 2012).

Occupy the DOE

> We are reclaiming our voice in education and putting the public back in Public school(s).
> (Occupy Education, 2010: capitalized in original)

From the US, Occupy the DOE called for less testing, smaller class sizes and more support for teachers.[5] This social movement provided the platform for many ongoing movements such as 'United Opt Out', a civil disobedience movement asking parents to opt their children out of standardized testing, to protest against 'corporate education reform' (United Opt Out, 2015). The lobbyists, in alignment with participating professional educators, argue that the constant emphasis on compulsory testing and reporting – often with harsh consequences for low results – detracts from quality teaching and learning experiences, adding to time spent on bureaucratic paper-pushing. This movement has grown since its emergence in 2011, with over 15% of students 'opting out' of standardized testing nationwide, despite being required to 'sit and stare' as a punishment (Kornhaber, 2015).

The backlash against corporate-backed educational reform is a common theme across the collective protests and agitations. '[We] dare the public school to serve student's passions instead of politicians and vendors coffers' writes #occupy education (2014) on their Tumblr and Facebook sites. There are far too many educational protests movements to iterate them all succinctly in this space. The majority (if not all) organize themselves online, utilizing *'technologies of resistance'* (Milberry, 2014: 53, emphasis in original). Whilst teacher activists protested in New York against corporate and for-profit education reforms, others occupied schools in locations across the US to rally against similar narratives – the mass closure of public schools, unaffordable and poor-quality public education, over-testing regimes and the mass termination of public school teachers (Picower, 2012; Cortez, 2013; Lipman, 2013; Stovall, 2013). I draw on an extended quote from Brian Jones, a New York City public school teacher, as reported in an interview during an Occupy Education protest:

> I used to teach in East Harlem, and my public school became invaded by a corporate chain of charter schools that was trying to spread and occupy more and more spaces in public school buildings, *where they could get space for free*. And so one of the things they did was they started advertising. They literally paid more than $1 million to a Madison Avenue advertising firm to create billboards, bus stop ads. Parents came to me having received ten or 12 glossy, high-color, foldable brochures in the mail. And so what's my public school to do? This is competition. Should we create a glossy brochure? Should we spend $1 million to retain a firm? In other words, should we spend more and more of the public school dollar on the competition between the providers?
>
> (The Real News, 2013)

The charter school has proven to be an efficient medium for the acquisition of existing public schools and corporate sector reform (Hursh, 2015). The US charter school is well supported and propped up by government funding, and still attached to the ideals of public schooling, theoretically speaking. This is routinely taken advantage of – many charter school advocates utilize language from the Civil Rights Movement to support their cause. However, the majority of charter schools are not required to hire registered teachers and actively fight and oppose the unionization of teachers. Furthermore, many charter schools hire unregistered and unqualified students from Teach for America – cheaper to hire due to their inexperience, without teaching degrees, who are learning on the job. Those involved in running and directing non-profit charter schools are generating sizeable incomes (Ravitch, 2011). From the *Huffington Post*, Singer (2014) reports that CEOs and managerial staff are earning well above their colleagues; for example, 'the head of the Harlem Village Academies earns $499,000 to manage schools with 1,355 students or $369 per student'. Compare this to their colleagues in public schools, where 'the highest paid New York City teachers with 22 years of experience can earn $100,000. A New York City high school principal with 22 years of experience as a principal earns $154,000 a year'.

The corporate backing of the charter school sector and the 'take-over' of existing public schools is effectively captured by the case of New Orleans (Buras, 2011, 2013, 2014b). Chicago is another city in the US which has experienced aggressive education reform and also widespread collective resistance in the form of strikes and occupations. Pauline Lipman describes Chicago as the 'neoliberal laboratory' of educational reforms, with a sustained assault against public schools and its teachers (see Lipman, 2010, 2011a, 2011b, 2013). I will touch on this subsequently, but first, a focus on hybrid relationships and policy networks.

Hybrid networks, philanthropic collectives and corporate backing

As Hursh (2015) writes, the 'public is increasingly aware that education policy is made by politicians, wealthy heads of foundations (for example, Gates, Walton, Broad), corporations (Pearson), and hedge fund managers' (88). Crucial decisions are made around schooling that have significant flow-on effects for schools, students and teachers, but the decisions are not made in democratic, accountable ways. Utilizing a 'network ethnography' approach, Ball and Junemann (2012) explore the 'messy hinterland' of global policy networks and the growing role of business and philanthropy in education reform, networks that cross nation-state boundaries (see Ball, 2016). In this context, we see the rise of global edu-businesses and philanthropic lobby groups – well versed as the 'perfect market-democracy hybrid' (Peters, 2004: 623). This is captured in numerous ways, such as the acquisition of schools by so-called 'public' entities but financed by private bodies, the involvement of big business in standardizing curriculum and testing, and the domination of multinational curriculum providers as a standard roll-out in schools (Windle, 2015). This inadvertently creates quite standardized, 'factory-produced' derivatives. The global calibration of education leads to a paradoxical post-capitalist version of schooling as anything but flexible and individualized.

I draw on a protest in the city of Chicago in order to further illuminate the confusion and 'messy hinterland' of policy networks (Ball and Junemann, 2012: 9). The teachers' strike in Chicago on September 10, 2012 which 'shut down every public school in the city' (Buras et al., 2013: 1) rallied against legislation introduced by the organization *Stand for Children*, a far-reaching lobby group in the US. Stand for Children positions itself as firmly pro-public schooling and supportive of public school teachers, utilizing language and imagery from the Civil Rights Movement. Stovall (2013) discusses the legislation,

> Recently, in Chicago, the organization Stand for Children introduced legislation that would limit the power of teachers to organize to address school conditions; this organization receives funding from major corporations such as Adidas, the Nike School Innovation Fund, and Intel. The legislation requires a 75% approval vote of union membership to authorize a strike.
> (41)

Lobby groups such as Stand for Children present perplexing and hybrid dictums, as philanthropic and non-profit organizations – but well supported by corporate bodies, asserting clear and unclear agendas. Nongovernment groups such as these routinely involve themselves in efforts to block teacher organization. In this instance, the teachers rallied to receive 90% approval by their membership to strike. This 'has never happened in the history of large-scale organized labor in Chicago' (Stovall, 2013: 41). The corporate economy, a concept I explore further in the final chapter, is dominated by networks and relationships between government and nongovernment, a growing 'number and diverse set of actors and organisations' (Ball and Junemann, 2012: 9). Clearly there is a vested interest in profit-making from schooling which underlines many of the policy movements.

The mass-produced and compulsory free school is marketed as outdated and outpaced by the entrepreneurial and flexible charter school, no longer managed by lagging government bureaucracy but staffed and funded by entrepreneurial policy actors. This means that 'social welfare measures which used to be relatively universal and guaranteed by the welfare state (but delivered by the local state) are now an arena of struggle, and are implemented in a fragmented fashion' (Mayer, 2008: 321).

The arena of struggle in New Orleans

In 2005, Hurricane Katrina hit New Orleans and in the days and months that immediately followed the disaster, hybrid networks and corporate alliances emerged to undertake 'perhaps the most revolutionary attempt at education reform in modern American history' (Uberti, 2015). Only three months following Hurricane Katrina, as the city was still 'submerged under water' (Buras, 2014b), the passing of Act 35 enabled 107 public schools to be converted to non-profit and profitable charter schools, on the basis of their standardized test results. These changes are documented by Buras (2014a), who writes,

> This was the occasion for passing Act 35, which changed the definition of a "failing" school from a performance score of 60 (on a scale of 200) to 87.4, just below the state average. This allowed the state-run Recovery School District to assume control of 107 of 128 public schools in Orleans Parish, enabling charter expansion on a scale never before attempted in Louisiana or elsewhere.

The majority of the schools deemed to be failing were dominated by African-American students and teachers. Charter school chains with wealthy backers – ranging from Walmart to hedge-fund billionaires – took over, as encouraged by federal tax credits and a range of government financial incentives. Reformers co-opted language from the Civil Rights Movement, claiming that the conversion of failing public schools to charter schools would empower African-American students and minority students from low-income backgrounds (Buras, 2014a, 2014b; Singer, 2014). Employees from the schools deemed to be 'failing' were immediately fired (approximately 7,500 in total), including 4,000 teachers[6] (Buras, 2011, 2013, 2014b). The newly converted charter schools hired predominantly white Teach for America employees (Kimmett, 2015).

Corporate-backed reform is invariably posited as innovative and yet in many of these cases, tends to undermine teacher professionalism and undercut public schooling. Teachers are experiencing ongoing and consistent attacks on their professionalization and job security, particularly in the form of casualization, introduction of merit pay and the stripping of teacher unions (Levine and Au, 2013; Lipman, 2013; Hursh, 2015).

The collapse of public schooling, but not the ideology

Whilst critics may argue that activism is perpetuated amongst the minority, clearly these expressions of collective dissatisfaction are pivotal for thinking about the more social aspects of policy in practice, illuminating these often conflicting points between free-market agendas and democratic participation. The citizen does express firm attachments to public education – these attachments have hardly been eroded through free-market reforms. These protests claim that 'Public education is a civil right' (e.g., Institute for Wisconsin's Future, 2012) and 'good education = good citizen = good society' (see, Bacon, 2010).

I refer to this as the citizen's narrative, because I argue that these movements construct symbolic representations of public education, important for the historical, social and cultural weight they carry. The volume and rigour of these movements suggest that the public school is ideologically emblematic for many citizens, held as a counterpoint for oppression or disadvantage. Shock therapy has not reduced the citizen's vision of public education. This is captured by Cortez (2013), writing about an occupation of a public school in Chicago:

> Public education is an entity that ideally enables communities to prosper culturally, intellectually, and economically. It is a public service that demands proper appropriation of resources, especially in disenfranchised communities. Its role to serve all communities is linked to the core principles of social justice – equality and solidarity. When local public schools lack proper resources to serve their students they violate social justice values.
>
> (8)

If I juxtapose these contemporary oppositions to the historical beginnings of the public school, there are common conflicts but also shared goals. Historically, the development of the public school in the US (originally known as the 'common school') was rife with controversy when a few common schools were first developed in the 1830s (Barnard, 1842). The proposal of a taxpayer-funded common school, in order to 'promote the common good' and 'even the playing field between the rich and the poor' (Jeynes, 2007: 142), received widespread political and parental opposition. But, after the American Civil War ended in 1865, common schools flourished in a bid to bring the country together (Jeynes, 2007). Proponents put forth that common schools were an essential pinnacle of democracy – justice, liberty, patriotism and Christianity – basically, everything we should aspire to. Whilst we may critique the meaning of public schooling (Labaree, 1997; Gerrard, 2015), it is undeniable that factions of the community are dissenting in response to what they claim is a fundamental attack on education, and in their dissent activists are mobilizing discourses of the public school and their claim to accessible, affordable and quality education.

Educational campaigns and protests are inherently political, just as they are intrinsically entangled within ontological and epistemological questions surrounding class, poverty and economic relationships. Marx and Engels originally envisioned class as an explanatory theory for collective political activity, for example, revolutions led by the proletariat to overthrow the government, redistribute property ownership and means of production. Herein, I turn to ask, what is the traction of traditional class theory for social movements and collective political action? I juxtapose traditional class theory with more contemporary theory in order to explore the role of social class in educational protestation.

The death of class

In their seminal text, *The Death of Class*, Pakulski and Waters (1996) contend the dissolution and irrelevance of class for the sociologist. If class is measured as Marx and Engels originally intended it to be measured, via means of production, ownership of property and economic relations, clear structures and formations of class are dissipated. The authors write,

> Class divisions are losing their self-evident and pervasive character . . . The good news [is] that class has collapsed and is decomposing, leaving only the merest traces of its effects . . . This means that sociologists cannot go on relating and reducing every social phenomenon, from feminine subordination to taste in music, to class. We must begin the search for a new theoretical *terra firma*.
> (Pakulski and Waters, 1996: 1, 7, emphasis in original)

The debate surrounding the sociological existence and value of class as a tool of measurement is long-standing and contentious. Nisbet's (1959) *The Decline and Fall of Social Class* was one of the first papers to challenge class as a category of measurement, and it preceded a debate that tended to be dominated by male scholars and more positivist perspectives. Goldthorpe (1983) famously argued that a woman's social class position can only be assessed via her husband. Clark and Lipset (1991) describe class as 'an increasingly outmoded concept' and that 'new forms of social stratification are emerging' (397). The traction of class has been fought across feminist, sociological and philosophical lines. Thus, it is important to *struggle* with class, to methodologically and epistemologically reposition or reframe the notion of 'class'. What makes up class? Who or what constitutes the middle class?

The debates around class tend to be intensifications and augmentations of the paradigm wars: interpretive versus positivist, qualitative versus quantitative. Pakulski and Waters (1996) describe class as a 'sociological chimera', something that we cling to more as a descriptive tool more so than an analytical tool. In other words, the notion of 'class' lacks objective substance, deeply diffused and dispersed within contemporary economic arrangements – a lack of groupness or 'statistical aggregates or taxonomic categories' (Pakulski and Waters, 1996: 10). For these scholars, the death of class is allegedly signalled by the lack of class conflict that challenges the status quo and the bourgeoisie. As financial growth increases and traditional hierarchies decline, so too does class conflict and 'support for social movements' (Clark and Lipset, 1991: 402). The 'socially distant' and 'exclusive' groupness, which are the 'enduring bases for conflict, struggle, and distributional contestation', loses its traction (Pakulski and Waters, 1996: 11).

There is a weak point here in claiming that struggle and contestation and social groupness will decline. Even though it is clear that class voting has steeply declined, social groupness has asserted itself with differing logics. For example, the Chilean Student Movement and the Occupy Movement, who claim 'we are the 99%' and 'we are the middle', demonstrate the continuity of social organization around political objectives, but perhaps not as clearly affiliated with a distinct left or right, and more so, resistance towards what the people perceive as inequality. Unequal class structures and stratification 'influence the formation of . . . collective actors seeking to bring about social change' (Hout et al., 1993: 21).[7] Although it may have shifted and evolved from an historical perspective (from revolutions overthrowing the government), there continue to be social movements that endeavour to challenge poverty, the existing status quo and continuing social inequalities. Certainly, many Occupiers argue that their movement does constitute a revolution, or the attempt to revolt (e.g., #World Revolution).

Do these political groups symbolize and reconfigure conceptualizations of class tensions and class struggle? Are they attempting to intervene, redress and challenge income differentiation and poverty gaps? Social movements, whilst not homogenous – operating in diverse ways and for divergent purposes – offer reimaginings of class conflict and class war within contemporary settings. They compel sociologists to take on divergent methods for thinking about and theorizing class conflict. These social movements demonstrate the significance of class, but clearly in generative ways. I use this discussion as a platform for utilizing class theory within this study, a point I explore further in the next chapter.

Conclusion

Whilst scholars have effectively mapped out the landscape of corporate-backed educational reform (Ravitch, 2011; Hursh, 2015; Schneider, 2015), there is still wide scope for critiquing and illuminating public response to educational reform. Indeed, many citizens respond via the way of school choice in escaping low-performing schools, whilst others allegedly 'neglect' important choice work; but in the public landscape, there is, arguably, a growing derision and dissent towards corporate-backed educational reform, and the lack of accessible, high-quality education.

In this chapter I have focused on social movements from the US and Chile; however this is only a partial glimpse of public education protests occurring on a global scale. The modification of requisite performance standards, the 'redefinition' of a failing school, and even the redefinition of a professional teacher and professional teaching standards are common threads throughout the protests and social movements. Activists pushing against these reforms frequently align with critical pedagogue Paulo Freire, indicating a shared vision of education as a necessary disjuncture from the technocratic model of education, burdened with an over-reliance on standardized testing and reporting. It is also a vision more closely aligned with exploratory or experiential pedagogy, a sense of belonging and satisfaction within the classroom.

This analysis suggests that the citizen is aware and responsive to privatization reforms, and mass protests occur in the *context* of profit-driven policy-making agendas. The narratives surrounding these campaigns share similar sentiments, whether in Melbourne, Santiago, New York City or Chicago. These are globalized narratives. In the midst of this countenance and discontent and a sense of dissatisfaction with accessible schooling provision, but also the corporate take-over of public schools, how is the affluent school chooser responding strategically? In the following chapter, I turn to examine parental campaigns and networks, challenging the government for a brand-new public high school. How do these parental groups, framed as public education advocacy, correspond with these social movements and the globalized policy reform agenda?

Notes

1 Whilst I am purposefully framing these as *movements*, I will refer to literature that utilizes both of these terms – collective action and social movement. The reason for this is due to a cross-over within the literature. Many theorists continue to use both terms within their work (Foweraker, 1995; Ellison and Martin, 2000; Brunsting and Postmes, 2002).
2 Declassified documents have indicated that the military coup was sponsored by the CIA and the US government, led by President Richard Nixon at the time (Kornbluh, 2016). The upper echelons of the US government regarded the Allende government as a threat because it was democratically elected and Marxist (Harvey, 2005).
3 A scientific autopsy in 2011 found that Allende died by self-inflicted gunshots and thus, Friedman was correct in this regard.
4 *Adbusters* Magazine. See their website: www.adbusters.org and https://www.adbusters.org/campaigns/occupywallstreet
5 See video of the Occupy the Department of Education, New York City: http://therealnews.com/t2/index.php?option=com_content&task=view&id=31&Itemid=74&jumival=10087. (Our Schools NYC, October 25, 2011; The Real News, 2013)
6 These figures are also cited in the federal civil rights complaint made by the Journey for Justice Alliance. The document is available in full (see Journey for Justice Alliance, May 13, 2014).
7 Also, see Devine (1997) for a useful discussion of this paper.

References

Anyon J. (2009) Progressive social movements and educational equity. *Educational Policy* 23: 194–215.
Auyero J. (2003) *Contentious Lives: Two Argentine Women, Two Protests, and the Quest for Recognition*, Durham & London: Duke University Press.
Bacon D. (2010) *David Bacon: California's Perfect Storm*. Available at: http://theragblog.blogspot.com.au/2010/10/david-bacon-californias-perfect-storm.html.
Ball SJ. (2016) Following policy: Networks, network ethnography and education policy mobilities. *Journal of Education Policy* 31 1–18.
Ball SJ and Junemann C. (2012) *Networks, New Governance and Education*, Bristol, UK and Chicago: The Policy Press.
Barnard H. (1842) Papers of Henry Barnard. *Manuscript Collection of Trinity College Watkinson Library*. Hartford, CT.
Barrionuevo A. (2011) *With Kiss-Ins and Dances, Young Chileans Push for Reform*. Available at: http://www.nytimes.com/2011/08/05/world/americas/05chile.html?_r=0.
BBC News. (2011) *Chilean President Seeks Answers on Protest Death*. Available at: http://www.bbc.com/news/world-latin-america-14705127.
Boler M, Macdonald A, Nitsou C, et al. (2014) Connective labor and social media: Women's roles in the 'leaderless' occupy movement. *Convergence: The International Journal of Research into New Media Technologies* 20: 438–460.
Brunsting S and Postmes T. (2002) Social movement participation in the digital age: Predicting offline and online collective action. *Small Group Research* 33: 525–554.
Buras KL. (2011) Race, charter schools, and conscious capitalism: On the spatial politics of whiteness as property (and the unconscionable assault on black New Orleans). *Harvard Educational Review* 81: 296–331.
Buras KL. (2013) 'We're not going nowhere': Race, urban space, and the struggle for King Elementary School in New Orleans. *Critical Studies in Education* 54: 19–32.
Buras KL. (2014a) *Charter Schools Flood New Orleans*. Available at: http://progressive.org/news/2014/12/187949/charter-schools-flood-new-orleans.
Buras KL. (2014b) *Charter Schools, Race, and Urban Space: Where the Market Meets Grassroots Resistance*, New York and London: Routledge.
Buras KL, Ferrare JJ and Apple MW. (2013) Grassroots educational organizing in an era of venture capital. *Critical Studies in Education* 54: 1–4.
Cabalin C. (2012) Neoliberal education and student movements in Chile: Inequalities and malaise. *Policy Futures in Education* 10: 219–228.
Catalano TA. (2013) Occupy: A case illustration of social movements in global citizenship education. *Education, Citizenship and Social Justice* 8: 276–288.
Clark TN and Lipset SM. (1991) Are social classes dying? *International Sociology* 6: 397–410.
Confederación Nacional de Estudiantes de Chile (CONFECH). (2011) *Demandas [National Confederation of Chilean Students]*. Available at: http://fech.cl/.
Cortez GA. (2013) Occupy public education: A community's struggle for educational resources in the era of privatization. *Equity & Excellence in Education* 46: 7–19.
Dawson MC and Sinwell L. (2012) Ethical and political challenges of participatory action research in the academy: Reflections on social movements and knowledge production in South Africa. *Social Movement Studies* 11: 177–191.

Della Porta D and Diani M. (2006) *Social Movements: An Introduction*, Oxford & Malden, MA: Blackwell.

Devine F. (1997) *Social Class in America and Britain*, Edinburgh: Edinburgh University Press.

Editors of Rethinking Schools. (2012) Occupy education. *Rethinking Schools* 26: 3. Accessed 3rd January, 2016. Available at: http://www.rethinkingschools.org/archive/26_03/edit263.shtml

Eichler A. (2011) *Occupy Wall Street Protesters Settle In, Despite Weather and Police Clashes*. Available at: http://www.huffingtonpost.com.au/entry/occupy-wall-street_n_987439.html?section=australia.

Elacqua G. (2012) The impact of school choice and public policy on segregation: Evidence from Chile. *International Journal of Educational Development* 32: 444–453.

Ellison G and Martin G. (2000) Policing, collective action and social movement theory: The case of the Northern Ireland civil rights campaign. *British Journal of Sociology* 51: 681–699.

Foweraker J. (1995) *Theorizing Social Movements*, London and Colorado: Pluto Press.

Franklin J. (2015) *Pinochet Directly Ordered Killing on US Soil of Chilean Diplomat, Papers Reveal*. Available at: http://www.theguardian.com/world/2015/oct/08/pinochet-directly-ordered-washington-killing-diplomat-documents-orlando-letelier-declassified.

Fraser N. (1997) *Justice Interruptus: Critical Reflections on the "Postsocialist" Condition*, London: Routledge.

Friedman M. (1974) Economic Miracles. *Newsweek (January 21, 1974)*.

Friedman M. (1982) Free Markets and the Generals. *Newsweek (January 25, 1982)*.

Friedman M. (2013) *Milton Friedman Speaking about His Involvement with Pinochet and Chile (Televised Interview, 1991)*. Available at: https://www.youtube.com/watch?v=dzgMNLtLJ2k.

Friedman M and Friedman R. (1998) *Two Lucky People: Memoirs*, Chicago & London: University of Chicago Press.

Gerrard J. (2015) Public education in neoliberal times: Memory and desire. *Journal of Education Policy* 30: 855–868.

Gewirtz S. (1998) Conceptualizing social justice in education: Mapping the territory. *Journal of Education Policy* 13: 469–484.

Goldthorpe JH. (1983) Women and class analysis: In defence of the conventional view. *Sociology* 17: 465–488.

Grayson J. (2005) Organising, educating . . . changing the world. *Adults Learning* 16: 8.

Greene B. (2011) How 'Occupy Wall Street' started and spread. *U.S. News & World Report News*. News & World Report.

Halvorsen S. (2015) Taking space: Moments of rupture and everyday life in occupy London. *Antipode* 47: 401–417.

Harvey D. (2005) *A Brief History of Neoliberalism*, Oxford and New York: Oxford University Press.

Hout M, Brooks C and Manza J. (1993) The persistence of classes in post-industrial societies. *International Sociology* 8: 259–277.

Hsieh C-T and Urquiola M. (2006) The effects of generalized school choice on achievement and stratification: Evidence from Chile's voucher program. *Journal of Public Economics* 90: 1477–1503.

Hursh DW. (2015) *The End of Public Schools: The Corporate Reform Agenda to Privatize Education*, New York & London: Routledge.
Institute for Wisconsin's Future. (2012) *Public Education Is a Civil Right*. Available at: http://wisconsinsfuture.org/public-education-is-a-civil-right-march-and-rally-to-be-held-in-milwaukee-on-sept-21/.
The Internationalist. (2011) The new battle of Chile for free, quality public education. *The Internationalist*. Demonstrators march on the Alameda in Santiago de Chile on second day of national strike, August 25. Photo: Víctor R. Calvano/AP.
Jeynes W. (2007) *American Educational History: School, Society, and the Common Good*, Thousand Oaks, CA: Sage Publications, Inc.
Journey for Justice Alliance. (May 13, 2014) *Federal Civil Rights Complaint*. Available at: http://b.3cdn.net/advancement/24a04d1624216c28b1_4pm6y9lvo.pdf.
Kellner D. (2013) Media spectacle, insurrection and the crisis of neoliberalism from the Arab uprisings to occupy everywhere! *International Studies in Sociology of Education* 23: 251–272.
Kimmett C. (2015) *10 Years after Katrina, New Orleans' All-Charter School System Has Proven a Failure*. Available at: http://inthesetimes.com/article/18352/10-years-after-katrina-new-orleans-all-charter-district-has-proven-a-failur.
Kirby P. (1996) The Chilean economic miracle: A model for Latin America? *Trocaire Development Review*: 66–85. Available at: https://www.trocaire.org/resources/policyandadvocacy/trocaire-development-review-1996.
Klein N. (2007) *The Shock Doctrine*, London and New York: Penguin Books.
Kornbluh P. (2016) *Chile and the United States: Declassified Documents Relating to the Military Coup, September 11, 1973*. Available at: http://nsarchive.gwu.edu/NSAEBB/NSAEBB8/nsaebb8i.htm.
Kornhaber ML. (2015) *Students Are Opting Out of Testing. How Did We Get Tere?* Available at: https://theconversation.com/students-are-opting-out-of-testing-how-did-we-get-here-40364.
Labaree DF. (1997) Public goods, private goods: The American struggle over educational goals. *American Educational Research Journal* 34: 39–81.
Letelier O. (1976) The Chicago boys in Chile. *The Nation (August 28, 1976)*.
Levine D and Au W. (2013) Rethinking schools: Enacting a vision for social justice within US education. *Critical Studies in Education* 54: 72–84.
Lipman P. (2010) Education and the right to the city: The intersection of urban policies, education, and poverty. In: Apple MW, Ball SJ and Gandin LA (eds) *The Routledge International Handbook of the Sociology of Education*, London: Routledge. 241–252
Lipman P. (2011a) Contesting the city: Neoliberal urbanism and the cultural politics of education reform in Chicago. *Discourse: Studies in the Cultural Politics of Education* 32: 217–234.
Lipman P. (2011b) *The New Political Economy of Urban Education: Neoliberalism, Race, and the Right to the City*, New York & Oxon: Taylor & Francis.
Lipman P. (2013) Economic crisis, accountability, and the state's coercive assault on public education in the USA. *Journal of Education Policy* 28: 557–573.
Long G. (2011) *Chile Recognises 9,800 More Victims of Pinochet's Rule*. Available at: http://www.bbc.com/news/world-latin-america-14584095.
Mayer M. (2008) Post-fordist city politics. In: Amin A (ed) *Post-Fordism: A Reader*, Oxford & Cambridge: Blackwell Publishers Ltd, 316–337.

Milberry K. (2014) (Re)making the internet: Free software and the social factory hack. In: Ratto M and Boler M (eds) *DIY Citizenship: Critical Making and Social Media*, Cambridge, MA: The MIT Press, 53–64.

National Turk. (2012) *Chile Students Education Protest, 3 Buses Burned, 49 Officers Were Injured*. Available at: http://www.nationalturk.com/en/chile-students-education-protest-3-buses-burned-49-officers-were-injured-23658.

Nisbet RA. (1959) The decline and fall of social class. *The Pacific Sociological Review* 2: 11–17.

Occupy Education. (2010) *Occupy Education: Reclaiming Our Voice in Education*. Available at: http://coopcatalyst.wordpress.com/blog-campaigns/occupy-education/.

Occupy Education. (2014) *#occupyedu*. Available at: http://occupyedu.tumblr.com/.

OECD. (2013) *PISA 2012 Results: What Makes Schools Successful? Resources, Policies and Practices*, Paris, France: OECD.

OECD. (2014) *Society at a Glance 2014: OECD Social Indicators*. Available at: http://dx.doi.org/10.1787/soc_glance-2014-en.

OECD. (2015) *Education Spending (Indicator)*. Available at: https://data.oecd.org/eduresource/education-spending.htm#indicator-chart.

Olssen M, Codd J and O'Neill A-M. (2004) *Education Policy: Globalisation, Citizenship and Democracy*, London: Sage.

Our Schools NYC. (October 25, 2011) *Occupy The DOE: People's General Assembly on Public Education (New York City)*. Available at: https://www.youtube.com/watch?v=YbmjMickJMA&feature=player_embedded.

Pakulski J and Waters M. (1996) *The Death of Class*, London, California & New Delhi: Sage.

Paley J. (2001) *Marketing Democracy: Power and Social Movements in Post-Dictatorship Chile*, Berkeley, CA: University of California Press.

PBS. (2000) *Commanding Heights: Interview with Milton Friedman (Transcript from Interview Conducted 10/01/2000)*. Available at: http://www.pbs.org/wgbh/commandingheights/shared/minitext/int_miltonfriedman.html#10.

Pepitone J. (2011) *Hundreds of Protesters Descend to 'Occupy Wall Street', September 17 2011*. Available at: http://money.cnn.com/2011/09/17/technology/occupy_wall_street/.

Peters MA. (2004) Citizen-consumers, social markets and the reform of public services. *Policy Futures in Education* 2: 621–632.

Picower B. (2012) Education should be free! Occupy the DOE!: Teacher activists involved in the Occupy Wall Street movement. *Critical Studies in Education* 54: 44–56.

Rambla X, Valiente Ó and Frías C. (2011) The politics of school choice in two countries with large private-dependent sectors (Spain and Chile): Family strategies, collective action and lobbying. *Journal of Education Policy* 26: 431–447.

Ravitch D. (2011) *The Death and Life of the Great American School System: How Testing and Choice Are Undermining Education*, New York: Basic Books.

The Real News. (2013) *Occupy the Department of Education*. Available at: http://therealnews.com/t2/index.php?option=com_content&task=view&id=31&Itemid=74&jumival=10087.

Rogers S. (2012) *The Occupy Map of the World*. Available at: http://www.theguardian.com/news/datablog/interactive/2012/sep/17/occupy-map-of-the-world.

RT Network. (2013) *Chilean Students Clash with Police in Protest for Free Education.* Available at: http://rt.com/news/chile-students-clashes-education-041/.

Schneider MK. (2015) *Common Core Dilemma: Who Owns Our Schools?* New York & London: Teachers College Press.

Singer A. (2014) *Big Profits in Not-for-Profit Charter Schools.* Available at: http://www.huffingtonpost.com/alan-singer/charter-school-executive-profit_b_5093883.html?ir=Australia.

Smaligo N. (2014) *The Occupy Movement Explained*, Open Court: New York.

Stovall D. (2013) Against the politics of desperation: Educational justice, critical race theory, and Chicago school reform. *Critical Studies in Education* 54: 33–43.

Stromquist NP and Sanyal A. (2013) Student resistance to neoliberalism in Chile. *International Studies in Sociology of Education* 23: 152–178.

Taylor A. (2011) *Student Protests in Chile.* Available at: http://www.theatlantic.com/photo/2011/08/student-protests-in-chile/100125/.

Tazreiter C. (2010) Local to global activism: The movement to protect the rights of refugees and asylum seekers. *Social Movement Studies* 9: 201–214.

Uberti D. (2015) *New Orleans' Switch to Charter Schools after Katrina: A 'Takeover' or a Success?* Available at: http://www.theguardian.com/us-news/2015/aug/27/new-orleans-recovery-school-district-charter-schools.

United Opt Out. (2015) *United Oot Out: The Movement to End Corporate Education Reform.* Available at: http://unitedoptout.com/uoo-opt-out-map-2015/.

Wiley BT. (2013) The 2006 Penguin revolution and the 2011 Chilean winter: Chilean students' fight for education reform. *Latin American and Iberian Studies.* Santa Barbara, CA: University of California.

Windle JA. (2015) *Making Sense of School Choice: Politics, Policies, and Practice under Conditions of Cultural Diversity*, New York: Palgrave Macmillan.

Young I. (1990) *Justice and the Politics of Difference*, Princeton, NJ: Princeton University Press.

Chapter 3

Campaigning for choice

Studies show that socially mobile parents, those with the resources, are willing to pay more for real estate that will enable access to a high-demand state-funded school-of-choice (Davidoff and Leigh, 2008; Dougherty et al., 2009; Fack and Grenet, 2010). So too, middle-class parents are willing to pay the direct fees to private schools, for perceivably 'better' or more 'prestigious' secondary schools. But, what happens when parents collectively agitate, lobby and pressure the government for a *brand-new* high school, one that is government-funded and theoretically freely accessible?

The chapter introduces the five-year ethnographic study (2011–2016) of long-term and organized parental groups and networks, which drives the subsequent chapters. The ethnographic mixed-methods study utilized multiple data sets, as influenced by Chicago School ethnographies (Deegan, 2001) and Bourdieusian theory, particularly around the measurement of class, participant observation and field-work. This study aims to be visual in its approach, and attentive to space and nuances of context (a comprehensive account of methodology and data can be located within the Appendix).

Parental networks

This study draws on data generated by local parent groups, and I refer to these parental networks as 'campaigns', each based in inner-city neighbourhoods in Melbourne, less than ten kilometres from the Central Business District. The exclusive goal of each campaign is to pressure and lobby the state government of Victoria for a brand-new, locale-specific public high school. The state government maintains the authority to initiate and fund new public high schools, which are largely dependent on government subsidies and provide relatively 'free' education. Similar to Hankins' (2007) US-based study, these 'family-oriented, middle-class' parents have organized to raise donations and gain state approval for the funding of their new school. However, unlike Hankins' (2007) study, the parents are organizing and lobbying for a *public* high school, as opposed to a neighbourhood *charter* elementary school.

Campaigning for choice 39

Their residential location is essential for considering and understanding the campaigners' consumption choices and preferences around schooling, and the following map shows the location of each parental campaign in relation to the proximity of surrounding schools (both government/public and nongovernment/private) and the city (see Figure 3.1).

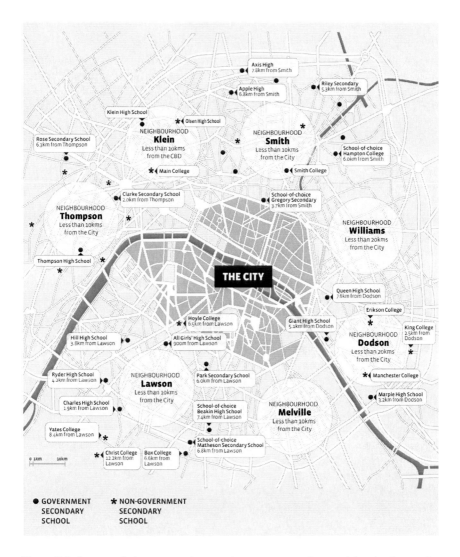

Figure 3.1 A map of the parental campaign groups as denoted by the inner-ring neighbourhood in which it is located, and proximity of surrounding high schools.

I generated the bulk of data for the campaigns located in the neighbourhoods of Lawson and Smith, and a relatively small amount of data relating to campaigns situated in Thompson, Klein and Dodson. Pseudonyms have been adopted for all people, neighbourhoods and schools.

I attended all meetings and events with the 'New School for Lawson' campaign as a participant observer, over an eighteen-month period (from September 2011 to March 2013). During this time, I conducted informal interviews, and formal interviews with ten campaigners from 'New School for Lawson'. For the campaigns located in the neighbourhoods of Smith and Thompson, data is generated in the form of maps and photographs, statistics, online material, published interviews in mass media and support letters written by the campaigners (for detailed information see Appendix, Table A.1).

These maps are useful for visualizing the spaces and yet they also point to the messiness of naming schools as public or private. As Figure 3.1 indicates, the neighbourhoods of Klein, Thompson and Smith retain a government (public) secondary school. Klein High School is 'public' although it offers single-sex education only, and enrolment is highly competitive.[1] Neighbourhood Thompson acquired a brand-new 'public' high school in 2011, a case I explore further in Chapter Seven, after a short campaign effort. As such, it represents a 'past' campaign. Neighbourhood Smith acquired a public high school in 2015, after a long and drawn out campaign; however the success of the campaign was arguably strongly attributed to the pre-existing 'public' school in the neighbourhood. The pre-existing school practiced select-entry enrolment and only educated the upper years of secondary school. Thus, the new school did not require substantial funding, simply expanding the enrolment years and removing the formal select-entry requirement.

I provide the maps in order to point to the importance of urban space within school choice. The campaigners argue that surrounding public high schools necessitate over five kilometres of travel from their residence, and therefore, the lack of an available public school impedes their democratic right to public schooling. My measurements, however, conflicted with the campaigners' measurements, and I found that – particularly for Lawson residents – that there were non-zoned and accessible public high schools within two kilometres (1.24 miles) from their neighbourhood. However, these schools are afflicted with 'conventional indicators' of bad choice (Reay et al., 2013: viii), including a location in a lower socioeconomic neighbourhood, higher levels of racial diversity and multiculturalism, in addition to a poor reputation amongst certain choosers.

The local and statewide newspapers are active in reporting on these campaigns. The parents are often pictured standing in their neighbourhood, holding their children, looking grave and solemn. The mass media tend to present the campaigns positively, especially the politically left-leaning papers, declaring the parental campaigns a sign of resurgence for public education and a commitment to the public good. This was announced by the press when the neighbourhood of Thompson received their brand-new public school in 2011 after a very short parental campaign, described by an involved parent as a 'vigorous grassroots campaign led by local parents who value local education' (Yale, 2014). One enrolled parent commented to the media, 'Why choose private?', referring to the new Thompson High. 'Why would you pay $25,000? That's the equivalent of an overseas trip to Paris every year'. After all, another parent said, 'We all have the right to public education' (Topsfield, 2011). Promptly following the opening of Thompson High School, the demand was so high that the enrolment zone was modified, effectively cutting out residents in a nearby, lower-income neighbourhood; and the newspapers reported that house prices and cost of rentals in neighbourhood Thompson were 'going through the roof'.

The urban space is decisive within these campaigns, and each location shares social, political and cultural commonalities. The majority of the campaigns are situated within inner-ring neighbourhoods and represent a politically left-leaning seat, particularly Lawson and Smith. Each campaign is located in a neighbourhood that previously held a public high school, but it was closed or merged during a period of mass privatization in the 1990s.

The privatization revolution

The state of Victoria experienced an intense history of protests for social services, including education, throughout the 1990s. There is a striking similarity between the reforms in this relatively small state in Australia, with those educational reforms playing out around the globe (Buras et al., 2013). The protests surged during the so-called 'privatization revolution' (from 1992 to 1999), responsible for the closure of 25% of all public high schools (ninety in total)[2] and the dismissal of 8,000 public school teachers. The revolution was part of a much wider social services reform in Victoria, aimed to transform and privatize a range of public services for profit-making, including education, public transport, roads, water and electricity (for example, see Seddon, 1994; Crooks, 1996; Hannan, 1996; Spaull, 1999; Rood and Tomazin, 2006).

The architects of the reforms, Don Hayward, a former lawyer and sales director of a car company, and Brian Caldwell,[3] a well-known advocate of self-managing schools, wrote in their later book that it would be the greatest education revolution in Victoria's history. 'A revolution is never easy. There has to be the one big, powerful idea . . . and the political power to make the idea work' (Caldwell and Hayward, 1998: 37). The small cabinet met each Friday – referred to as Black Friday by the schooling sector – to determine the fate of public high schools, issuing a closure notice to the school's management, often with very little time to respond. The demolishment team would move in shortly afterwards. Many reports indicated that over $150 million was cut from education. Caldwell writes that the schools were closed due to low enrolment numbers and to improve the 'educational opportunities of the students through giving them access to a broader curriculum' in a bigger school (Caldwell and Hayward, 1998: 41). Unlike charter or private schools, in which a small size can be regarded as highly marketable, public schools must consistently prove their economic feasibility.

Whilst the large-scale school closures and sacking of teachers echo the global landscape, the collective public response is markedly analogous. The media described the public response in Victoria as 'the biggest battle over education in more than a decade' (Painter, 1993a). Thousands of protestors took to the city, marching and rallying, and others took over closed schools, establishing non-violent yet resistant occupations, setting up complex rotation schedules over a twenty-four-hour basis, to make demolishment of the building impossible. Some of the occupiers lasted only a few days, whereas other activists lasted months (Crooks, 1996). At the closed Richmond Secondary College, activists occupied the closed school for over a year, setting up a 'rebel school', and police were finally sent in to forcibly extract the protestors (Jolly, 1996).[4]

This is an important context for the study, located in the state of Victoria, Australia. In the scope of nationwide policies, the state of Victoria has led the way with school decentralization, adopting formalized legislation in 1998 (*Education Self-Governing School Act*) (Parliament of Victoria, 1998). The purpose of the Act was to enable public high schools to be self-managing and operate autonomously from government sectors. The majority of public schools developed independent charters and elected independent school councils (effectively becoming 'charter schools'). Ideally, these councils would appoint business leaders to facilitate competitive engagement within a market environment and more efficient use of budgets (approximately 90% of the public school budget was decentralized) (see Spaull, 1999). Despite the so-called autonomy of public schools, the state of Victoria continues to maintain a well-funded Department of Education, with the reported remuneration of 78 executives totaling approximately 16.8 million AUD per year (Tomazin and Preiss, 2015). Public secondary school teachers in Victoria are amongst the lowest paid in Australia.

Many years following the 'privatization revolution', the state of Victoria records the second-lowest proportion of students enrolled in the public sector, in comparison to all states and territories in Australia (see Figure 3.2).

These are the latest figures available at time of writing. As evident on this graph, the Australian Capital Territory records the highest proportion of full-time secondary school students enrolled in private schools, followed closely by Victoria, with nearly half of the population enrolled in private high schools.[5]

Neighbourhood transformations

Whilst these neighbourhoods each had a local public high school in the 1990s, they also share a working-class socio-historical narrative, which is common for most inner-city neighbourhoods in Melbourne. Fast-forward approximately ten years following the closure of the local public school, after the neighbourhood has experienced a considerable gentrification overhaul, and a parental campaign for a local public high school has emerged. To illustrate this point, I refer to an economic profile of the neighbourhood of Lawson, from the period 2001 to 2006 (see Figure 3.3 on page 44).

Campaigning for choice 43

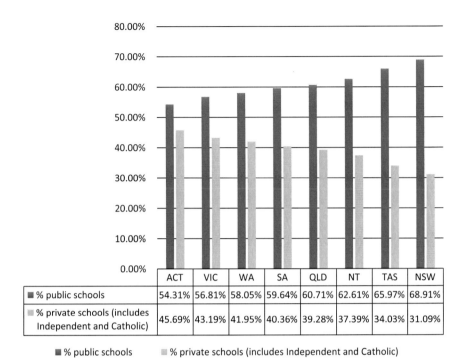

Figure 3.2 Secondary school enrolment divided by sector and state/territory in Australia (2015): includes all states and territories in Australia. Full-time secondary school students only.

'New School for Lawson' emerged during this period (2003) and the relationship between gentrification and organized, collective lobbying for educational services is evident – a pattern that is reflected throughout the campaigns. The neighbourhood shows a statistical increase of persons with university educational qualifications, who speak English only and identify with 'no religion'. There is a decline of traditional religions, such as Catholicism or Christianity, and non-English speakers.[6] Indeed, utilizing the neighbourhood as a central methodological lens is useful for capturing school choice and parental organization around urban schools. 'High status parents' as Holme (2002) puts forth, clearly look at the urban movements and residential choices of other high-status parents, particularly when choosing public schooling.

The urban space is also decisive in terms of how it directs and commands the purpose of the campaign. I draw on interview data with participants from the 'New School for Lawson' to point to their central goal:

E: What are the purposes of the group, in your own words?
Matthew: The purposes really are . . . to get a local high school.

44 Campaigning for choice

Harry: You know [our purpose] is to ask for a local high school, umm ... and local means, close enough that, you know, people can walk or cycle there ... you know, get there easily, as part of their own community.

The celebration of community schooling is routinely evoked by the campaigners, and the public school tends to serve as a proxy for progressive values, relating to politics, religion and ideology. The parents stress the importance of proximity

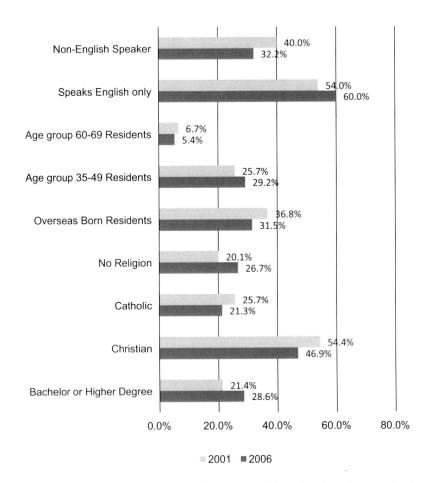

Figure 3.3 Economic profile of the Lawson neighbourhood and gentrification, from 2001–2006.

Source: Raw data obtained from an economic profile of the Lawson neighbourhood, available from the City Council, in 2008 and 2012.

and an ability to access the school easily. The matter of proximity and residential address is particularly relevant for public schools in Australia, generally considered free and accessible, but those public high schools considered 'high-demand' or 'popular' enforce strict catchment areas and turn away potential students who reside outside of the catchment area. This is overt selection of students, but there is also the more covert selection of students. Parents can still apply for public high schools outside of their catchment area – or choose a low- to high-fee private school, of course – however, enrolment in a popular public high school will depend on the parents' (and students') ability to meet the school's criteria. The popular schools may select a small proportion of 'out of catchment area' pupils on the basis of standardized test results, extra-curricular activities, such as whether the student is learning a musical instrument, is the captain of a cricket team, or speaks a second language. The school can also request that a student complete a special examination (schools such as Thompson, Hampton and Klein High each utilize this strategy). Using Windle's (2015) terms, the popular schools are 'socially restricted', whereas the rejected schools are 'socially exposed', demonstrating the 'opposite poles within the logic of social restriction that frames school choice, recognizing that schools may be differently positioned between these poles' (2).

If the campaigners do not achieve the local public high school within their neighbourhood (and catchment area), there are 'popular' and preferred public high school choices located in the surrounding neighbourhoods. The popular schools are labelled as 'school-of-choice', indicated on close-up maps of neighbourhoods Lawson and Smith (see Figures 3.4 and 3.5).

The 'schools-of-choice' are routinely mentioned in written letters, interviews and community meetings, despite their further distance from the neighbourhoods.[7] The residents are only too aware of the strict catchment areas that keep their children out of these schools. In the earlier years of the study, from 2011, I found that one-third of potential applicants were denied enrolment into the schools-of-choice (Beakin, Hampton, Matheson) on the basis of their residential address; however this sharply increased towards the latter stages of the study. An estimated two-thirds of potential applicants are annually denied entry into Matheson Secondary, and an estimated half of potential applicants are denied enrolment to Hampton and Beakin on the basis of their residential address. Even if parents had younger children in these schools, accessed many years earlier before a surge of popularity, this wasn't enough to acquire enrolment for the siblings, if they resided outside of the catchment area. Like private schools in Melbourne, Hampton College requires enrolment applicants to pay a non-refundable application fee of $270, regardless of whether their enrolment is accepted or not.

Rather than relocate for these schools, or simply attend a school without an enforced catchment area, the campaigners are committed to pressuring the state government for a brand-new government-funded high school. There are

46 Campaigning for choice

Figure 3.4 'New School for Lawson' is located in the neighbourhood of Lawson. This map shows the proximity of surrounding high schools.

clear tensions surrounding the campaigners' inability to choose the surrounding schools, considering the relative proximity (see Figure 3.1). The campaigners are well aware of these tensions, and maintain an emphasis on proximity, parental involvement and community schooling.

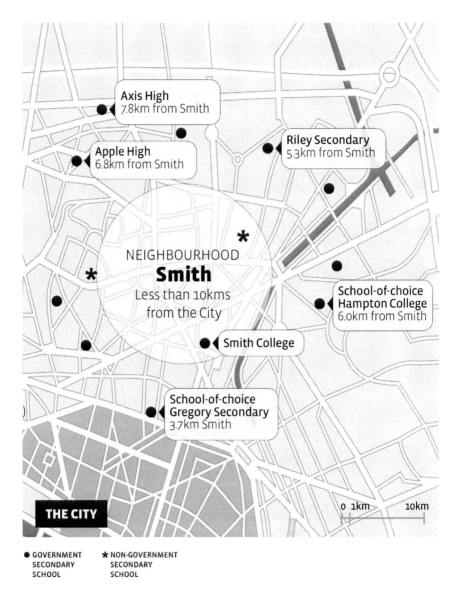

Figure 3.5 The Smith High Campaign is located in the neighbourhood of Smith. This map shows the proximity of surrounding high schools.

Political and professional alliances

Emerging in 2003 by a number of local families and currently ongoing, the 'New School for Lawson' campaign is relatively active within the public landscape in Melbourne, Victoria. With 1,200 members reportedly, this group holds bi-monthly meetings that are open to the public and annual protest events, such as 'walk to no school day', a walking protest through the neighbourhood that routinely involves their children. This protest is annually replicated in the Smith campaign also. The following image is an adaptation of a photograph from a 'New School for Lawson' campaign event (see Figure 3.6).

Figure 3.6 'We want a local high school', New School for Lawson event (2012). This image is an adaptation of the original photograph.

Local politicians bidding for re-election in the seats of Lawson or Smith routinely utilize the campaigns for political leverage, publically declaring their allegiance and commitment to the campaign goals. For example, at a meeting for the Smith High Campaign, a politician representing the 'Socialist Alliance' party declared to the press, 'There is no need for further investigation and more taskforces . . . Smith High Campaign has established the facts, we now just need to build the school' (Topsfield, 2010). Whilst the left side of politics is predominantly represented, the campaigns themselves firmly (and regularly) assert their bipartisanship status, refusing to attach to a political party or affiliation – and this is part of their official charter available on their website.

The decision to denounce a political alliance offers the campaigns adaptable leverage with both sides of politics, and there are numerous discussions regarding political strategies. 'New School for Lawson' regularly discusses strategies for increasing the strength and volume of their political reach and weight, how to attract more support, and generate pressure on political representatives to lobby for their campaign. Campaigner Steven expresses that he is confident they can do so by utilizing their numerous contacts. Many members of the campaign retain contacts or are employed within high-level professional and managerial positions, citing the power to utilize this power network if necessary.

Despite their commitment to bipartisanship and independence, there are glaring similarities across the campaigns, such as their mutual celebration of community and community schooling, with the inner-city described here as a 'village' (see Figure 3.7).

The Smith High Campaign has a full-time spokesperson and a reported 1,500 members, and like the Lawson campaigners, the majority of activists in the neighbourhood of Smith own their home, are university educated and predominantly white. They are adept with social media and maintain an active online profile, advertising all of their public meetings and events through Twitter, Facebook and their own website, and utilizing their online profile to generate and distribute research. For example, the Smith group used Facebook to generate a thirty-six-page survey that included 267 responses to four questions (Smith High Campaign, 2013). The report was compiled by their spokesperson (a time-consuming task) and distributed via social media. 'How would you like the new school to be?', the first question asked. The most popular responses centred on the notion of community, 'community-oriented and community focused', and that it needs to be a 'good public high school', academically rigorous, with a smart uniform. Respondents asked for a worm farm, an environmentally conscious building, solar panels and bike sheds. Their environmental awareness – coupled with their political activism – is indicated in the following image, photographed in the neighbourhood of Smith in 2012 (see Figure 3.8). The fence borders an empty, discarded block of land where the demolished Smith High used to be located. The spray-painted fence reads, 'High school not high rise' (ballot box ticked) (see Figure 3.8).

In similarity, 'New School for Lawson' is active in generating independent reports and surveys which they provide for various stakeholders. 'New School for Lawson' participant Mark, who holds a PhD in political science and considers himself

50 Campaigning for choice

proficient with technology, tells me during his interview that he designed the campaign website and spends time every week maintaining it. Mark has been involved in the campaign for seven years, and discusses the first meeting he attended:

Mark: I knew there was political influence in the committee.
E: A political clout?
Mark: I knew that it was political. So, I figured it was worthwhile, I guess that's what I'm getting to . . . I knew that it wasn't just a bunch of rabble. You know. It actually had structure, and it had some political influence. The first meeting I attended . . . a federal politician [Nicola Roxon] was there . . . a federal member!

Figure 3.7 'This village needs a high school', Smith High Campaign event (2012). This image is an adaptation of the original photograph.

Campaigning for choice 51

Figure 3.8 'High School, Not High Rise' (Ballot Box ticked). Photograph by Elisabeth Devereux, in the neighbourhood of Smith (2012).

Indeed, during my time as participant observer within 'New School for Lawson', I observe a well-organized and structured collective with political reach and influence. The local political representatives regularly attend general meetings, particularly before the elections. The first time I attend a meeting, they are voting in the official working party, including a president and treasurer. The mayor arrived in his suit, introduced himself to the group, and proceeded to formally run proceedings. The campaigns elicit attention from bureaucratic agencies, such as the Department of Education, and during my research with 'New School for Lawson', the official working party was meeting monthly with representatives from the Department. These meetings are also routinely advertised by the Smith group. Independent research companies are annually commissioned by the state government in order to carry out feasibility studies to determine whether there are sufficient anticipated enrolment numbers in the new school.

The campaigns develop mutual interest relationships with local private enterprises to raise funds, suggesting quite savvy, well-organized and professional networking strategies. During one meeting, 'New School for Lawson' discusses how they should use a $1,000 donation from a local bank. The Smith group raised $28,000 in one year alone, receiving donations from a real estate agent ($2,000) and a pharmacist ($2,500). They originally received $10,000 from a property development group, but this grant was retracted and the business named as 'no longer a partner' on their website. Both groups raise funds through community appeals and sell merchandise at their campaigning events.

52 Campaigning for choice

Drawing on these campaigns in relation to middle-class school choice and publishing this data has proved to be highly contentious over the years. Some may see it as an attack on the campaigns, or an overall attack on public education. My research has been positioned in a range of different ways by the media, but also conservative think tanks. One well-known Australian academic advised me to remove the pseudonyms for each campaign, otherwise my study would have little purpose or meaning. Meanwhile, another US-based academic argued that the level of anonymity afforded to the campaigns needed to be significantly extended, to protect the 'vulnerable' campaigners. Evidently, there are many different ways to interpret or read this data and diverse methods of framing the campaigns and participants: as public education activists and social justice campaigners, as middle-class school choosers. Ultimately though, it is not my purpose to ascertain whether the neighbourhoods require a new school or not, and rather, I draw on the campaigns as a sociological lens to examine the economy of urban school choice in a globalized marketplace, and to rethink middle-class school choices. These parental networks and actions – highly sophisticated and highly organized – provoke an historical and critical contract-shift in signaling the reorientation of consumer-citizen relations, and the demand to reassess conventional understandings of public schooling and public provision (Hankins, 2007).

Participant observation: Mapping the role of researcher-participant

Field-notes from the 'New School for Lawson' General Meeting, October 8, 2012:

I sit in a circle of chairs at a 'New School for Lawson' general meeting, led by Karen, the working party member. She hands around a document clearly marked 'Confidential'. It is the official report from a feasibility study, conducted by an independent research company but commissioned by the state government.

('New School for Lawson' received a negative response. The report concluded that the proposed high school would attract insufficient enrolment numbers. The campaigners refute the methodology that was utilized in the study, arguing that a higher proportion of residents in their neighbourhood choose public schools, in comparison to the State median percentage that was utilized in the study).

There are multiple copies of the report, and Karen encourages everyone to take a copy. I reach out to take a copy. Karen shifts in her seat uncomfortably. I say to her, 'Do you mind if I take a look?'

She pauses. 'Well you can have a look (*nervous laugh*) . . . I do trust you Emma . . . but probably best not to take a copy'.

The above extract, recorded one year into observation, seeks to demonstrate the frequently troublesome relationship I experienced as participant observer within the 'New School for Lawson' campaign, from September 2011 to March 2013.

This reflects work by Vaughan (2004), in which she describes a 'fragile' and complicated role of participant observer, within an alternative school facing forced closure by the Department of Education. What she describes is an uncomfortable and disquieting experience in which she struggles with conflicting pressures, demands and inner ethical conflicts pertaining to the agenda or purpose of her research. The fundamental conflict that is evoked by Vaughan's study is: what is the purpose of my research? Vaughan's perception of purpose is very different to her participants and she says that 'the imperative for me to produce a victory narrative about [the school] was quite strong' (393).

Like Vaughan, I felt pressure to produce a victory narrative about the campaign, or at least help the campaigners to achieve victory. I first made contact with the Smith High campaign by attending a public meeting (held in their local library), but they were hesitant in allowing me formal access to their meetings as a participant observer. The campaigners believed my involvement might detract from their primary goal. With this uncertainty on my mind, I attended another public meeting, this time held by 'New School for Lawson' at their local pub. The meetings were advertised on their websites, open for all interested persons to attend. On this night, 'New School for Lawson' were voting in the official working party, and I nominated myself for a non-descript (lowest-tier) role within the working party. The role wasn't prized by the other attendees and my nomination was easily accepted. During the meeting, the newly elected president (Harry) asked everyone to sign up or renew their campaign membership and contribute their annual membership fees, and possibly make an optional donation. The newly elected treasurer (Matthew) gave out a tax invoice for the donation. They looked over at me, the new person, the lowest-tiered working party stranger. I felt inclined to hand over my twenty dollars.

Eventually, after a lengthy negotiation process,[8] I was graciously granted consent to record field-notes at all 'New School for Lawson' events, in addition to pursuing one-on-one interviews with the campaigners. However, I was asked to formally resign in writing from my working party post, with members believing it would complicate matters.

Collective actions

I refer to the parental groups as types of collective action, which 'broadly refers to actions undertaken by individuals or groups for a collective purpose, such as the advancement of a particular ideology . . . or the political struggle with another group' (Brunsting and Postmes, 2002: 527). My purpose for selecting the term, collective action, is twofold: to describe the differences between '*soft* and *hard* actions' (Brunsting and Postmes, 2002: 527) and to thematically include an emphasis on individual motivation and individual action.

I utilize the notion of *collective action* in this study as theoretically distinct from social movements, as discussed in the previous chapter, and to describe a *soft* action – not to imply superiority of one to the other but rather to describe differences in 'nature and intensity' (Brunsting and Postmes, 2002: 527). A collective action is an interconnected act which consists of multiple individuals to achieve a 'collective good' (Jordan, 1996: 164). In this case, the 'collective good' is subjective in that it is debatable whether the local public high school will be beneficial for the collective good, or just a select group. Thus, the term 'collective action' refers to:

> More individualistically perpetrated acts as *collective*. For example, sabotage, civil disobedience, and letter writing can all be thought of as collective in nature in the sense that they serve a collective purpose in the struggle between different groups and, hence, can be intended and used as means of achieving a collective outcome. Thus, what distinguishes collective action from individual action in this broad definition is that a collective action is, essentially, an intergroup act.
> (Brunsting and Postmes, 2002: 527, emphasis in original)

The campaigns in this study demonstrate forms of individual action conducted as an intergroup act in order to obtain a collective interest that is beneficial for the individual and the collective. It is debatable whether this interest is beneficial for broader citizenship interests. In order to obtain this collective interest, members individually sign petitions, write letters to members of parliament and the State Minister of Education, meet as a collective and with officials from the Department of Education. Campaigners explicitly state their political bipartisanship and neutrality, and their aim to avoid conflict with external stakeholders or controversy (Field-notes – August 26, 2012; Field-notes – May 7, 2012). At a 'New School for Lawson' event, I posed the question at a public meeting: 'Would you resort to any of the Occupy tactics? Like setting up a protest tent outside the Department of Education, or something like that, to get attention?'

> Karen replied, 'No, no we wouldn't use those . . . do those types of things. We want good, working, strong relationships with the Department'.
> 'Yeah, we don't want to piss them off', Steven said.

This is a *soft* action, as it looks to avoid severe hardship or conflict, even though it is long-term, hard-working and committed. I also refer to the individuals engaging in collective action as campaigners. In alignment with collective action, a campaign consists of more than one individual lobbying in a deliberate and purposeful manner to acquire a certain product, service or object.

Indeed, there are divergences between various protest actions, parental-led activism, grassroots movements and social movements. However, there are also parallels. Whether it be via occupation of schools or mass protests, hunger strikes, 'walk to no school day' or writing letters to politicians and signing petitions, at the heart may be a sense of dissatisfaction with educational equity, accessibility and provision. Certainly, conceptualizations of equity and accessibility (and how equity translates in practice), depending on the level of resources and capital that an individual has, may wildly differ. Typecasting the protests as necessarily vulnerable and requiring advocacy, via the 'victory narrative', may avert the more complex and interesting contradictions and convergences. Applebaum's (2003) work is relevant here, in that we need to critique matters of power when evaluating freedom of speech and social participation. Freedom of 'expression is democratic only on the grounds of an equal playing field' (160). Thus, a collective action may operate as dialectic: it can represent a struggle for freedom of expression and democracy, one that is engaged in matters of social justice; however, it may simultaneously perpetuate the marginalization of weaker voices.

Movements inside, in between and outside

Research indicates that it is 'increasingly difficult' to obtain ethical clearance for participant observation. Despite the contentious and contested nature of participant observation, it arguably 'yields more information' in comparison to only conducting interviews (Tope et al., 2005: 471). However, if participant observation is the sole method of data collection, a researcher is unlikely to 'report the negative aspects of their subjects' personalities and lives' (DeWalt and DeWalt, 2010: 95).

There is a third space beyond the binary contentions, between the biased and the unbiased, the ethical and unethical. As participant observers, we move in between the covert and the overt, at times shifting between the two. This is well demonstrated by Li (2008) in her covert-to-overt study of female gamblers, and Calvey (2008) in covertly exploring the hidden world of bouncers. The highly contentious – yet also acclaimed – ethnographic studies by Carolyn Ellis (1984, 1995) and James Patrick (1973) stand out. Ellis secretly observed and recorded people during the time she lived in an isolated fishing village, and her research was only 'outed' to the 'participants' after she had widely published and her publications were read aloud to the villagers (as most were illiterate). There is a sense of contempt that Ellis shows towards her 'participants' in secretly writing about them, and in her later work when she 'returns to the field' (1995), she writes about her feelings of shame, guilt and sense of loss – but continues to critique and record the 'participants' without their permission.

The process of note-taking during observation highlights the physicality of insider/outsider politics. I attended all public meetings, armed with a notepad and pen. During their conversations, I was very conscious of my 'note-taking' activities that physically accentuated a differing objective to those of the campaigners. At many times, particularly during conversations that were potentially contentious, controversial or secretive, I withheld note-taking and notes were recorded subsequently (Emerson et al., 2001). To explore this slippage, I draw on the following extract from my field-notes, recorded six months into observation:

> Field-notes from 'New School for Lawson' campaign event (February 11, 2012):
>
> > I arrive at the Lawson Community Festival, an annual day of celebration in the suburb of Lawson. I'm on the roster to help out with the 'New School for Lawson' stall. I volunteered at the general meeting last Wednesday.

They seemed hesitant to write my name down, but since I asked twice, I think they wanted to avoid an uncomfortable situation.

So here I am, armed with my pen and notebook, half campaigner, half researcher. I approach the stall – which is wearing a loud banner, 'New School for Lawson' – and signs are posted around their stall reading, 'We want a local school'. The campaigners have printed out several large maps, to highlight the lack of a public high school in their local neighbourhood.

Several of the campaigners seem wary of me, as I pull out my pen. The mayor (who is running for re-election) arrives at the stall and shakes my hand, introducing himself by his first and last name. I don't yet have informed consent to observe or record the mayor's comments.

I ask the mayor about his involvement with the campaign. He says, 'This is the longest running pressure group that comes to my mind . . . we've been running for eight years now . . . our first meeting was in . . . our first meeting was in 2006'.

I ask, 'And why did the pressure group get started?'

Robert says, 'I got it started because the issue was there . . . When I did my door-knocking [as mayor] that's what everyone was telling me, that's what the issue was you know – they all wanted a local high school'. A couple arrives at the stall and the mayor leaves to speak with them. He introduces himself, using his full name.

Apart from Robert's assertion that he started the group in 2006, a view that conflicts with his fellow campaigners, the extract also alludes to several ethical dilemmas that I experienced as a participant observer. Fine (1993) writes that these so-called 'dilemmas' that we experience as ethnographers should more so be understood as 'lies' and the conceals that we hide behind. I obtained the mayor's informed consent *following* this conversation and therefore, my observation operated covertly, at the time. Field-notes were not taken on the spot, and error is more likely when dialogue is recorded several hours following the incident (Emerson et al., 2001). The campaigners were running a stall to promote their cause and I attended, primarily for my own purposes to record field-notes and talk with campaigners. Nor did I have informed consent to observe the constant flow of people passing by the stall, and whilst most enthusiastically supported the petition and initiated lengthy conversations with Matthew and Robert, others were outspoken, hostile and critical. When I asked Matthew about this, he shrugged and said, 'It happens. Some people feel . . . threatened'.

Tope et al. (2005) write that 'participation is also invaluable for achieving "insider status" as someone who is trustworthy' (473). The issue of whether I was trustworthy – with a focus squarely on whether I was 'for' or 'against' the campaign – were arguably strongly related to the affronts 'New School for Lawson' received from residents living in neighbouring locales. There was a distinct impression of stark juxtapositions, in terms of whether you were an *ally* of 'New School for Lawson', or whether you were *against* the campaign. To augment this point, I refer to online responses to a local newspaper report. The online forum was open for any individuals to make a statement, about 'New School for Lawson':

> I am a non-Lawson person writing to the Lawson campaigners: I hope [your reasons for a school in Lawson] do not include socio-economic measures. That would make you a rather ugly elitist of a certain variety given the demographics. If you feel that way, shell out for private schooling & leave local government schools to we unbigotted [sic] people. We wouldn't want your sort at our egalitarian schools.
>
> Mahony writes: There are some 'pinch points' for public school provision in the wider Lawson region – but Lawson is not one of them. [But] Let's not let the facts get in the way of a good fear campaign from people who just want a culturaly [sic] and socio-economicaly [sic] insular education for their children.
>
> (Twining, 2012)

Very early on, I was aware of these critiques towards their campaigns. The critiques, though, could be described as subdued – they did not seem to occupy central stage. They were made in the online 'comments' section (does anyone really read these?), or off-hand comments by people walking past the stall, or by a solo attendee at a campaign meeting. Perhaps understandably, some of the campaigners were wary of my involvement – not rushing to write my name down for the stall, self-censoring and halting their conversation. Even though I made every attempt to be friendly, genuine and trustworthy, I frequently observed campaigners self-censoring themselves in my presence. Participants are not naïve to the critical nature of research, but rather savvy in the way they are reading the interaction.

Whiteness

It was approximately six months into my observation that I realized we were all white. I felt embarrassed by my ignorance, or possibly, the ease in which I shared in the construction of tacit privilege (Rivière, 2008). It was all too comfortable. My membership in the lobby group came almost effortlessly: white, university-educated, an 'inner-city type' with young children. I ticked all the boxes. Gillan and Pickerill (2012) argue that the participant observer selects 'social movements' that are aligned with their political left-leanings and thus, the process of complex reciprocation is comfortable and compatible with the scholar's self-identity (136). The 'ugly movement' tends to be avoided, such as pro-life campaigns or those associated with fundamentalist religion (136). An interruption to my own comfort increased my sense of discomfort and, over time, transpired into quite a heavy feeling of tension. In part, reasons for my discomfort are the bonds of friendship that I formed with the campaigners. They welcomed me to meetings;

they agreed to interviews during their own time and in their own spaces; I met their children and their partners, and at times, I was exposed to personal information about private lives. I was invited to social gatherings, outside of 'official' campaign meetings (for example, a 'Eurovision night' at Steven's house, complete with costumes and projector – I did not attend). Campaigners inquired into my personal life, and I inquired into theirs. These are the shades of ethical complexities that participant observation – and the process of reflexivity – produces (Pillow, 2003; Kenway and McLeod, 2004). Participant observation imposes a personal, bodied intrusion onto both the researcher and the researched. Vaughan (2004) describes it: 'that dominion or field of play took a thoroughly embodied form in me – a heavy feeling in my stomach, a sense of unrelenting boredom, and physical discomfort throughout the day' (397).

Drawing on Hage (2012), I employ the notion of 'whiteness' as opposed to 'white people' or 'Anglo-Saxon' throughout this text. Whiteness is an 'important field of investigation' in the US, yet it 'remains highly under-developed in Australia' (Hage, 2012: 20). I need to be clear as to what I am referring to as 'whiteness' and I develop this further in the following chapter. I take up the notion of 'whiteness' as a theoretical lens, more than a prescriptive application of race or ethnicity. A 'central characteristic of whiteness is a process of "naturalization" such that white becomes the norm from which other "races" stand apart and in relation to which they are defined' (Gillborn, 2005: 489). Like many white-colonized countries, Australia maintains an in-depth history of white nationalism and the 'fantasy of white supremacy' (Hage, 2012), evident by the celebration of British colonization, etched onto our national flag, and conversely, the violent displacement and murder of Indigenous people, anti-immigration policies and the 'Yellow Peril', and contemporary 'dialogue' surrounding long-term imprisonment of asylum seekers in offshore detention centers. Discourses of whiteness and modes of 'new racism' routinely impose restrictions and conditions of entry upon those not privileged to 'whiteness', under the guise of nationalism (Romm, 2010). The cultural landscape of Australia is fraught with contemporary identity politics surrounding race – conjuring territorialized imaginations and fantasies of Australia as inherently white – rather than international in scope, with a constant flow of international migrants, forced onto the country's first people, and predominantly coming from Britain, India, Asia, Europe and New Zealand. In Australia, and according to the most recent available Census statistics, 69.8% of people were born in Australia, followed by England (4.2%) and New Zealand (2.2%).

How is class measured?

The ten interview participants from the 'New School for Lawson' campaign lend themselves to Reay et al.'s (2013) 'new middle-class' in that the majority are relatively affluent and upper-median income earners, but do not represent the most elite networks or 'old money'. The interview participants are inner-city home-owners who are paying a mortgage rather than a lease. The only exception is interview participant Michelle, a self-described 'single mother' of two school-aged children, and she is renting (or leasing) her home in neighbourhood Lawson. The majority of interview participants are university-educated, except for Steven and Adam, and all participants are employed in 'white-collar' or 'pink-collar' professions, upper managerial or professional positions. Five of the interview participants have postgraduate qualifications, one with a doctorate (see Appendix, Table A.2).

There were more male interview participants (60%) than female (40%), and this reflected the overall campaign. This would suggest that male parents are highly engaged in choice work, and possibly more active in comparison to female parents, which conflicts with how previous studies have positioned the 'mother' in choice work (Reay, 1998, 2005). This study did not set out to inquire into gender-based differences in choice work and I have not sought to make this a key contribution. As based on this small sample, the data more so points to the notion that female and male parents are highly involved and active in choice work, but male parents are particularly representative in institutional settings. By institutional, I am referring to the campaigns and their institutional relationships with the Department of Education, businesses and nongovernment stakeholders. In these settings, the male participants are highly represented and active. The female parents are engaged in choice work, but they are not as visible at the collective meetings, as many were looking after children at home.

All of the participants are Australian-born and speak English as their first language. Adam is the only interview participant whose parents were born in another country, and speaks another language in addition to English at home. All of the interview participants have children, with many pre-school or in the early years of primary school. The majority of interview participants are newcomers to the neighbourhood of Lawson, having purchased a home with their young family in the past few years. The neighbourhood has many bike paths, a train station and public buses that frequently run through it, and it is only two stops from the city via the train. It is accurate to describe the neighbourhood as *connectedly* cosmopolitan, although the neighbourhood itself has a higher proportion of Australian-born residents, in comparison to the state median (see Appendix, Table A.4).

Throughout the interviews, participants introduced the concept of class and identified as 'middle-class', even though I did not introduce or utilize language around 'class' (see Rowe, 2015). Certainly, Savage et al.'s (2001) concepts of 'ordinary, ambivalent and defensive' class identities were evident. This attachment to the ordinary middle class, fastened around the 'neighbourhood' is highlighted by Cucchiara's (2013) study of urban gentrification and school choice in the US, with affluent, upper-middle families tending to refer themselves as simply middle-class. From Australia, a large-scale survey found that 92% of Australians consider themselves as either working or middle-class (Sheppard and Biddle, 2015).

In our small-scale study of school choice, we found that upper-income earners still positioned themselves within this rather broad 'middle' category (Rowe and Windle, 2012). This is significant as a broad category of 'middle class' can undercut important stratification differences, in terms of the amount of capital that an individual can utilize in appropriating advantage. As I have written previously,

> Class as a concept is equally disowned and embraced by its very performers. There is a mutual distaste of class operating simultaneously with the utilization of class power. This is a struggle of identity, but so too it becomes a struggle of methodology; individuals question how class is measured or validated (Savage et al., 2001). Indeed, for many 'class is an embarrassing and unsettling subject' (Sayer, 2005: 1).
>
> (Rowe, 2015: 7)

Whilst the majority of participants self-identified with the 'ordinary' middle, and felt that the collective or the 'community' as a whole were middle-class with 'similar values', only two participants self-identified with the working-class or blue-collar. These two interview participants, Steven and Adam, are also the only two participants without university education. The possession of higher or college education is used as a marker of class, to draw distinctions between the working and middle (Pusey, 2003).

Indeed, interview participants tended to talk about class when they were discussing the neighbourhood, or the community. The increasingly spatially orientated configuration of class, and how this relates to urban school choice, is a theme that I will follow through in subsequent chapters, a theme which is evident in both theory and method, with the incorporation of more spatial data sets, such as detailed maps. The maps endeavour to *visually* portray class as the hierarchal 'drawing of boundaries' (Ball, 2003: 158) and production of value within these boundaries. In presenting the neighbourhood in this way, it aims to be representational or metaphorical, in outlining the importance of space within school choice movements. This space is underpinned by class histories, race and religion, contemporary political leanings and income classifications. Educational research requires a rethinking of class along spatial lines, in order to recognize the significance of residential location in contemporary measures of class and urban school choice.

In this study, I take up class along constructivist, interpretivist and descriptive lines. I gesture towards traditional class theory, incorporating economic relations (occupation and means of production, house ownership and locality), and endeavour to link this to more subjective analyses around 'cultural communities and groupness' (behaviour and collective political action) (see Pakulski and Waters, 1996: 11). Although we may have shifted and evolved from Marx and Engel's historical conceptualization of class, there continue to be remnants of their scholarship, and perhaps it more so resembles a *class bricolage*, a taking and borrowing from a wide range of influential class theorists.

Conclusion

In speaking to these collective actions, each based in the inner-city of Melbourne, Australia, a reader may wonder about the overall importance of these campaigns and why they matter for broader educational reform and policy. Australia's private school sector is larger than many other OECD neighbours, including England and Wales, New Zealand, the US and Sweden, with a large proportion of students who attend private schooling and a well-funded, largely unregulated private sector (Whitty et al., 1998). As such, a focus on the micro-politics of school choice within this geographical landscape offers cogent input for contemporary matters surrounding the provision of schooling. I argue that these collective actions can make strong contributions for education policy and reform agendas in cross-national contexts.

In this study, the contemporary urban middle class is idiosyncratic of the socially aware, socially mobile chooser, squeezed and pressured by economic gaps and disparities, whilst at the same time, exerting their own pressure in the social, cultural and policy landscape. I describe the school choosers as both reactors and actors, asking whether they are informing and inscribing policy, or simply reacting to policy. In the following chapter, I take up the notion of *glocalization* in order to explore global education reform in context – the local education market.

Notes

1 Readers may question why certain schools are not named on this map. The unnamed schools reflect the invisibility of these schools as viable choices for the participants, and within the data sets, in this study. The unnamed schools were never discussed within the data. It is necessary to note that 'All Girls' High School' is the closest school to neighbourhood Lawson, but it does not appear in the analysis as it educates single-sex only and practices select-entry enrolment processes. This chapter has provided very brief information regarding methodology and data sets. For a more comprehensive explanation (e.g., how were distances calculated) see Appendix.
2 This figure was sourced from Australian Bureau of Statistics (raw figure of the total number of government secondary schools, 1992 through to 1999). Australian Bureau of Statistics indicate that a total of ninety public high schools in the state of Victoria were closed. Reports often cite a figure of 300 to 351 schools, but this figure also includes schools that were merged and is inaccurate.
3 Brian Caldwell is a global policy actor, playing a role in many self-managing school reforms in Australia and New Zealand, but he has also been involved with OECD, UNESCO, UNICEF and World Bank (see Caldwell, 1996, 1998).
4 These protests and protest actions were widely reported in the state newspapers. These archives are available online: (Pegler and Easterbrook, 1992; Lewis, 1993; Muller, 1993; Muller and Mangan, 1993; Munro, 1993; Painter and Magazanik, 1993; Painter, 1993b; Pegler et al., 1993; Jolly, 1996; Muller, 1993; Muller and Mangan, 1993; Farouque et al., 1994; Conroy, 1996; Jolly, 1996; Forbes, 2000; Pegler et al., 1993; Pegler and Easterbrook, 1992; Lewis, 1993; Munro, 1993; Conroy, 1996). Also, see Stephen Jolly's (1996) *Behind the Lines* regarding the protest of Richmond High.

5 These figures were collected from the Australia Bureau of Statistics, from the most current statistics available at time of writing. The data was collected for each state and territory (full-time secondary students only) and converted to percentages by the author.
6 These figures were obtained from an economic profile of the Lawson neighbourhood (Lawson City Council, 2008, 2012). These figures were published previously in my own work (see Rowe, 2014).
7 The schools-of-choice have been coded as 'popular, rejected and balanced' choices within the data sets (Seppánen, 2003). The coding has been explained in further depth, see Appendix.
8 After the first meeting with 'New School for Lawson', I approached the newly elected president (Harry) to discuss the possibility of entering his campaign as a 'participant observer' and a lengthy negotiation process ensued after that discussion. I was eventually requested to attend a meeting with the working party, one-on-one, or more precisely, myself and the six members of the working party. Over the course of the meeting, I was asked several questions from each of the members, similar to a round table or interview, and the members pressed the importance of secrecy (see Mitchell, 1993).

Despite the shared goals and parallel strategies, the campaigns operated independently until 2014, the year in which they formed an alliance. This alliance was announced via mainstream media, in the form of radio interviews, a new website and press releases. The alliance currently maintains eighteen parental groups, with the same goal (to obtain a brand-new public high school in their immediate neighbourhood). At the time I met with 'New School for Lawson' though, and also my brief discussions with Smith, it was conveyed that confidentiality and discretion was paramount; it was vital that campaign strategies and tactics were not shared with neighbouring, competing campaigns. The reader may be concerned in regards to confidentiality, particularly when it comes to these publications. I repeatedly disclosed and communicated to the campaigners my intention to publish the data from the campaigns. During participant observation, I communicated to the participants that I was submitting to a journal for potential publication, and again asked for permission. The campaigners granted me permission to publish, provided that participants are anonymous (although, not all participants wanted to be anonymous).

References

Applebaum B. (2003) Social justice, democratic education and the silencing of words that wound. *Journal of Moral Education* 32: 151–162.
Ball SJ. (2003) *Class Strategies and the Education Market: The Middle Classes and Social Advantage*, London: RoutledgeFalmer.
Brunsting S and Postmes T. (2002) Social movement participation in the digital age: Predicting offline and online collective action. *Small Group Research* 33: 525–554.
Buras KL, Ferrare JJ and Apple MW. (2013) Grassroots educational organizing in an era of venture capital. *Critical Studies in Education* 54: 1–4.
Caldwell B. (1996) *Beyond the Self Managing School: Adding Value in Schools of the Third Millennium*, Jolimont, Vic.: Incorporated Association of Registered Teachers of Victoria.
Caldwell B. (1998) *Beyond the Self-Managing School*, London: FalmerPress.
Caldwell B and Hayward DK. (1998) *The Future of Schools: Lessons from the Reform of Public Education*, London: Falmer Press.

Calvey D. (2008) The art and politics of covert research: Doing 'situated ethics' in the field. *Sociology* 42: 905–918.
Conroy P. (1996) Baton charge police praised. *The Age*. Melbourne: Fairfax Digital.
Crooks ML. (1996) 'To market, to market': The radical right experiment with Victoria's state education system. In: Webber M and Crooks ML (eds) *Putting the People Last: Government, Services and Rights in Victoria*, South Melbourne: Hyland House Publishing Pty Ltd, 170–205.
Cucchiara MB. (2013) *Marketing Schools, Marketing Cities: Who Wins and Who Loses When Schools Become Urban Amenities*, Chicago: University of Chicago Press.
Davidoff IAN and Leigh A. (2008) How much do public schools really cost? Estimating the relationship between house prices and school quality. *Economic Record* 84: 193–206.
Deegan M. (2001) The Chicago school of ethnography. In: Atkinson P, Coffey A, Delamont S, Delamont, S, Lofland, J., Lofland, L. (eds) *Handbook of Ethnography*, London: Sage, 11–26.
DeWalt KM and DeWalt BR. (2010) *Participant Observation: A Guide for Fieldworkers*, Plymouth, United Kingdom: AltaMira Press.
Dougherty J, Harrelson J, Maloney L, et al. (2009) School choice in Suburbia: Test scores, race, and housing markets. *American Journal of Education* 115: 523–548.
Ellis C. (1984) Community organization and family structure in two fishing communities. *Journal of Marriage & Family* 46: 515–526.
Ellis C. (1995) Emotional and ethical quagmires in returning to the field. *Journal of Contemporary Ethnography* 24: 68–98.
Emerson R, Fretz R and Shaw L. (2001) Participant observation and fieldnotes. In: Atkinson P, Coffey A, Delamont S, et al. (eds) *Handbook of Ethnography*, London: Sage, 352–369.
Fack G and Grenet J. (2010) When do better schools raise housing prices? Evidence from Paris public and private schools. *Journal of Public Economics* 94: 59–77.
Farouque F, Painter J and Dunlevy L. (1994) *Locked-Out Northland Students to Try Again*. Available at: http://newsstore.fairfax.com.au/apps/viewDocument.ac?page=1&sy=age&kw=richmond+secondary+school&pb=all_ffx&dt=enterRange&dr=1month&sd=1992&ed=1994&so=relevance&sf=text&sf=headline&rc=10&rm=200&sp=adv&clsPage=1&docID=news940126_0165_3474.
Fine GA. (1993) Ten lies of ethnography: Moral dilemmas of field research. *Journal of Contemporary Ethnography* 22: 267–294.
Forbes M. (2000) Richmond protestors to receive $300,000. *The Age*. Melbourne: Fairfax Digital.
Gillan K and Pickerill J. (2012) The difficult and hopeful ethics of research on, and with, social movements. *Social Movement Studies* 11: 133–143.
Gillborn D. (2005) Education policy as an act of white supremacy: Whiteness, critical race theory and education reform. *Journal of Education Policy* 20: 485–505.
Hage G. (2012) *White Nation: Fantasies of White Supremacy in a Multicultural Society*, Hoboken: Taylor and Francis.
Hankins KB. (2007) The final frontier: Charter schools as new community institutions of gentrification. *Urban Geography* 28: 113–128.
Hannan B. (1996) Lying low: Education under Kennett. In: Webber M and Crooks ML (eds) *Putting The People Last: Government, Services and Rights in Victoria*, South Melbourne: Hyland House, 140–169.

Holme JJ. (2002) Buying homes, buying schools: School choice and the social construction of school quality. *Harvard Educational Review* 72: 177–205.
Jolly S. (1996) *Behind the Lines*, Richmond: Global Books.
Jordan B. (1996) *A Theory of Poverty and Social Exclusion*, Cambridge: Polity Press.
Kenway J and McLeod J. (2004) Bourdieu's reflexive sociology and 'spaces of points of view': Whose reflexivity, which perspective? *British Journal of Sociology of Education* 25: 525–544.
Lawson City Council. (2008) *City of Lawson Community Profile: 2006 and 2001 Enumerated Census Information for Lawson*, Lawson: id.consulting Pty Ltd.
Lawson City Council. (2012) *Economy Profile*.
Lewis J. (1993) *Kennett Defends Baton Charge*. Available at: http://newsstore.fairfax.com.au/apps/viewDocument.ac?page=1&sy=age&kw=richmond+college+and+police&pb=all_ffx&dt=enterRange&dr=1month&sd=1993&ed=1997&so=relevance&sf=text&sf=headline&rc=10&rm=200&sp=adv&clsPage=1&docID=news931215_0056_6264.
Mitchell RG. (1993) *Secrecy and Fieldwork*, Newbury Park, California & London: Sage.
Muller D. (1993) Radical changes ahead for 40% of state schools. *The Age*. Melbourne: Fairfax Digital.
Muller D and Mangan J. (1993) Merger another blow for battlers. *The Age*. Melbourne: Fairfax Digital.
Munro I. (1993) Baton complaints force inquiry. *The Sunday Age*. Melbourne: Fairfax Digital.
Painter J. (1993a) Cuts could continue, education protesters told. *The Age*. Melbourne: Fairfax Digital.
Painter J. (1993b) Schools lay down their arms. *The Age*. Melbourne: Fairfax Digital.
Painter J and Magazanik M. (1993) Teacher protest strike. *The Age*. Melbourne: Fairfax Digital.
Pakulski J and Waters M. (1996) *The Death of Class*, London, California & New Delhi: Sage.
Parliament of Victoria. (1998) *Education (Self-Governing Schools) Act 1998*, Melbourne, Victoria: Parliament of Victoria.
Patrick J. (1973) *A Glasgow Gang Observed*, London: Eyre Methuen.
Pegler T, Dunlevy L and Johnston N. (1993) Police warn picketers after clash. *The Age*. Melbourne: Fairfax Digital.
Pegler T and Easterbrook M. (1992) Reprieve for two schools faced with closure. *The Age*. Melbourne: Fairfax Digital.
Pillow W. (2003) Confession, catharsis, or cure? Rethinking the uses of reflexivity as methodological power in qualitative research. *International Journal of Qualitative Studies in Education* 16: 175–196.
Pusey M. (2003) *The Experience of Middle Australia: The Dark Side of Economic Reform*, Cambridge: Cambridge University Press.
Reay D. (1998) Engendering social reproduction: Mothers in the educational marketplace. *British Journal of Sociology of Education* 19: 195–209.
Reay D. (2005) Mothers' involvement in their children's schooling: Social reproduction in action? In: Crozier G and Reay D (eds) *Activating Participation*, Stoke-on-Trent: Trentham Books, 23–38.
Reay D, Crozier G and James D. (2013) *White Middle-Class Identities and Urban Schooling*, London: Palgrave Macmillan.

Rivière D. (2008) Whiteness in/and education. *Race Ethnicity and Education* 11: 355–368.
Romm N. (2010) *New Racism: Revisiting Researcher Accountabilities*, The Netherlands: Springer.
Rood D and Tomazin F. (2006) Baillieu backs Kennett school closures. *The Age*. Melbourne: Fairfax Digital.
Rowe E. (2014) The discourse of public education: An urban campaign for a local public high school in Melbourne, Victoria. *Discourse: Studies in the Cultural Politics of Education* 35: 116–128.
Rowe E. (2015) Theorising geo-identity and David Harvey's space: School choices of the geographically bound middle-class. *Critical Studies in Education* 56: 285–300.
Rowe EE and Windle J. (2012) The Australian middle class and education: A small-scale study of the school choice experience as framed by 'My School' within inner city families. *Critical Studies in Education* 53: 137–151.
Savage M, Bagnall G and Longhurst B. (2001) Ordinary, ambivalent and defensive: Class identities in the northwest of England. *Sociology* 35: 875–892.
Sayer A. (2005) *The Moral Significance of Class*, Cambridge: Cambridge University Press.
Seddon T. (1994) Assessing the institutional context of decentralised school management: Schools of the future in Victoria. *Discourse Studies in the Cultural Politics of Education* 15: 1–15.
Seppánen P. (2003) Patterns of 'public-school markets' in the Finnish comprehensive school from a comparative perspective. *Journal of Education Policy* 18: 513–531.
Sheppard J and Biddle N. (2015) *Social Class in Australia: Beyond the 'Working' and 'Middle' Classes*. Available at: http://politicsir.cass.anu.edu.au/sites/politicsir.anu.edu.au/files/ANUPoll-social-class-sept-2015.pdf.
Smith High Campaign. (2013) Towards a new high school in 2015: A survey of parents.
Spaull A. (1999) The end of the state school system? Education and the Kennett government. In: Costar B and Economou N (eds) *The Kennett Revolution: Victorian Politics in the 1990s*, Sydney: University of New South Wales Press Ltd, 214–224.
Tomazin F and Preiss B. (2015) *Education Executives Get Bonuses as School Performance Declines*. Available at: http://www.theage.com.au/victoria/education-executives-get-bonuses-as-school-performance-declines-20151113-gkywjk.html.
Tope D, Chamberlain LJ, Crowley M, et al. (2005) The benefits of being there: Evidence from the literature on work. *Journal of Contemporary Ethnography* 34: 470–493.
Topsfield, J. (2010). The neighbourhood of Smith calling for a new high school. *The Age*. Melbourne: Fairfax Digital.
Topsfield J. (2011) Thompson high. *The Age*. Melbourne: Fairfax Digital.
Twining J. (2012) Have your say: Secondary issues in schools. *The Leader Newspaper*.
Vaughan K. (2004) Total eclipse of the heart? Theoretical and ethical implications of doing post-structural ethnographic research. *Discourse: Studies in the Cultural Politics of Education* 25: 389–403.
Whitty G, Power S and Halpin D. (1998) *Devolution and Choice in Education: The School, the State, and the Market*, Melbourne: Open University Press.
Windle JA. (2015) *Making Sense of School Choice: Politics, Policies, and Practice under Conditions of Cultural Diversity*, New York: Palgrave Macmillan.
Yale M. (2014) *Local Is Best*. The Age. Melbourne: Fairfax Digital.

Chapter 4

Glocalization and evocations of whiteness in the local education market

Scholarship surrounding global education reform tends to be detached from the local context in which these conditions manifest, and in which the consumer engages. To study the global, we need to return to the local: concepts such as 'white flight', homogeneity and heterogeneity, are mutually anchored in the local, as Beck (2002) writes,

> . . . Globalization is about globalization. This isn't true. Globalization is about localization as well. You cannot even think about globalization without referring to specific locations and places. One of the important consequences of the globalization thesis is the recovering of the concept of place . . . Therefore sociology can investigate the global locally.
>
> (23)

As Beck shows in this paper, globalization tends to be understood within a spatial lens, through concepts such as de-territorialization, 'time-space compression' and de-nationalization (27). However, within the educational market place, time-space is compressed and magnified in dual forms; on one hand, proximity of schooling is negotiable and fluid, but on the other, certain spatial distances are impossible to overcome, disproportionately magnified in the context of the urban schooling circuit (Ball et al., 1995). I argue that these spaces are disproportionally magnified via race-based differentiations, and in this chapter I explore how whiteness is carved out in the cosmopolitan urban schooling market. As a concept, whiteness is slippery, tenuous and in-flux and yet is simultaneously valorized in the educational market, 'supported by material practices and institutions' (Leonardo, 2002: 31). I explore the socio-historical narrative of the community, before examining how the neighbourhood is conceptualized within more current social imaginaries. Social imaginaries 'differ from social theory in that they are held by large groups of people and often communicated in stories and anecdotes' (Hursh, 2015: 27).

Thinking glocally

Robertson (1995) initially introduced the concept of glocalization to argue for a radical rethinking of globalization as singularly interested in the universal, or the 'bigger is better' social imaginary. The neighbourhood may merely represent a locality within a larger city environment, and in the global sense, these are miniscule spaces, but this points to the paradox of urban space within the globalization thesis (Beck, 2002). Urban spaces are reduced and magnified in equal measure, in the demand for public resources. They are reduced to the more romanticized sense of space (community and village) and yet they are magnified in the sense that certain surrounding neighbourhoods represent intractable distances. Indeed, this speaks to the meaning and power of segregation on the grounds of income and race, played out via schools and neighbourhoods, feeding into a narrative around how we take up identity.

Adam is the only participating campaigner who grew up in the neighbourhood of Lawson, attending the local Charles High as a teenager. I met him for the first time at a campaign meeting – he is irresistibly loud and tactile, approaching me afterwards, vigorously shaking my hand and regaling me with stories of the campaign. I later contact him via email, asking for an interview, and we meet at his house – just one of them, he tells me – during his lunch break. Throughout the interview, Adam speaks extensively about the neighbourhood, a mix of the past and the present, to explain his involvement with the parental campaign. As he speaks of his childhood, his memories and recollections, of the space itself and also the people who filled that space, his stories portray quite a rich sense of identity:

> Adam: The place [Lawson neighbourhood] has changed from what I remember it, to what it is today . . . it's two different places . . . If I reflect back to my childhood, when I was going to this same school here . . . Lawson primary school right here . . . I reflect back, the park was a . . . *quarry*. The park that you see out there with the green grass, it was *a quarry with car bodies*. Aah, rabbits, horses were free to run, motorbikes were up and down . . . there was no greenery . . . and I remember the bridges that are concrete today, we had a wooden footbridge in the same place, that was about a metre away from where it was originally . . . it was a wooden footbridge that was missing planks so you had to hold onto the sides to get around . . . to get over to the school.

Adam's parents were born in Macedonia and they immigrated to Melbourne before he was born, settling in the neighbourhood of Lawson. Adam continues to live in the neighbourhood, now with his wife and two young school-aged children, and is employed full-time as a business manager. Throughout the interview, Adam routinely shifts between his more provincial identity – in that he has spent his whole life within the neighbourhood – to a more transnational 'ethnoscape' identity. Appadurai (1990) describes an ethnoscape as the 'landscape of persons who constitute the shifting world in which we live: tourists, immigrants, refugees . . .' (297). Adam fluctuates between feeling part of the community, to locating his identity as a 'wog', a label that he received throughout his schooling years, from teachers and students, and at other times, he seems to take on the label almost proudly as a type of 'defensive identity' (Savage et al., 2001).

Adam stands out in many ways, both in his ability to provide a rich, historical backdrop of the neighbourhood, but also in how he speaks about community. Whilst many of the campaigners speak about the 'new' community, in fond, often romantic ways, Adam seems more detached and nostalgic. Despite Adam's long-term residence and childhood roots in the neighbourhood, his description of community is far removed from that of other participants. He says,

> I take my son to oz-kick [football], um . . . if you had a-caught me twenty, twenty-five years ago, I woulda known 95% of the people that went there, now I go there and I'm the only person I recognize (*laughs*) . . . I don't recognize anyone! *There's no one left!*

Adam elucidates the contrasting and perhaps disagreeable undertones of gentrification. Like many inner-city Melbourne neighbourhoods, Lawson was poorly regarded through the inter- and post-war years, firmly working-class, dominated by an influx of European immigrants. Adam describes this: 'You had . . . the Masos [people from Macedonia], the Greeks, the Italians against the Aussies, which hated us all, called us wogs, at school, teachers used to call us wogs and that's the way it was'. Adam feels that this fundamentally shifted in the 1980s,

> when the Asians came in, the influx of Vietnamese, Cambodians, all those people who came from Asia and the war-torn countries over there, suddenly they [the Aussies] were against the Asian populates. Suddenly the Aussies accepted the wogs. As wogs. Common cause you know.

Adam is referring to the 'common cause' of whiteness. He was accepted into the social fabric on the basis of a 'new', feared foreigner. Many 'groups that at one time or another have been defined as outside whiteness have at other times been redefined and brought within the privileged group' (Gillborn, 2005: 489). Adam's racial identity was clearly identified *for* him, and in contemporary Lawson, it is questionable to what degree he feels part of the collective whole. He tends to associate more with the earlier generations,

> The neighbourhood was *completely different* . . . the generation that was here was an ethnic mix . . . there was blue collar . . . Foley Street was all lined up with factories, so when the ethnics, or the wogs, we all came here in the sixties, they went to where the blue-collar operations were, so they ended up [in other inner-city neighbourhoods] and some ended up here in Lawson to work in all the James Street factories and all those factories down the road . . . you had . . . the abattoirs . . . the Riley Street abattoirs, a lot of Masos, Greeks all ended up here . . . 'cause that's what they knew, they were all farmers . . . so that's what the culture was here once, but it's not here anymore, it's *different*. . . . It's a more professional, more organized, more . . . cultured, educated, bunch of people . . . You couldn't give these

houses away thirty years ago; now you cannot buy into the area unless you are professional or a high earner.

The concept of white flight fails to capture the complex and distinct manoeuvrings and sense of groupness within the urban space. As Adam elucidates, the collective migration away from the working-class, factory-ridden inner-city neighbourhood has evolved to reverse white flight, as the white middle class flocks back to the inner-city. In this resettlement of the urban space, the once distasteful factories are converted to 'warehouses', ultra-hip and fashionable, and highly sought after within the housing market. For the incomers, the neighbourhood *develops* distinctiveness, character and social identity (Winters, 1979; Cole, 1985; Bridge, 2001). The migrant socio-historical narrative largely plays out as an abstract backdrop, in that the neighbourhood offers cosmopolitanism and 'multiculturalism without migrants' (Hage, 2012: 99).

Participant Steven also experienced this shift, having purchased in neighbourhood Lawson in 1995 as a self-described struggling musician returning from Europe. He now has two school-aged children and I meet him regularly throughout my observation, but his involvement in the campaign is more so related to his role as a local politician. This was an issue of contention during the interview – his partner endeavoured to end the interview, believing that it may be detrimental to Steven's political interests, but he chose to continue the interview. He speaks extensively about a 'monumental shift' in the population, but also the neighbourhood since he moved in:

> The biggest change is simply tertiary educated . . . for the first time really. 'Cause it's always been . . . a . . . a factory fodder population around here . . .
>
> E: And you've been here since 1995?
> *Steven:* Yeah I've sort of . . . I saw the end of it yeah, yeah . . . because I know even these factories along the river all cut their work forces hugely and you know . . . because this was . . . I mean (*laughs*) [the wider Lawson region] used to be called . . . what was it . . . in the 30s it was called the ah, *Birmingham of the South*, they really pride themselves on being this sort of manufacturing industrial centre you know, they were the Midlands of Australia, of Melbourne type thing you know . . . so um . . . and that's why it's always attracted the migrant population because um . . . there's always a place to get a job if you can speak the language.

Steven refers to neighbourhood Lawson as '*Birmingham of the South*', a city in England, and the metaphor is useful in capturing the spatial motifs of class. It also captures the importance of context in conceptualizing and understanding consumption within local education markets. Steven attributes the population shift to the inner-city locale and the 'still affordable' house prices. To put this affordability into perspective, when Steven purchased his three-bedroom house in 1995 he paid $105,000. According to Steven, his neighbours were bewildered by the amount he paid, and told him that he was 'robbed'. Twenty years later in 2015, when the neighbourhood is marketed as a 'unique and gentrified inner-city village', consumers can expect to pay a median price of $888,000 for a three-bedroom house, a price that steadily increases. The migration of the middle class has resulted in increased pressure for more public services, but also the rise of house prices and points of exclusion.

In modern-day Lawson, there is a sharp division between the neighbourhood and many of the surrounds. Walking through the streets, the neighbourhood reflects only the remnants of its industrial past. It is physically disconnected from surrounding neighbourhoods by busy highways, railway lines and obtrusive bridges. So too, the racial make-up sharply differs. The next-door neighbourhood of Charles is well known for its diverse population, particularly refugees from the continent of Africa, many drawn to the inner-city locale, affordable rentals and proximity to universities. The neighbourhood offers pluralistic tastes, from its restaurants to the cafes. In this way, the two neighbourhoods are not only physically disconnected, but also visibly differentiated in terms of its population and consumer choices. A trip to neighbourhood Charles will offer the best of Ethiopian or Vietnamese fare – often in modest or unpretentious surrounds – whereas a visit to the neighbouring Lawson serves up Scandinavian-oriented breakfasts and 'creative' brunches. Karen describes Lawson neighbourhood as the 'latte crowd', replete with hip cafes, book clubs and sculpture artworks.

Across the other side of the city in the neighbourhood of Smith, residential segregation is played out in similar ways, albeit with differing racial populations. This is most evident in terms of dominant religious affiliations – surrounding catchment areas, particularly those that contain the rejected schools for the Smith residents, contain higher proportions of individuals who affiliate with Islam, according to the Australian Census. This difference is quite steep: for example, 24% of the population living within the catchment area of Riley High identify with Islam, or Apple High (16%). This is compared to the popular Hampton or Beakin High, where only 1% of the population identify with the Islamic faith (see Appendix, Table A.5).

The neighbourhoods of Lawson and Smith can be described as dominantly representing a largely affluent, Australian-born and secular population. In similarity to each of the neighbourhoods (and catchment areas) that contain a 'popular' public high school for the campaigners, and according to the Australian Bureau of Statistics, the neighbourhoods of Lawson and Smith earn higher levels of gross household income in comparison to the state median; they represent a higher proportion of individuals who identify with 'no religion' in comparison to the state median; and, they represent a higher proportion of residents born in Australia and the United Kingdom (see Appendix, Table A.3 to A.5). Conversely, the catchment areas that contain a 'rejected' public high school represent lower median incomes in comparison to the state median; a lower proportion of

Australian-born and United Kingdom–born residents; and a higher proportion of individuals who identify with 'other' religions, such as Hinduism, Buddhism and Islam. To put this in perspective, I provide a table that lists each catchment area, according to country of birth and arranged from lowest to highest according to the percentage of Australian-born residents (see Table 4.1):

As evident on the table, residential segregation is visible and in some cases inverted. The Vietnamese-born population in the catchment area of Park is twenty-one times greater than the catchment area of Beakin. So too, the Indian-born population of Charles and Box is more than three times the proportion of Smith and Lawson. Individuals who affiliate with the Census category of 'born elsewhere/country of birth not stated' is higher in the catchment areas with 'rejected' public high schools, including Apple and Axis, Park and Charles.

Whiteness then, is played out within the local education market as an essential constituent for leveraging advantage and collectively evading differences. Beck and Levy (2013) write that 'modern collectivities are increasingly preoccupied with debating, preventing and managing risks' (3). If racial diversity is rendered as risky, then local collectives are clearly risk-averse within the global 'ethnoscape'. This is paradoxical in an era which has experienced higher levels of transnational migration than ever before, and also for idealized notions of cosmopolitanism. Cosmopolitanization implies an 'interactive relationship between

Table 4.1 Country of birth and proportion of residents by school catchment area. The table is organized from lowest to highest based on the proportion of Australian-born residents (2012 data).

Popular, Rejected or Balanced Choice?	Catchment Area	Australia	UK	Vietnam	Born Elsewhere/ Country of Birth Not Stated	India	China
R	Park Secondary	38%	1%	21%	20%	5%	3%
R	Charles High	41%	2%	9%	22%	7%	5%
R	Box College	45%	2%	11%	20%	7%	2%
R	Riley Secondary	47.4%	1.0%	1.0%	16.0%	3.0%	1.0%
R	Apple High	54.0%	2.0%	1.0%	14.0%	5.2%	2.0%
R	Axis High	55.9%	2.0%	2.0%	12.0%	4.0%	3.0%
P	Matheson Secondary	57%	4%	1%	12%	1%	6%
N/A	Smith	60.3%	2.0%	1.0%	11.0%	2.0%	2.0%
B	Gregory Secondary	61.0%	3.0%	1.0%	12.0%	2.0%	2.0%
N/A	Lawson	66%	4%	3%	10%	2%	1%
P	Hampton College	68.9%	4.0%	1.0%	8.0%	2.0%	2.0%
P	Beakin High	74%	7%	0%	7%	1%	0%

the global and the local' (Beck and Levy, 2013: 6) – and yet cosmopolitanization is strained within the schooling market, with schools offering a type of modern collectivism – one that excludes the *other*.

Newcomers, identity and contours of racism

The majority of interview participants (80%) are newcomers or strangers to the neighbourhood, moving to Lawson from another inner-city location in the period 2001–2006. The only outliers are Steven and Adam. During the public meetings with 'New School for Lawson', the significant number of 'incomers' to the neighbourhood, and their involvement with the campaign, is a theme that I regularly note. During the often drawn-out introductions, when attendees introduce themselves around the table, individuals frequently speak at great lengths about their recent move to the neighbourhood with their young family, how much they enjoy the neighbourhood, some even stating how 'middle-class' the neighbourhood is. One participant tells the group that she moved to the neighbourhood with her husband, buying a house on Stott Street, when they discovered she was pregnant. She feels it is a good place to raise a family, and discusses the drug and crime problems of the inner-city neighbourhood in which she used to live: 'I'm glad that we don't have those sorts of problems here [drugs and crime], it is very middle-class here'.

The interactions and lengthy self-introductions are sometimes personal and self-reflective – one participant shares about a recent divorce, another participant Michelle describes herself to the group as a 'single mother'. Through these interactions and introductions – at times, quite revealing – and their discussion of family life, their reasons for particular choices around residential location, and their reasons for attending the meeting, the individuals are 'negotiating' and 'affirming' their self-identities and consumption choices within a like-minded community (Cucchiara and Horvat, 2014: 490). The authors write about 'Darcy Group' meetings, a group of middle-class parents organizing around a local public school in the US,

> Each meeting of the Darcy Group began with introductions . . . Notably, the introductions were quite extensive and regularly took up a more than a third of the 90-minute meetings. Such lengthy introductions, in which parents spoke far more about themselves and their experiences, beliefs and goals than they did about their children, were evidence of the importance parents placed on affirming and communicating their own identities in relation to the choice process.
>
> (Cucchiara and Horvat, 2014: 490)

In the contemporary market, and particularly for the more affluent and well-resourced chooser, selecting a school is a means to establish a sense of class collectivism. On one hand, this may be 'reclaiming' social democracy and progressive values, but on the other, it is fiercely individualized and territorialized.

For many of the incomers to the neighbourhood, the presence of 'education' makes all the difference in transforming the culture and class-status. Indeed, Bourdieu's scholarship around the cultural activities and social behaviour of collective class groups, gains traction here. In *Distinction* (1984), Bourdieu utilizes surveys to look for associations between cultural activities and education levels. This is more so a *performance* of class, as Skeggs (1997) stipulates, and thereby the construction of collective behaviour and class. This comes through in how Robert speaks about the neighbourhood: 'We keep importing people who are, you know . . . highly educated. Why wouldn't you come here? Cheap land, fantastic-sized blocks, close to the city. The neighbours have got your value system. The people in this area are well educated'. The presence of university education is regularly utilized as a marker of sorts, to ascertain class status and 'groupness' within the neighbourhood. Steven also points to this, saying, 'It was *such* a working-class area and . . . and it's quite the opposite now I'd say . . . probably the majority would be tertiary educated now and that's probably the biggest change, the education level'. However, whilst levels of tertiary education are routinely discussed, racial population changes are rarely noted, except by Adam. To put these changes in perspective, in 2001 only 58.1% of the Lawson population were Australian and United Kingdom–born, whereas in 2011, 70% of the population in Lawson are Australian or United Kingdom–born. The Vietnamese-born population has more than halved, from 7.5% to 3%. The reluctance to identify these racial changes within the neighbourhood may suggest a broader proclivity to deny the role that whiteness plays in territorializing space and leveraging class-status. This is reflected in scholarship by Leonardo (2002), who writes that 'whiteness is characterized by the unwillingness to name the contours of racism . . . the minimization of racist legacy, and other similar evasions' (32).

Adam and Steven are the only interview participants without university education, something they both independently bring into the interview. Steven pauses, leans in conspiratorially, and I almost expect him to reveal a family secret, when he says, 'I didn't get an education, you know. I'm the only one in my family who didn't go'. Steven attended an elite secondary school and it was clearly a family disappointment that he did not 'get an education'. However, Steven is employed in a professional role, a position he acquired through his extensive musical abilities. He also maintains a leadership role within the community as a political representative.

Adam, on the other hand, quite proudly denounces university education. He knows I work at one. He spends quite a bit of time talking to me about the 'uselessness' of higher education, that it is clearly 'a waste of time' – particularly if you 'want to make any money in the world'. To illustrate his point, he tells me a story of two friends:

> I've got a cousin . . . this is a person who started off as a mechanic, biggest bludger on earth . . . and he says, I got my education at Charles High School and he quit school . . . got an apprenticeship . . . and he says, I've got five houses now . . . I've got another friend – same age group – went to medical school, a doctor today, *hasn't got one house, got a mortgage to the hilt, and*

no matter what his wage is, will *never* catch this guy that *dropped out of school early in 1988!* So my cousin says, look at him, look at me! I'm earning as much as him, through, just . . . going through things . . . Uneducated, no degree, *he just talks shit all day*! (*Laughs*) But see he is a person, with no education, and he is ahead of the game than some who have gone through ten, fifteen years of education . . . so you know, it is where you want to be . . . it's all through luck, the right people . . . and these people can take you places . . . you know I see people every day, the people I employ, I see them go to uni [university] to waste their time.

Adam's view of university education, and the value of university education, is far different to his fellow campaigners. Adam describes school as a 'business', consisting of 'inputs and outputs' and at the end of the day, it is about '*who you know, not what you know*'.

Community schooling

The purpose of the parental campaigns is to acquire a 'local' community school, one that they can walk or ride their bike to, a theme that overrides the campaigners' publications and also the interviews. In a sense, the campaigners elicit old-fashioned ideas around their locality in the context of a relatively high-density urban locale. The space itself takes on a variety of identities, from 'this village needs a high school' (see Figure 3.5) to an inner-city cosmopolitan 'vibrant' neighbourhood. Adele seeks to capture the goals of 'New School for Lawson':

> We are a tight-knit community, and we want a *local, community* school. That's our wish list. When we sat down and did a workshop with the Department [of Education], we told them, it's a community school; it would be a learning community, a hub of learning.

The parents maintain direct communication with the Department of Education, in similarity with campaigners from the Smith group, and in these meetings 'New School for Lawson' does endeavour to define what they mean by 'local' in terms of quantitative measurements. In their regular surveys they design, distribute and publish on their website, the working party asserts that a local community high school needs to be less than two kilometres from their place of residence. While the campaign has defined the meaning of 'local' for itself, this position conflicts with wider policy-making, and the view of the Department of Education, with whom the campaigners regularly meet. This is indicated during a general meeting:

> The campaigners are discussing local schools. Elizabeth asks, 'What is local, how do you define local anyway?'
> 'Does the Department stipulate a definite proximity of local?' asks Greg.
> Steven responds, 'No, no, no . . . they don't unfortunately . . . they don't say what a reasonable distance is'.

Glocalization and evocations of whiteness in the local education market 75

In her study based in the city of Detroit, Bell (2009) identifies geographic sets for school choosers, with the average parent selecting a school 'that was 4.9 miles from home' (502) equivalent to 7.88 kilometres. In their study based in Auckland, Lubienski et al. (2013) define a 'reasonable walkable distance as two kilometres' (95). I point to the map of the Lawson neighbourhood and surrounding schools, in order to further elucidate these distances for the reader (see Figure 4.1).

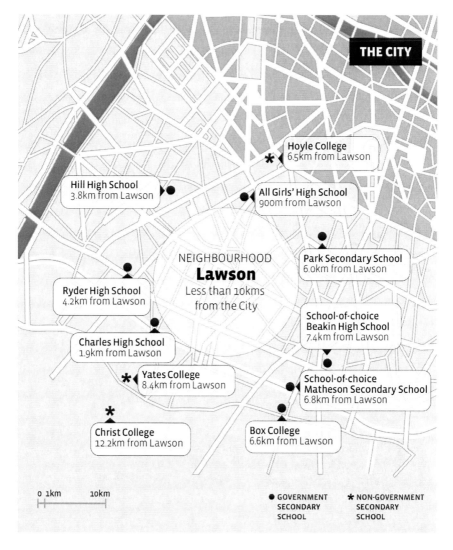

Figure 4.1 'New School for Lawson' is located in the neighbourhood of Lawson. This map shows the proximity of surrounding high schools.

As the reader can discern, for the Lawson residents, there are numerous schools in surrounding neighbourhoods with Charles High School a little over one mile from the neighbourhood. As Bell (2009) writes, geography is 'operationalized through variables such as distance, commute time, and the availability of transportation. It is measured in miles and minutes' (495). Thus, it is necessary to consider these distances not within an empty space, but in terms of contextually loaded variables. As an inner-city neighbourhood, there is wide availability of both buses and trains. There is a public bus service that runs from the neighbourhood of Lawson, to neighbourhood Charles, another to neighbourhood Beakin. The bus service to Charles is three times quicker in minutes, as opposed to neighbourhood Beakin. But the surrounding schools are also willing to help out, as indicated by Adele:

> I also met with a few of the principals in the area . . . two or three principals from Park Secondary and they were very keen to, you know, to encourage children to progress down there, to the point of . . . we can move a whole grade six class and make that a year seven class and we can help bus them down to our school etcetera . . .
>
> E: Oh right, they were very keen to have you there?
> *Adele:*   *Absolutely.* Yeah.
> E: Why do you think that is?
> *Adele:*   They've got the capacity, absolutely.

Adele is the only participant who has visited the surrounding schools and met with the principals. While she admits that surrounding schools are eager to enrol children from the Lawson neighbourhood, and are even willing to implement a free-of-charge bus service to facilitate and promote this movement, this doesn't seem enough to eradicate the spatial gaps. The complementary bus service is not a new idea. It was previously implemented by the state government, only to be stopped due to lack of interest.

Clearly there are frictions and tensions in the campaigners' agitations for a brand-new public school, and whilst the campaigners may identify boundaries and borders – distances that are too far and over-subscribed schools – some of the surrounding schools, the rejected schools, are keen to overcome the 'friction of distance' (Harvey, 1973: 14). However, this is not readily disclosed or advertised by the campaigns. Adele's anecdote is almost confessional-like; it is a position that conflicts with the New School for Lawson's emphasis on lack of capacity and the tyranny of distance. 'We have always been supportive of the existing public schools in the region,' their working document states. 'They are just too far away'.

It is little surprising that surrounding schools are eager to attract the attention of the well-resourced campaigners. This is a predominant theme across the literature, regardless of the country context. Cucchiara (2013) identifies the well-funded business initiative to revitalize the urban city schools in an urgent bid to market the schools to higher-income or upper-middle-class consumers. In her study of urban public schools in California and the collective strategies of white middle-class parents, Posey (2014) suggests 'school gentrification' as the school is remodelled and redesigned to appeal and attract the more discerning and affluent consumer.

The campaigners' emphasis on location and proximity is understandable. The literature demonstrates the importance of convenience for the school chooser (Bell, 2009; Windle, 2015). However, the well-resourced chooser tends to overcome distances if necessary, and the local public school has predominantly been connected to the working-class or disconnected school chooser (Reay and Ball, 1997; Reay and Lucey, 2004). The school chooser's emphasis on location sits uneasily in terms of their resources and commitment they are willing to bring to schooling, but also in the context of the 'time-space' compression (Beck, 2002). It is clear then, that questions of proximity and distance within the urban schooling market tease out sociological questions surrounding race, class and inequality.

Theorizing space in relation to the urban schooling circuit

David Harvey (1973) writes in *Social Justice and the City*, that

> There are various ways in which we can think about space. It is crucial to formulate a proper conception of it if we are to understand urban phenomena and society in general; yet the nature of space has remained something mysterious to social enquiry.
>
> (13)

Harvey (2006, 1973) argues for a tripartite division of space, thinking about space as relational, absolute and relative.[1] Indeed, scholars posit a variety of ways to formulate space, as experienced, conceptualized and lived (Lefebvre, 1991). Influential scholar Doreen Massey (2005) pushes against space as uniformly equated with representation, space as closed and static. She argues for space as open, composed of multiplicity and dynamic (or 'lively'). Many scholars debate the distinctiveness of place versus space, but Massey positions place and space as integrated concepts. This is reflected throughout her text, *For Space*, as she pushes against 'space on the one hand and place on the other' (6). Space is a 'surface on which we are placed' (7).

Harvey's projection of space as 'absolute' is useful for educational research in that it enables a rethinking of how space becomes commodified, in the context of a public school choice 'circuit' (Ball et al., 1995). A public school is supposedly 'non-selective' but obviously one that is experiencing high demand will define inclusion and exclusion points. These points are based on a geographical grid – often arbitrarily or seemingly haphazardly designed, blocking out one part of the neighbourhood whilst enrolling the other – and inclusion within the grid can be a highly fraught, panic-filled, investment for some parents. This notion of 'bounded' space is effectively explored by Reay, et al. (2013) in their study of *White middle-class parents and urban schooling*:

> Harvey (1989, 1993), for example, has argued that in contemporary society the urban dweller frequently becomes defensive, territorial and competitive about their urban space, creating spatial barriers or 'bounded space' . . . the middle-class inhabitants tended to relate to their locale in terms of Harvey's 'bounded space'
>
> (1993: 56)

Spatial barriers and the notion of relating to a locale as a 'bounded space' are fitting in this study, in which the location of the school is of primary importance. Indeed, a 'significant attribute of the middle-classes is the ability to erect boundaries, both geographically and symbolically' (Reay et al., 2013: 12).

Scholars have argued that a consequence of globalization will be the eradication of community life, 'no longer determined solely or even primarily by location' (Beck, 2002: 31). Whilst distances are clearly quite fluid for school choosers in their ability to overcome boundaries for desirable schools, boundaries are also 'chosen and interpreted . . . redrawn and legitimated anew' (Beck, 2002: 19).

Spatial inscriptions of class

Harry: I think [in school-of-choice] if there's a good mix of the kids born to the parents of this area, then that would be fantastic because I think they would be good kids and good people.

Residential address within a neighbourhood is utilized as an important proxy for class identity and social rank, and as Harry suggests, feeds into how an urban public school is measured as desirable. Comparable themes are reflected in a broad number of studies. In Cucchiara's (2013) study, whether a pupil or family were 'neighbourhood' or 'non-neighbourhood' was a weighty and symbolic substitute for 'broader social status, namely membership within the [predominantly white] middle- or upper-middle-class' (104). This is substantiated in Posey-Maddox's (2014) study of urban middle-class choosers in California, and also Holme's (2002) earlier paper, *Buying Homes, Buying Schools*. Holme writes that school choices of high-status parents are largely predicated by the choices of other high-status choosers, as signalled by residential address within certain neighbourhoods, and therefore socially constructed as desirable, good choices. Ho (2011) and colleagues (Ho et al., 2015) explore the 'cultural polarisation' of public schools in Australia, deeply divided on the basis of race and ethnicity. Arguably, this is how absolute space becomes *operative* as a commodity: even though boundaries are nebulous and changeable, the neighbourhood grid (and the people who fill this neighbourhood grid) is perceived as knowable and largely absolute.

A class-identity is mapped out via the neighbourhood in which we live, and this underscores consumption choices around schooling, and yet this concerns far more than logistical issues surrounding proximity. Savage et al. (2005) argue that, 'rather than seeing wider social identities as arising out of the field of employment it would be more promising to examine their relationship to residential location' (207). Participants frequently refer to themselves as 'middle-class' and usually in relationship to where they live and the community. For example, Matthew says,

E: The idea of community is raised all the time, why do you think community is so important to this campaign?

Matthew: The particular area here . . . a lot of families have come over here in the past ten years, or even more recently, and they are at a similar stage of their lives . . . they've got young kids . . . and they're all, in a sort of, a like-mind . . . they've got, I suppose, a similar profile, they tend to be middle-class, similar values . . .

Matthew's remark is a common theme in many of the interviews. The urban neighbourhood tends to be imagined in homogenous ways, captured as an 'educated' community with shared values. This essentially denies difference and I would argue, is rooted in an evasive sense of whiteness. A relationship to residential address is markedly significant for the ways in which the urban middle-class chooser identifies and engages with school choice, as the public school is mobilized as the purchase of identity, 'the similarities or shared attributes around which group members coalesce' (Cerulo, 1997: 386). This is contentious for how the local school would potentially organize and territorialize *white* identity and this is marked out in a number of ways, but perhaps the most pointed way, is via a strong provocation and claim to community schooling.

Bounded space

Robert: A lot of people from the [surrounding neighbourhoods] have . . . a view of the world that is . . . tantamount to . . . what's best described as the law of accident. Things happen to them. They're like a cork in many ways. They see themselves as corks on an ocean. And wherever they wind up, that's where they wind up. The value systems of people in the Lawson [neighbourhood] are more in line with the laws of cause and effect. They believe that if you put in then you'll get out. Now it may not be what you want, but you'll get a lot better than thinking of leaving it to chance. So . . . that's a fundamental difference in terms of values and understandings. Some people believe that there's nothing they can do, some people think there's not much that can be done.

My interview with Robert, a previous mayor, was held at the local town hall. Sitting in his office, he insisted that I use his full name for the interview, rather than a pseudonym, adamant that 'everybody knows me in this town'. I knew this would place difficulties on the anonymity of the campaign and it was discomfiting to push back against this.[2] Robert tends to regard 'New School for Lawson' as a type of leverage for his own political aspirations, consistently arriving at meetings and events in his business suit, announcing his title and shaking people's hands. Despite his presence at the campaign, he has no personal ambition to send his own children to the proposed high school, even though he very unhappily designates this as his 'ex-wife's decision'. He has his sights firmly set on Klein High School, 'the only public school in Melbourne with rowing in their curriculum'. Although Klein is listed as a public school, it is far from accessible.

Whilst my contact with Robert was often experienced as discomfiting – I met him several times over the course of my participation – his description of the lower-income surrounding neighbourhoods sat awkwardly for me, also. For Robert, there are strong associations between an individual's residential location and their neoliberal aptitude, which Nikolas Rose (1996) describes as, 'choice, personal responsibility, control over one's own fate, self-promotion and self-government' (335). The surrounding neighbourhood residents' inability to self-govern and be 'active' citizens, merely 'corks on an ocean', is a sense of failure and attributed to a lack of hard work. This is an act of class power and the 'reclassification' of taste:

> Those with social power have a monopoly over ways of seeing and classifying objects according to their criteria of good taste. The ability to create new systems of discernment is class power. Gentrification can be seen as one such reclassification (away from the working-class city and the desirability of the middle-class neighbourhoods) in which inner urban living became once again invested with ideas of status, style and cosmopolitanism.
>
> (Bridge, 2001: 92)

For the middle-class gentrifiers, 'the local' becomes valuable but only in so far that it enables better consumption of capital, and reinforces social and cultural distance from the *other*. It is through this lens that the notion of community (or perhaps, the celebration of community) gains traction. Community schooling is routinely celebrated and utilized as a positive term across the political spectrum, a common feature of Third Way political discourse (Rose, 2000). Dewey (1927) originally evoked the term to celebrate accessible education as the 'great equalizer' within civic society, and Warren and Mapp (2011) argue for community organization to create educational change. The notion of community tends to be bilaterally promoted in educational discourse, endorsed by the charter school movement, and as a new means of governance, but also taken up by the left-of-centre to speak to grassroots movements and parental involvement, a positive delineation of a group of people living side by side and sharing common concerns. This is augmented by Williams (1983), who describes community as one of the only 'social organization' terms that is consistently used favourably:

> **Community** can be the warmly persuasive word to describe an existing set of relationships, or the warmly persuasive word to describe an alternative set of relationships. What is most important, perhaps, is that unlike all other terms of social organization (*state, nation, society*, etc.) it seems never to be used unfavourably, and never to be given any positive opposing or distinguishing term.
>
> (76, emphasis in original)

Whilst there are positives to schooling for the community – parental involvement, togetherness and collectiveness, a 'possible antidote' to the individualistic, neoliberal thesis (Rose, 1996: 332) – the active production and consumption of community schooling highlights how the educational market place is entangled within the process of reproducing racial segregation. Whiteness becomes deeply valorized within the community schooling market, particularly in policy conditions that do not actively work to increase racial and socio-economic schooling integration (Roda and Wells, 2013).

Conclusion

The agitation for renewed public schools, from an informed and relatively resourceful middle class, retains encouraging signs for a post-welfare economy. For the 'squeezed' middle class, depicted as anxious and fearful of their fraught economical position (Reay et al., 2013), the desire to reclaim the public school may suggest a pivotal cultural turn. The participants in this study are pushing for greater funding of the public sector, but at the same time, may be taking the little-available funding from established schools nearby, schools that are dominated by lower-income residents.

Evidently there are tensions in parents campaigning for a brand-new public school, in utilizing strategies to influence educational policy and provision, but this also represents divergences in terms of the dominant trends and patterns playing out across the education market. On the surface, the campaigners demonstrate contrary 'anti-market' choices, but on the other hand, the parents are 'working the market' and only further bolstering racial divides. In the following chapter, I consider the wider segregation of the public schooling sector, differentiations in funding levels, and build profiles for each school within the data set.

Notes

1 I apply David Harvey's theories to school choice elsewhere, see Rowe (2015).
2 I later realized that using his correct name would reveal the identity of the campaign, and with further correspondence, he eventually agreed to a pseudonym, when I advised him that his interview would have to be cut.

References

Appadurai A. (1990) Disjuncture and difference in the global cultural economy. *Theory, Culture & Society* 7: 295–310.

Ball SJ, Bowe R and Gewirtz S. (1995) Circuits of schooling: A sociological exploration of parental choice of school in social class contexts. *The Sociological Review* 43: 52–78.

Beck U. (2002) The cosmopolitan society and its enemies. *Theory, Culture & Society* 19: 17–44.

Beck U and Levy D. (2013) Cosmopolitanized nations: Re-imagining collectivity in world risk society. *Theory, Culture & Society* 30: 3–31.

Bell C. (2009) Geography in parental choice. *American Journal of Education* 115: 493–521.

Bourdieu P. (1984) *Distinction: A Social Critique of the Judgement of Taste*, London, Melbourne and Henley: Routledge & Kegan Paul.

Bridge G. (2001) Estate agents as interpreters of economic and cultural capital: The gentrification premium in the Sydney housing market. *International Journal of Urban and Regional Research* 25: 87–101.

Cerulo KA. (1997) Identity construction: New issues, new directions. *Annual Review of Sociology* 23: 385–409.

Cole DB. (1985) Gentrification, social character, and personal identity. *Geographical Review* 75: 142–155.

Cucchiara MB. (2013) *Marketing Schools, Marketing Cities: Who Wins and Who Loses When Schools Become Urban Amenities*, Chicago: University of Chicago Press.

Cucchiara MB and Horvat EM. (2014) Choosing selves: The salience of parental identity in the school choice process. *Journal of Education Policy* 29: 486–509.

Dewey J. (1927) *The public and its problems*, New York: Henry Holt and Company.

Gillborn D. (2005) Education policy as an act of white supremacy: Whiteness, critical race theory and education reform. *Journal of Education Policy* 20: 485–505.

Hage G. (2012) *White Nation: Fantasies of White Supremacy in a Multicultural Society*, Hoboken: Taylor and Francis.

Harvey D. (1973) *Social Justice and the City*, London: Edward Arnold Ltd.

Harvey D. (1989) *The Condition of Postmodernity: An Enquiry into the Origins of Cultural Change*, Oxford: Basil Blackwell.

Harvey D. (1993) From space to place and back again: Reflections on the condition of postmodernity. In: Bird J, Curtis J, Putnam T, Robinson G, Ticker L (eds) *Mapping the Futures: Local Cultures, Global Change*, London: Routledge, 3–29.

Harvey D. (2006) Space as a keyword. In: Castree N and Gregory D (eds) *David Harvey: A Critical Reader*, Oxford: Blackwell Publishing, 270–295.

Ho C. (2011) Respecting the presence of others: School micropublics and everyday multiculturalism. *Journal of Intercultural Studies* 32: 603–619.

Ho C, Vincent E and Butler R. (2015) Everyday and cosmo-multiculturalisms: Doing diversity in gentrifying school communities. *Journal of Intercultural Studies* 36: 658–675.

Holme JJ. (2002) Buying homes, buying schools: School choice and the social construction of school quality. *Harvard Educational Review* 72: 177–205.

Hursh DW. (2015) *The End of Public Schools: The Corporate Reform Agenda to Privatize Education*, New York & London: Routledge.

Lefebvre H. (1991) *The Production of Space*, Oxford & Cambridge: Blackwell.

Leonardo Z. (2002) The souls of white folk: Critical pedagogy, whiteness studies, and globalization discourse. *Race Ethnicity and Education* 5: 29–50.

Lubienski C, Lee J and Gordon L. (2013) Self-managing schools and access for disadvantaged students: Organizational behaviour and school admissions. *New Zealand Journal of Educational Studies* 48: 82–98.

Massey D. (2005) *For Space*, London: Sage Publications.

Posey-Maddox L. (2014) *When Middle-Class Parents Choose Urban Schools: Class, Race, and the Challenge of Equity in Public Education*, Chicago, IL: University of Chicago Press.

Reay D and Ball SJ. (1997) 'Spoilt for choice': The working classes and educational markets. *Oxford Review of Education* 23: 89–101.

Reay D, Crozier G and James D. (2013) *White Middle-Class Identities and Urban Schooling*, Basingstoke and New York: Palgrave Macmillan.

Reay D and Lucey H. (2004) Stigmatised choices: Social class, social exclusion and secondary school markets in the inner city. *Pedagogy, Culture & Society* 12: 35–51.

Robertson R. (1995) Glocalization: Time-space and homogeneity-heterogeneity. In: Featherstone M, Lash S and Robertson R (eds) *Global Modernities*, London: Sage, 25–44.

Roda A and Wells AS. (2013) School choice policies and racial segregation: Where white parents' good intentions, anxiety, and privilege collide. *American Journal of Education* 119: 261–293.

Rose N. (1996) The death of the social? Re-figuring the territory of government. *Economy and Society* 25: 327–356.

Rose N. (2000) Community, citizenship, and the third way. *The American Behavioral Scientist* 43: 1395–1411.

Rowe E. (2015) Theorising geo-identity and David Harvey's space: School choices of the geographically bound middle-class. *Critical Studies in Education* 56: 285–300.

Savage M, Bagnall G and Longhurst B. (2001) Ordinary, ambivalent and defensive: Class identities in the northwest of England. *Sociology* 35: 875–892.

Savage M, Bagnall G and Longhurst B. (2005) *Globalization & Belonging*, London, Thousand Oaks & New Delhi: Sage.

Skeggs B. (1997) *Formations of Class & Gender: Becoming Respectable*, London, California & New Delhi: Sage.

Warren MR and Mapp KL. (2011) *A Match on Dry Grass: Community Organizing as a Catalyst for School Reform*, Oxford: Oxford University Press.

Williams R. (1983) *Keywords: A Vocabulary of Culture and Society*, Oxford: Oxford University Press.

Windle JA. (2015) *Making Sense of School Choice: Politics, Policies, and Practice under Conditions of Cultural Diversity*, New York: Palgrave Macmillan.

Winters C. (1979) The social identity of evolving neighborhoods. *Landscape* 23: 8–14.

Chapter 5

Private versus public schools

This chapter is titled 'private versus public schooling', but this is with a hint of irony. Despite the widespread dilution of the public sector, in many OECD countries, the rhetoric between private versus public schooling continues to be used as a blunt instrument to fuel a popularized debate. Within any given newspaper, any day of the week – from *The Guardian*, to *Huffington Post*, or *The New York Times* – even the list of bestsellers on Amazon, the slogan of 'private versus public schools' is a strong seller. The public is clearly attentive to this debate. This debate occurs in the context of post-welfare policy conditions, a schooling market, that essentially pits schools against each other, rather than framing schools as a collective entity with similar goals.

This chapter focuses on the Australian secondary school, generating comprehensive statistical analyses of the private and public sector, in terms of enrolment and funding differentiations. I explore how significant policies have shaped and driven consumer engagement for each of the sectors. It includes an in-depth profile of each public secondary school within the data set, aiming to make broader contributions in identifying sharp levels of segregation within the public schooling sector.

Segregation is increasing across schooling sectors – private and public – aggravated by competitive policies and inequitable funding levels, undercutting fairness, inclusion and the opportunity to learn for lower socio-economic status students. Secondary schools are important for establishing pathways for students, from employment to further study, and in Australia the secondary school is essential for facilitating access to higher education.[1] The more prestigious degrees at university require high entrance scores on final examinations. This chapter concludes by examining the scholarship surrounding the 'private school advantage' and academic differences between the sectors.

The consumption of secondary schools in Australia: Statistical data

Australia's private sector consists of two separate sectors: the Independent and the Catholic sector, even though many schools in the Independent sector are also aligned with the Catholic faith. Australia maintains a high proportion of religious schools in comparison to other OECD countries, with 30% of all schools religiously affiliated. This is contrasted to Sweden, where less than 2% of all schools are religious, or the US where 'less than 10% of all schools' are religious schools (Buckingham, 2010: 8, 9). The majority of religious schools represent the Christian or Catholic faith, and there is ongoing cultural backlash and hostility towards Islamic schools (Jamal Al-deen and Rowe, 2016).

High-fee and exclusive secondary schools in Australia tend to be part of the Independent school sector. This is typically understood as the 'elite' school sector, although there are wide variations. The private Catholic school generally charges quite low fees and emphasizes accessibility. The majority of lower socio-economic status students are educated within public schools with the exception being the select-entry public school, which students can access via academic examination (Ho, 2011). Australia maintains a well-funded and resourced private sector, and a higher percentage of students attend private schools in comparison to many other OECD countries (35% of Australian students attend private schools, higher than the OECD average of 18%) (see OECD, 2011). The percentage of enrolment by school sector is shown here (see Figure 5.1).

These figures are routinely reported in the media and by external stakeholders (e.g., OECD, National Commission Audits), although they can be misleading when assessing secondary school enrolment. A greater proportion of parents

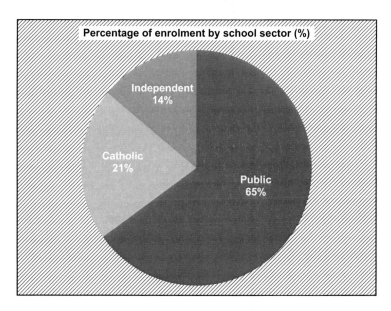

Figure 5.1 Total percentage of enrolment by school sector in Australia (%): Independent, Catholic and Public (2015 figures).

86 Private versus public schools

enrol their child in public primary schools, and there are differences on the secondary level. This sector is far more entangled within the politics of choice.

To illuminate this further, the following figure *excludes* primary school enrolment and shows the proportion of full-time secondary students enrolled in government (Public), Catholic and Independent schools in Australia. This includes all states and territories in Australia. The graph draws on raw statistical data from the Australian Bureau of Statistics, rather than secondary sources[2] (see Figure 5.2).

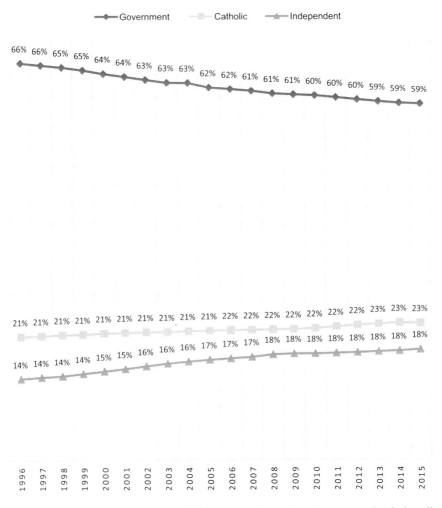

Figure 5.2 Full-time students enrolled in secondary school by sector (includes all states and territories in Australia), 1996–2015.

When examining the data, it is evident that the Independent sector has experienced the largest proportional increase in enrolment from 1996 to 2015 (4%). The government (public) school has recorded the largest proportional decrease during this same period (7%). Evidently there is a consistent pattern of growth within the Independent sector and a regular pattern of decline, in terms of enrolment levels, within the public sector. It would be simplistic to argue that this is simply a matter of demand, rather than complicated by many other factors including economic, social and cultural shifts. As education reforms increased funding for the private sector, enrolment levels in the private sector increased at a similar rate and time period. I will discuss this further in the following section.

The consumer growth of the Independent school becomes much clearer if we examine the increase in enrolments within the Independent secondary school sector since 1980 (see Figure 5.3).

In Australia, the Independent school sector has grown exponentially since 1980 (see Figure 5.3). This sector has increased their enrolment from 6% of the total enrolment in secondary school to 18% of the total enrolment (an increase of 12%). The public school has decreased from 74% to 59% during this same period (a decrease of 15%). The Catholic school sector has fluctuated far less and eventually recorded a very similar proportion of enrolment since 1980 (a difference of 4%). Evidently, in correlation with the proportional increases, the number of Independent schools has grown; conversely, the number of public schools has dwindled.

The cost of schooling

The Independent secondary school has experienced this significant consumer growth in spite of the high tuition fees. Albeit, there are 'affordable' or lower-fee Independent secondary schools, however the most expensive schools in Australia are those within the Independent sector, emphasizing academic results and charging the highest tuition fees.[3] Watson and Ryan (2010) write, in regards to the private school, 'it would appear that charging relatively high tuition fees is not a barrier to growth' (90). For example, Scots College in Sydney annually charges $33,098 for a senior student; the Sydney Church of England Girls Grammar School charges parents $33,627 annually for a senior student (Kimmorley, 2015).[4] To put this in perspective, sending one child to this school represents almost half of the gross median household annual income in Australia, cited as $80,717.[5] One year of secondary school at an elite Independent school is far more expensive than most university undergraduate degrees and out of reach for many. For example, enrolment per year in an undergraduate medicine or law degree at the University of Melbourne (one of the highest-ranking universities in the world, according to QS rankings) currently costs $10,440 per year.

Mainstream media often print articles exhorting parents to save for secondary school as soon as they *conceive*. At the point of conception, a savvy couple will begin stockpiling finances in order to guarantee quality, elite schooling.

88 Private versus public schools

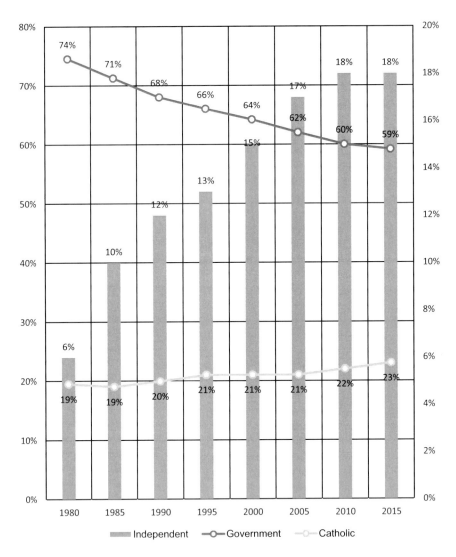

Figure 5.3 Full-time students enrolled in secondary school by sector (includes all states and territories in Australia), 1980–2015.

For example, Marcelle and her husband, photographed as a smiling couple with their new baby, are reported in *The Age* newspaper, 'Marcelle, 36, and her husband were already clients of a financial adviser before [baby] Cruz came along. They raised the issue of education with their adviser when Marcelle was pregnant' (Collett, 2016). But the cost of schooling may have already exceeded their savings. In Australia, education 'is one of the fastest rising components of the

Consumer Price Index (CPI)'. During the past ten years, the cost of education for consumers has risen at almost 'twice the rate of inflation' (ASG, 2011). To be precise, recent figures from the Australian Bureau of Statistics show that education costs are outstripping inflation. From December 2014 to December 2015, the cost of education for the consumer increased by 5.5%, compared to general inflation of 1.5%, as measured by the consumer price index (ABS, 2015). According to these calculations, Scots College, for example, whilst currently charging $33,098 for a senior student, in twelve years' time will annually cost parents $55,938 for one student, if it continues to rise at 5.5% each tax year.

The high cost of secondary schooling is exploited by private interests, such as banks and scholarship saving funds, like the Australian Scholarship Group (ASG) (2011), who advise parents to take a 'proactive approach' to their children's schooling.

> Therefore, Australian Scholarship Group encourages parents to take a proactive approach to their children's education early in their children's lives. This enables parents to have greater choice and peace-of-mind.
>
> (Profile page)

The Group offers financial rewards to parents only if their child goes onto study higher education. In Australia, the cost of secondary schooling is rising rapidly. Alongside the purchasing of a home, the secondary school may be one of life's major financial outlays. For these reasons, there are many consultancy firms offering advice for school enrolment and saving funds. Parents can also apply for tuition scholarships for private schools, sit examinations for select-entry public schools, or relocate for 'desirable' public high schools. It is important to keep in mind that many public secondary schools still retain a high level of accessibility and affordability, even for students living outside of the neighbourhood. However, for many parents, these schools are simply not an option.

Independent private schools have clearly been successful in the market, in terms of convincing the consumer of the superiority of their product. It is noteworthy that the private school has commanded this consumer growth, in spite of the largely free or inexpensive schooling options available. Indeed, these decisions are not purely economic, and certain private schools may be more desirable for parents on the basis of ideology or religion (Watson and Ryan, 2010). I will argue in the following section that government policy has played an important role in marketing and providing consumer incentives for parents to choose Independent schools.

Policy and funding levels per sector

Whilst neoliberal policies frequently claim to create 'small government' with little regulation and intervention, laissez-faire approaches construct certain policy conditions for the consumer, influential in meaningful ways. Post-welfare policy conditions or the 'market-oriented' position (Bunar, 2010) tends to privilege funding subsidies for private schools, incentivizing consumer demand and activity. In Australia, as evident in Figure 5.3, the private Independent school recorded significant consumer growth between 1980 and 1985 (4% increase) and then again from the period 1995–2005 (4% increase), however the growth has been consistent. The public school recorded almost similar proportional decline, in the period 1980–1985 (3% decrease) and 1995–2005 (4% decrease) and again, the decline is constant.

In tracing a brief policy history, federal government grants were first provided for private schools in 1964 (*States Grants Act 1964*). These were intended as one-off capital grants for struggling Catholic schools to purchase science blocks. The introduction of recurrent per-student grants for private schools in 1970 (*States Grants (Independent Schools) Act 1969*) significantly reoriented the market, but it would be many more years before a large proportion of parents began to view private schools as a viable option. The introduction of the recurrent grants for private schools was partly offset by the federal Whitlam government in the 1970s, which allocated additional funding and grants for public schools. Whilst funding increased for public schools, it also grew for the private sector. The *States Grant Act* was broadened in 1973 with an injection of twenty million dollars into private schools.

This injection of federal funds for private schools was amplified and extended during the 1990s, under the conservative federal Howard government (1996–2007). The policy shifts reflected the emphasis on privatization and competition, and the federal government removed the *New Schools Policy* to encourage direct competition between private and public schools. With the elimination of this policy, private schools were now permitted to build near a public school, thereby increasing the market competition between private and public schools. However, the negative rhetoric surrounding public schools also grew (Kenway, 1987, 1990). A chief of staff within the government wrote a book titled, *Why Our Schools Are Failing* (referring exclusively to public schools), blaming left-wing and 'politically correct' teachers and unions for widespread failure (Donnelly, 2004). The Prime Minister weighed in on the conversation, arguing that public schools were dominated by politically correct teacher unions and were far too 'values-neutral' and progressive (Crabb and Guerrera, 2004). The government of the day attributed the increased parental choice of Independent schools to ideological preferences, as opposed to market influences.

The Howard federal government continually encouraged parents to make better schooling choices and in 2001, introduced the socio-economic status-funding model (referred to as the SES funding model). This funding model reflected the earlier recurrent funding schemes in the 1970s, but modified how funding was calculated for private schools. The SES funding model was described as 'exceedingly opaque' (Dowling, 2008), complex and wholly lacking in transparency (Vickers, 2005). Private schools were now funded on the basis of the socio-economic status of the student, calculated by linking a student's residential address to Census information, thereby allocating an average SES score for each school (based on parental income, occupation and education). This needs-based approach initially sounds positive, and yet analyses indicated that private schools generated significantly increased funds, in real terms, from as much as 5:1 ratio in favour of private schools (Vickers, 2005; Windle, 2009). In certain cases, elite Independent schools, many of which charge upwards of $30,000 annually per student, received sizeable injections of taxpayer funds. The Independent Schools Lobby argued that it is a fairer system of funding, as many of the schools, even the elite schools, are educating a greater proportion of lower socio-economic status students than previously realized. However, research consistently indicates that Independent schools which educate large proportions of low SES students are rare (Watson and Ryan, 2010; Gonski et al., 2011). Lamb (2007) notes the 'real shift in expenditure in favour of private schools' in the 1990s and that Australia's method

> ... of supporting private provision in schools through public funding is quite rare internationally because the funding from governments is provided without any regulations or conditions governing use and without any accountability requirements.
>
> (7)

In the wake of the school funding controversy in the early 2000s surrounding the sizeable funding of private schools, the succeeding left-of-centre government initiated a review of school funding, commonly referred to as the 'Gonski report' (Gonski et al., 2011). This report found that the Independent sector receives a total of 45% of its net recurrent income from combined forms of government. This equates to 8.2 billion dollars to educate 14% of the population.[6] Watson and Ryan's (2010) analysis stipulates that students enrolled in private schools attracts a 'government subsidy worth between 15% and 70% of average estimated student operating costs, determined on a needs basis' (86). The high funding of Independent schools 'sets it apart from many OECD countries' (Gonski et al., 2011: 11).

The continuous closing of public schools is also linked to funding, and clearly connects with consumption choices. Throughout the 1990s and beyond, public schools were consistently closed or merged across various states and territories. This undoubtedly establishes a sense of instability for the consumer, and whilst the overall number of full-time secondary students grew, by 2011 the availability of public schools had declined. The total percentage of public schools in Australia had decreased by 2%. On the other hand, the percentage of private schools had increased by 1% of the total number of schools.

As a percentage of GDP Australia spends less on secondary education, in contrast to other OECD countries such as the US, but more than the OECD average (OECD, 2015). However, this figure includes private sources, such as philanthropy, parental contributions and fundraising, which boost the overall average. Private sources constitute a higher percentage of per-school funding, in comparison to the OECD average, which effectively means that parents are allocating more of their personal income for schooling, in addition to their tax.

There are three different 'types' of grants for schools, referred to as recurrent, capital and targeted funding, and the different grants come from various sources. Productivity commissions that report on school funding tend to exclusively report the net recurrent funding per student, and *exclude* levels of capital funding for the school (for example, Australian Government Productivity Commission, 2014). This Productivity Commission report, for example, indicates a funding ratio of 2:1 in favour of government schools. However, this is not an accurate or conclusive indicator of funding levels, obfuscated by different types of funding (recurrent, capital and targeted grants) and also the different sources (state, federal and private sources). Reported funding levels tend to conceal the inflated capital funding (for new capital works, such as gymnasiums or swimming pools) that private schools receive. Capital grants have increased for the private sector, but this can also be attributed to the rise of students within this sector. Transparent indicators of government school funding are further masked by a heavy reliance on private sources.

Government subsidies have not alleviated the barriers for lower socio-economic-status students in accessing private schools, particularly within the Independent sector. More so, research would indicate that government subsidies have only aggravated and further entrenched the accessibility barriers. The Independent school sector reflects the most affluent and advantaged families, and 'parents from higher socio-economic groups are more likely to choose private education than parents from lower socio-economic groups' (Watson and Ryan, 2010: 86). According to the Gonski et al. (2011) report, the public sector educates 36% of students who represent the lowest socio-economic-status bracket in Australia. This is contrasted to the Independent sector, which educates 13% of the lowest socio-economic-status bracket.

> Of all students in the lowest quarter [including the lower and middle two tiers] of socio-educational advantage, almost 80 per cent attended government schools . . . Government schools provide for a high proportion of Indigenous students and students with disability. In 2010, 85 per cent of all Indigenous students attended government schools . . . Seventy-eight percent of students with a funded disability attended government schools.
> (Gonski et al., 2011: 10)

The laissez-faire deregulation of competition between private and public schools has stimulated market principles and increased equity gaps. Segregation on the basis of income, country of birth and religion is palpable across the Australian schooling system, and public schools educate the majority of students within the lowest quarter of socio-educational advantage.[7] The Independent School Council of Australia, an organization that lobbies the federal government on behalf of the Independent school sector, repeatedly affirms its commitment to cultural diversity, social inclusion and equity. In actuality their diversity is limited. Indigenous students and students experiencing a disability tend to be 'quartered off' – enrolled within the 'Other' schools, including 'special schools, Indigenous schools and community schools', which make up 2.4% of the Independent school sector in Australia.

Whilst many advocates of choice policies argue that lower-income students attend private schools, the lower-income students are the minority within these schools, and this is strongly reflected across the data. In their research that investigated international determinants of private school attendance, the authors found that students from higher socio-economic status backgrounds were more likely to attend private schools (Rutkowski et al., 2012).[8] The authors write,

> In fact, of 44 countries that classified some of their schools as privately managed and publicly funded, 36 countries exhibited a significant and positive relationship between a more advantaged student background and choosing a privately managed, publicly funded school.
> (Rutkowski et al., 2012: 383)

However, educational policy has not sought to alleviate this segregation by regulating tuition fees or requiring that private schools educate a certain proportion of students from a lower socio-economic-status background. As I pointed to previously, despite the rising government subsidies for private schooling, the cost of private schooling has only increased for the consumer. Advocates of choice argue that parents have the right to choose expensive and elite schools, if they are prepared to pay for it – although it is clear that high tuition fees eliminate this choice for many consumers. Government subsidies for private schools, in addition to the high tuition fees, and political rhetoric that favours private schools have enabled private schools to leverage and consolidate a robust advantage in the market. Watson and Ryan (2010) write,

> We find that Australian private schools have used government subsidies to increase the quality of their services (that is, to reduce student:teacher ratios) rather than to reduce their fees. As a consequence, the socio-economic composition of private schools has remained above average while a higher proportion of public school students now come from low socio-economic status (SES) backgrounds.
> (86)

There is clearly a division between private and public schools. However, in the following section, I will demonstrate the levels of segregation occurring within the public schooling sector, and stark differentiations based on government subsidies and student composition. By drawing on the schools within the data set, the following analysis examines levels of social exclusion within the public school sector – a sector commonly understood as accessible and democratic.

Segregation within the public school sector: Statistical school profiles

The following analysis identifies and highlights sharp levels of segregation within the public schooling sector, by socio-educational advantage and disadvantage. The following graphs utilize statistical and financial data from the *My School* website[9] (2012 data) in order to demonstrate gaps and differentiations between schools. Levels of advantage and disadvantage – and how this is marked out by individual schools – is measured via the Index of Community Socio-Educational Advantage (hereby referred to as ICSEA).

The ICSEA is calculated by utilizing direct data (students' family backgrounds) and indirect data (school-level factors). The student's family background includes parental occupation, parental levels of school education and non-school education. The school-level factors include a school's geographical location (i.e., remoteness) and the proportion of Indigenous students (see ACARA, 2010). The third measure shown on the graphs is the school ICSEA score, with a higher score (over 1000) indicating a more advantaged school cohort, and a lower score (under 1000) equating to a more disadvantaged school cohort. This score takes into consideration the percentage of students within the bottom, middle two tiers and highest socio-educational advantage quarter.

In the following analysis, the schools have been coded as 'popular, rejected and balanced' (Seppánen, 2003: 513) to indicate whether the school is coded within the data sets as a popular, rejected or balanced choice for the participants. This categorization is signified in each figure by utilizing the symbols (P), (R) and (B). Seppánen's (2003) 'popular, rejected and balanced' categories are useful for rejecting the dualism of choice, even though preferences can be considerably weighted in a particular direction, and are typically not based on empirical data as related to test scores. The qualitative data suggests that certain public high schools are, for the vast majority of parents living in these catchment areas, far more desirable than others.[10] Whilst the popular schools are identified as 'high-demand' and 'heavily zoned' by many participants, there are shortcomings in arguing that all residents living in the neighbourhoods of Smith and Lawson desire or prefer these particular high schools, and moreover, that all parents living in these zones are white and affluent. Even though the majority of residents living in these catchment areas, and responding to the Census, represent a higher socio-economic status, and are Australian-born with higher educational qualifications, it is important to be cautious in generalizing the consumption choices for all residents. Rather, I argue that there are majority or dominant socio-demographic characteristics within each of the neighbourhoods and school catchment areas, and dominant school preferences; however, there also outliers.

For the public high schools in the surrounding catchment areas, there is clearly an inverse relationship when considering levels of disadvantage and advantaged student cohorts. Unsurprisingly, the schools identified as 'popular' within the data set serve the most advantaged student cohorts. The following figure is

Private versus public schools 95

organized by its ICSEA score, by the schools identified as the most disadvantaged to the more advantaged schools – a low to high ICSEA score (see Figure 5.4).

Originally this graph included fifteen schools, and the reader can see the complete data set in the appendix.[11] This graph includes ten schools only for the

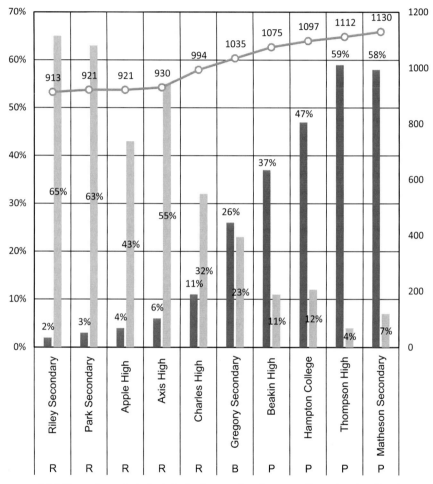

Figure 5.4 A profile of surrounding public high schools within the data set, ranked from the lowest to highest ICSEA score. The higher ICSEA score equates to a more advantaged student cohort.

purpose of brevity and clarity. Across the data set there are strong correlations between popular schools for the choosers in the study and advantaged student cohorts, with the popular schools strongly inverted between advantage and disadvantage. This is even further pronounced when visualizing it another way (see Figure 5.5).

Data indicates that differentiations between school-level advantage and disadvantage are clearly marked out and tangible. Rather than a mixed or diverse cohort of students, public schools are largely serving homogenous student cohorts, defined by advantaged or disadvantaged student bodies (see Figures 5.4 and 5.5). For example, Riley Secondary, the school with the lowest ICSEA score

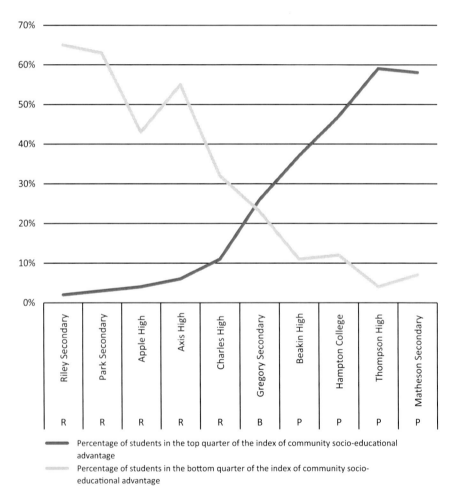

— Percentage of students in the top quarter of the index of community socio-educational advantage

— Percentage of students in the bottom quarter of the index of community socio-educational advantage

Figure 5.5 Public high schools and inverse levels of advantage and disadvantage according to their ICSEA score.

Private versus public schools 97

(913) and positioned only 5.3 kilometres from neighbourhood Smith, has only 2% of students in the top quarter of the measure of socio-educational advantage and 65% of students in the bottom quarter.

The following figure shows the percentage of students with a Language Background Other than English (LBOTE), in addition to the ICSEA school score (see Figure 5.6).

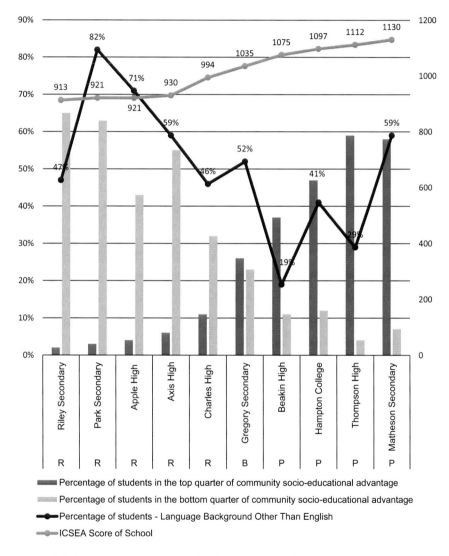

Figure 5.6 A profile of schools by ICSEA score of school and percentage of students who are from a language background other than English (LBOTE).

The majority of the popular schools report a lower percentage of students from a LBOTE; however, Matheson Secondary is the outlier in this regard. As stated previously, the percentage of students from a LBOTE is not a reliable measure of school-level disadvantage, as it neglects to consider wider variables, including parental education and occupation. Matheson Secondary enrols a higher percentage of students from a Chinese-born background and achieves in the top ten of the state for university entrance examination results. Matheson Secondary maintains a sense of exclusivity and most of the campaigners mention Matheson as a school preference. However, none have actually visited the school, except for Michelle, who says, 'I have visited Matheson Secondary, but I was put off by the elitist academics, and it seems to be half Asian'. Other participants stipulate Matheson as a school preference, even though they have never visited the school and seem unaware of its location. Naomi says, 'What about Matheson? I don't know much, but I still like it!' As the campaigners emphasize the importance of proximity, Matheson Secondary is a contrary preference.

Financial profiles of each public high school

The following figures utilize ten different sets of data to generate detailed financial profiles for ten public high schools within the data set.[12] Before turning to these figures, they require a brief explanation. The complete data set generated financial profiles for fifteen different schools and it is available in the Appendix; the subsequent graphs focus on the ten schools previously profiled. The graphs depict ten different sets of financial data for each school. This consists of (a) Australian government recurrent funding and (b) state/territory government recurrent funding, and the level of funding was collected over two separate years (2012 and 2013), as it differs for each year. This funding was calculated to a total sum (c–d) for each year and (e) for both years combined. The financial school profile also shows (f) fees, charges and parent contributions and (g) other private sources. This was collected over two separate years (2012 and 2013), and again this is calculated to a total sum (h–j). All of these calculations are based on net recurrent income *per student*, rather than the total sum received by the school. This enables a more accurate analysis, allowing for broad differences in the enrolment size of the school. The final marker that is included in the financial profile is total capital expenditure attributed to the school, over five years (2009–2013). This figure is *not* divided by the number of students, and rather it is based on the total amount of funding that was allocated to the school, exclusively for capital expenditure (e.g., a new gymnasium or library). This amount is separate from the funding received in the indicators (a) and (b) in that the total capital expenditure is in *addition* to this funding.

The following graph (see Figure 5.7) shows the grand total of income per student, according to each school, as generated by government funding and private sources. This figure emphasizes levels of government funding, from lowest to highest (sources a–j).

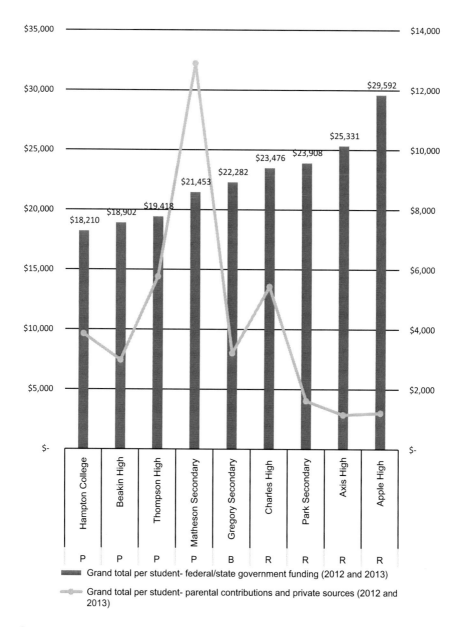

Figure 5.7 Financial profile of public high schools from sources a–j: includes private/parent sources, and government funding. It shows government funding from lowest to highest (2012–2013).

100 Private versus public schools

It is promising that the schools with a more disadvantaged student cohort received higher levels of funding from both forms of government in 2012 and 2013 (shown here as a total figure). However, the level of funding received from the government does not resemble the 'hockey stick' effect that was visible in the socio-economic composition of the schooling cohort (see Figure 5.5). For example, Park Secondary received a total of $23,908 from both levels of government, compared to Matheson Secondary's $21,453 funding level. But, the private sources and contributions at Matheson Secondary is three times the proportion of Park Secondary and the schooling cohort is completely inverted. Park Secondary enrols 63% of students in the bottom quarter of community socio-educational advantage, in comparison to Matheson Secondary with 7% in the bottom quarter (and 58% in the top quarter).

Figure 5.8 utilizes identical data, but displays this graph as based on parental contributions and private sources from lowest to highest.

With the exception of Charles High, the majority of popular schools for the campaigners receive a much higher proportion of funding per student from private sources and parental contributions, reflecting the wealthier and more socially advantaged student cohort. Indeed, the proportional differences are sizeable. The total proportion of private funding generated by the schools considered to be 'popular' and 'balanced' within the data set generated almost three times the proportion of funds generated by the 'rejected' within the data set ($28,677 compared to $10,724), and this relates only to 2012 and 2013 (see Figure 5.7). These contributions clearly have a substantial impact on the resources that the school is able to garner and generate.

These figures also conceal the level of government funding for total capital expenditure that each school receives. Figure 5.9 on page 102 shows the total capital expenditure (2009–2013) for each school, and this figure includes funding for new capital received from both forms of government. Thompson High is not included in this graph as the figures are not available.

The levels of total capital expenditure that each school received within this period is spread out between the popular schools and rejected schools. Park Secondary, also one of the most disadvantaged, received the highest level of capital funding, but Apple High (with an ICSEA score of 921, the second lowest) also received the least amount of funding for capital expenditure. If these figures are compared to Figure 5.8, which shows Apple High as recipients of the highest amount of per-student funding (2012–2013), this is visibly levelled out due to the very low level of capital grants received by the school. Hampton College (the first preference for Smith campaigners) and Beakin College (the first preference for Lawson campaigners) received the lowest level of government funding per student, however these schools obtained considerable capital investments and upgrades within their schools.

Finally, to obtain a more conclusive account of the differences in funding levels, the following graph is arranged from lowest to highest on the basis of net

Private versus public schools 101

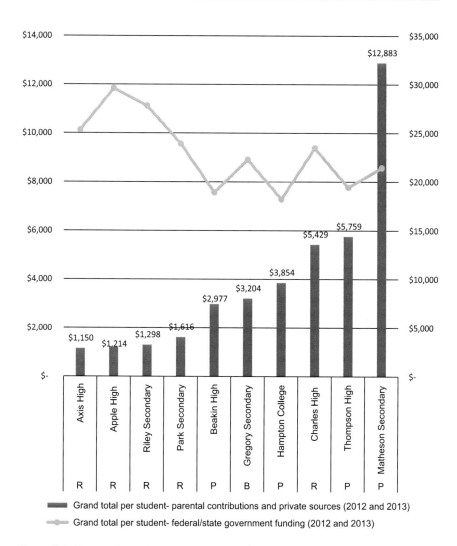

Figure 5.8 Financial profile of public high schools from sources a–j: includes parental/private sources, and government funding. It shows parental/private sources from lowest to highest (2012–2013).

recurrent income per student (calculated as an average, 2009 to 2013). The line indicates financial subsidies that the school received from the government for capital expenditure in the same period (see Figure 5.10 on page 103).

Data indicates that funding for public schools is complex and at times, illogical. Certain schools with lower ICSEA rankings, such as Gregory and Park, schools that are acknowledged as serving a disadvantaged cohort, receive less funding than schools with a far more advantaged cohort. The level of net recurrent

102 Private versus public schools

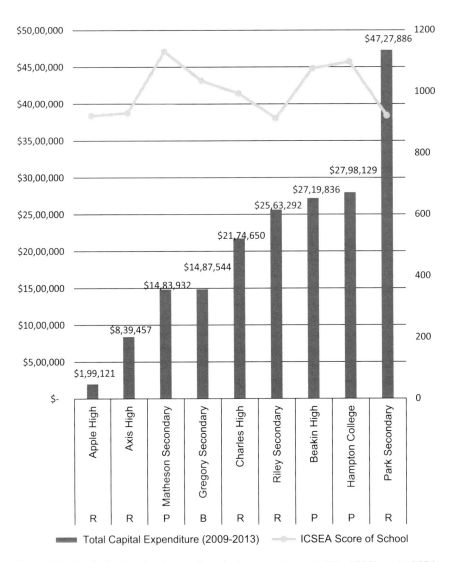

Figure 5.9 Public high schools: total capital expenditure (2009–2013) and ICSEA score of school.

income between schools is relatively similar, despite the contra differences in socio-educational advantage and disadvantage. For example, Apple High, with an ICSEA score of 921 and the second most disadvantaged within the data set, reported a net recurrent income per student of $15,468 (see Figure 5.10). This is slightly higher than the most advantaged Matheson Secondary (ICSEA score

Private versus public schools 103

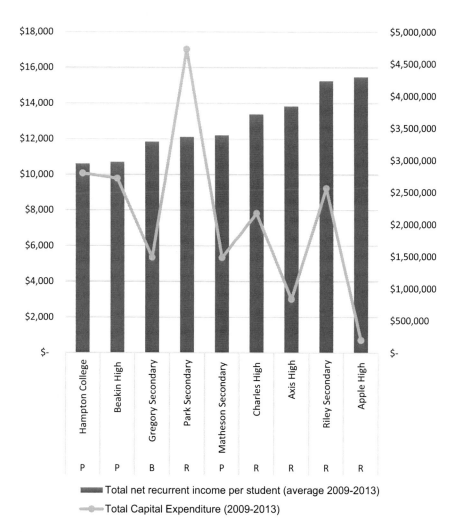

Figure 5.10 School financial profile: includes net recurrent income per student from lowest to highest (2009–2013) and capital expenditure (2009–2013).

of 1130), with a reported net recurrent income per student of $12,206. However, the differences in capital expenditure are overly substantial – Apple High ($199,121) in contrast to Matheson Secondary ($1.5 million).

There seems to be very little logic behind these variances, although many policy documents available through the *My School* website advocate against readers making 'direct funding comparisons' and that capital expenditure varies significantly, due to the wide range of programs that are available at each school. However, due to an overall lack of transparency, and using all resources that are available to the public, the calculations indicate that, at times, the government allocates greater levels of funding for more advantaged school cohorts. Furthermore, this small-scale analysis would suggest that more affluent families are clustering within particular public high schools and there are sharp differences when it comes to levels of advantage and disadvantage between public high schools. This is critical for notions of educational equity and desegregation within the public school, highlighting a critical need for government policy to arrest gaps at the school-level and construct policy conditions that aim to desegregate, rather than segregate.

Driving distinction and entrenching disadvantage

Policies have not only exacerbated the growth of the private sector, but also intensified segregation between schools, with many characterized by concentrated disadvantage. Lamb (2007: 189) refers to these schools as 'residualised' schools, routinely located in high-poverty neighbourhoods and serving lower-income families. This affects staff retention, recruiting and sustaining high-quality and experienced teachers, generating high-calibre resources within the school, and having the capacity to meet the needs of a disadvantaged population (Lamb et al., 2015).

Curriculum differentiation is also a key issue for lower socio-economic-status schools (Perry and Southwell, 2014; Schmidt et al., 2015). Schmidt et al. (2015) found this to be a 'cross-country phenomenon', occurring in a broad range of global contexts, in that 'the most affluent students generally receive more rigorous opportunities to learn important mathematics' (381). Lower socio-economic schools 'offer students less access to the core academic curriculum subjects that are important for university entry' (Perry and Southwell, 2014: 467). Schools are essentially 'tracking' students based on family income and social advantage into certain pathways, whether it be higher-tiered universities and prestigious courses, such as medicine or law, or vocational further education and apprenticeships. Lower socio-economic schools also record higher proportions of students who 'drop out' early and do not graduate (Keating, 2009). Schools create networks of opportunities, certain expectations for future life-chances, and prepare students for career pathways. However, these pathways are far from democratic or equitable; they are stratified and highly informed by individual school differences and concentrated levels of advantage or disadvantage.

The importance of a mixed cohort for academic and social outcomes was identified many decades ago by the Coleman Report (Coleman et al., 1966). Whilst many topics are still under debate within the field of education, the influence of socio-economic status on a student's opportunity to learn, but also their academic achievement outputs, results on standardized tests, higher likelihood to complete secondary education and access university, is consistently demonstrated within the international literature (Perry and McConney, 2010, 2013).[13]

The socio-economic status of the student, which contributes to the larger socio-economic status of the school overall, affects learning outcomes, because 'any individual student outcome is correlated not only with that individual's own social background, but also with the social background of other students in the same school' (Field et al., 2007: 42). The school that a student attends can be incredibly influential for academic outcomes or standardized test results, decisive for access to higher education and employment, however the degree of influence will differ depending on the country in which you live. This is well demonstrated by Perry and McConney (2013) in their comparison of Australia and Canada PISA results to examine the relationship between school socio-economic status and student outcomes in reading and mathematics. Attending a high SES school is more important in Australia than it is in Canada, and

> educational equity in Canada does not come at the expense of privileged students: high SES students perform the same in both countries, while low SES students generally perform higher in Canada than in Australia
> (Perry & McConney, 2011; 2013: 136)

Research indicates that different countries are more effective in ameliorating educational disadvantage and reducing the gap between high and low achievers, particularly those that reduce between-school variance, academic selection of students and pathway tracking (OECD, 2012; Perry and McConney, 2013). This opens up a crucial and essential debate surrounding the policies that structure and organize educational systems. A school that is characterized by poverty and concentrated levels of disadvantage, and further exacerbated by funding neglect, is a considerable risk for educational equity. It creates distinct segregation, played out between schooling sectors – the private versus the public – but also geographically, within the residential housing market, as parents compete to access certain high-demand public schools. As the more privileged clientele grows within a public school, it tends be an ongoing cycle, and the more privileged and exclusive it becomes. The clientele generates higher levels of funding in the way of private sources and contributions, either by fundraising or through their professional contacts (Posey-Maddox, 2016). For example, some of these more privileged public schools within the data set, such as Matheson Secondary, hire professional event managers, comedians, bands and hosts for their annual school fete, generating thousands of dollars in profits. However, it is not only the private funding that grows, and government funding is far from stagnant for these affluent schools.

In the data I have analyzed in this section, I have focused on public schools, highlighting the problematic and distinct segregation between public schools. To conclude this chapter, I will briefly explore the 'private school advantage'. This will scaffold the following chapter regarding the urban middle class and the 'cultural turn' to public education.

The private school advantage

Without any methodological controls, private schools tend to achieve higher results on standardized tests in comparison to public schools across many country contexts (see Braun et al., 2006; Coulson, 2009; OECD, 2011; Rutkowski et al., 2012; Lubienski and Lubienski, 2013; Marks, 2015). However, the difficulty comes in that private schools tend to educate the more affluent or wealthier students and research shows that students who represent a more advantaged background typically achieve higher results on standardized tests or university entrance examinations (OECD, 2012). Therefore, it is critical to control for socio-economic factors, such as parental level of income, occupation and education when examining standardized test results. The PISA index of economic, social and cultural status (ESCS) utilizes three indices, including highest occupational status of parents, highest educational level of parents and home possessions, such as the number of books in the home (OECD, 2013).

Many studies argued, through the 1970s to 1990s, that even after controlling for socio-economic factors including family levels of education, occupation and income, that nongovernment schools achieve higher results on standardized tests or university entrance examinations. This was termed the 'private school effect' (Coleman et al., 1981; Coleman and Hoffer, 1987), and there grew a consensus that the greater autonomy of private schools, and the ability of private schools to be more resourceful, accountable and responsive to parents, led to higher academic results. This effectively boosted the flight of white, middle-class parents to the private sector.

The differentiations in academic performance became particularly contentious in the 1990s, during the introduction of charter schools and vouchers in the US (see Chapter One). Many scholars argued that the implementation of large-scale reforms, under the belief that private schools out-perform public schools, demanded rigorous research supporting or validating the reforms. Ravitch (2011) provides a useful account and review of the research literature during this period, which were largely initiated and funded to either provide leverage for charter school advocates, or charter school adversaries. Witte (1992) found that, after controlling for student background (amongst other controls), statistically significant differences between private and public academic outcomes are trivial and uncertain. Charter school advocates sought to discredit Witte's findings, on the basis of his appointment by a well-known opponent of charter schools. Overall, results were mixed, but private school lobbyists did not ultimately receive the results they were hoping for (Rouse, 1998; Ravitch, 2011). Some studies continue to suggest (or make strong claims for) the 'private school effect' in achieving higher outcomes than public schools, in various country contexts (Kingdon, 1996; Coulson, 2009; Tooley et al., 2011).

US-based studies demonstrate that private schools outperform the public school in the area of reading, but the effect is nil to negative in the area of mathematics (Braun et al., 2006). Referring to this study in a subsequent publication, Braun (2007) writes

> Specifically, we found no difference in reading in grade 4 and a private school advantage of about seven points in grade 8 reading. The reverse occurred in mathematics for grade 4, with public schools having an advantage of about four points. There was no difference between public and private schools in grade 8 mathematics.
>
> (24)

These findings are supported by additional studies. Sarah Theule Lubienski and Christopher Lubienski from the US found that even after controlling for student background, fourth-grade and eighth-grade mathematics results are 'statistically significantly higher' in the public school sector. Their earlier results (2005, 2006) were substantiated in the later book entitled *The Public School Advantage* (2013). The Lubienskis again draw on mathematics results from the National Assessment of Education Progress (NEAP), writing,

> The large, nationally representative ... data set indicates that, after accounting for the greater advantages of students served in private schools, public school fourth and eight graders' mathematics achievement is higher, on average, than that of students in private schools.
>
> (82)

The Lubienskis (2013) argued that the higher achievement levels in the area of mathematics could be attributed to a greater willingness on behalf of the public sector to be innovative and responsive to curriculum changes, and more proactive in taking up contemporary pedagogical practice. These arguments, and indeed their findings, were both contentious and celebrated (Ryan, 2013; Strauss, 2013). The National Association of Independent Schools criticized the study for its methodology (Chubb, 2013), claiming that the methods utilized to measure socio-economic status are flawed. This critique is not surprising, given their own stakeholder interests. Certainly, the bulk of the debate that has been generated towards the public school or the 'manufactured crisis' (Berliner and Biddle, 1995) is undoubtedly linked to fiscal concerns and stakeholder interests.

Many believe that enrolment in a private school will lead to a more satisfying and higher remunerated career. Indeed, this is difficult to substantiate given the variables, but a report published by the London School of Economics (Green et al., 2010) endeavours to do so. Their calculations argue that consumers can expect a 7%–13% average net return for their investment in a private school, with the return higher for day students as opposed to boarding students. These findings were issued with many caveats, and were based on the argument that private school graduates go on to achieve higher-paid employment over their lifespan. This is potentially due to the networking opportunities that are available to private school students, rather than increased merit. Certainly, many studies argue that public school graduates achieve higher results in university and lower 'drop-out' rates, as compared to private school graduates (Win and Miller, 2005; Birch and Miller, 2007).

Moreover, when it comes to educational effectiveness, research suggests that there are more important aspects than the governance of the school, whether it is private or public. There are two characteristics that are consistently emphasized in the literature: first, teacher quality, and second, the socio-economic status (SES) of the student and school, or the economic, social and cultural status (see OECD, 2013). The politics of educational reform is routinely played out via the relentless division and debate between the importance of teacher quality versus the SES composition for achieving higher outcomes. Whilst a great depth of research continues to mutually identify the importance of teacher quality and SES composition, they are frequently positioned in opposing ways in policy agendas and policy shifts. For example, Hattie's (2003) widely promoted paper declares that teachers make all the difference, but 'schools barely make a difference to achievement' (2), a view that has resulted in highly influential roles for Hattie within the educational landscape, in Australia and overseas. Many New Right ideologues will strongly argue that SES composition has very little to do with educational effectiveness, and teacher quality supersedes the importance of SES composition. Policy documents tend to focus on the importance of teacher quality and disregard the second aspect of educational effectiveness (Skourdoumbis, 2013). The ongoing and relentless opposition between these two policies, frequently highlighted in popular culture and the media, demonstrates the politics of educational reform. It is curious as to why both of these characteristics cannot be acknowledged as legitimate, valid and influential in the pursuit of educational effectiveness.

Conclusion

This chapter highlights acute levels of segregation between public schools, to the point that levels of advantage and disadvantage are exceedingly concentrated in particular schools. However, this is not reflected in funding levels and differentiations between schools, and many of the schools serving advantaged student cohorts received inflated government subsidies for capital works. The majority of schools educating disadvantaged cohorts received the lowest level of capital expenditure, and government subsidies tend to favour the more affluent clientele, although there are exceptions. Sharp levels of segregation within the public schooling sector is significant for conceptualizing public education as equitable, accessible and high-quality for all individuals, regardless of their parents' income, educational levels and occupation.

The data suggest an ongoing trend for parents to choose the Independent private school, despite the ever-growing cost of many schools in this sector. The high tuition fee charged by certain private schools is the foreclosure of inclusion for low-income earners, and clearly helps for brand management, selling a more 'exclusive' and affluent label, enabling access into elite class networks. Indeed, many high-powered politicians in OECD countries such as Britain and Australia attended the most elite schools.

As Watson and Ryan (2010) point out, public schools are increasingly educating students from lower socio-economic-status backgrounds. The savvy middle- to upper-middle-class consumer may be seeking out alternative and strategic ways to avoid those schools characterized by disadvantage and funding neglect, whilst simultaneously looking to avoid the onerous pressure of private school fees. I will take up this discussion further in the following chapter with a focus on white flight and the repopulation of the urban public school.

Notes

1 In Australia, the secondary (or high) school educates the upper years of schooling, approximately ages twelve to seventeen, with slight differences between states and territories.
2 See the Appendix for further information about how these figures were calculated: see Chapter Five: Parental Choice in Australia: enrolment levels per sector.
3 Private education is also expensive in the US and England. In the US, the national average cost for parents is estimated to be $9,505 USD per year. However, the cost of private school tuition varies greatly across the country, with some states such as Connecticut recording an average of $21,876 USD per year, compared to the state of Nebraska ($3,726 USD).
4 All dollar figures in this book are reported in Australian Dollars (AUD) unless specifically stated otherwise.
5 This is the most recent figure available at time of writing (release date: 03/30/2016). This figure represents median gross household income. See ABS (2016) '6523.0 - Household Income and Wealth, Australia, 2013–14'. Author Accessed 05/24/2016. http://www.abs.gov.au/AUSSTATS/abs@.nsf/Lookup/6523.0Main+Features312013-14?OpenDocument
6 This figure includes net recurrent income plus capital expenditure. These are 2009 figures. This includes the primary and secondary sector only.
7 Socio-educational advantage is similar yet slightly different to 'socio-economic' and this measurement is derived from the Index of Community Socio-Educational Advantage (ICSEA) measurement. I explain this further in this chapter; see 'Segregation within the public school sector'. Also, see Appendix.
8 This paper excludes Australia from the analysis, and therefore this finding does not relate to Australia.
9 The *My School* website is authored and published by the Australian Curriculum Assessment and Reporting Authority (ACARA) and is available from www.myschool.edu.au. This data reflects the year 2012 only.
10 The schools were coded as 'popular, rejected and balanced', drawing on Seppánen's (2003) categories. The schools-of-choice were coded within the qualitative data by frequency. At times, participants explicitly stated that certain schools were preferable choices, whereas at times it was subtle and nuanced. I acknowledge the subjectivity within this coding. Subsequently, I contacted the schools deemed to be 'schools-of-choice' within the data set, to ascertain potential application figures, and collected this data each year (2011–2015). The number of potential applicants increased slightly each year for the popular schools (Hampton, Beakin, Matheson) and Gregory is balanced. The complete list of methods

utilized to generate data for coding schools is included within the Appendix (see Table A.1).
11 This data set is available in full in the Appendix. It includes fifteen public high schools. See Table A.6 in the Appendix.
12 The complete data set (fifteen schools in total) is available for further reading, in the Appendix (see Tables 9.7–9.10). These are the most recent available figures at time of writing. See the appendix for further details regarding methodology and calculations.
13 See the extensive literature around the relationship between socio-economic status and educational outcomes (Blossfeld and Shavit, 1993; Renzulli and Park, 2000; Perie et al., 2005; McConney and Perry, 2010; OECD, 2012, 2014; Lubienski and Lubienski, 2013; Lamb et al., 2015; Schmidt et al., 2015).

References

ABS. (2015) *6401.0 — Consumer Price Index, Australia, Dec 2015*, Canberra: Australian Bureau of Statistics.
ABS. (2016) *4221.0- Schools, Australia, 2015*. Available at: http://www.abs.gov.au/ausstats/abs@.nsf/mf/4221.0.
ACARA. (2010) "My School": About ICSEA (accessed 15th March, 2010).
ASG. (2011) *ASG Profile*. Available at: http://www.asg.com.au/resources/.
Australian Government Productivity Commission. (2014) *Report on Government Services 2014: School Education*. Australian Government.
Berliner DC and Biddle BJ. (1995) *The Manufactured Crisis: Myths, Fraud, and the Attack on America's Public Schools*, Reading, MA: Addison-Wesley.
Birch ER and Miller PW. (2007) The influence of type of high school attended on university performance. *Australian Economic Papers* 46: 1–17.
Blossfeld HP and Shavit Y. (1993) Persisting barriers: Changes in educational opportunities in thirteen countries. In: Shavit Y and Blossfeld HP (eds) *Persistent Inequality*, Boulder, CO: Westview, 1–24.
Braun H. (2007) Are private schools better than public schools? *Principal* 86: 22–25.
Braun H, Jenkins F and Grigg W. (2006) *Comparing Private Schools and Public Schools Using Hierarchical Linear Modeling*, Washington, DC: National Center for Education Statistics.
Buckingham J. (2010) *The Rise of Religious Schools. The Centre for Independent Studies*. https://www.cis.org.au/images/stories/policy-monographs/pm-111.pdf.
Bunar N. (2010) Choosing for quality or inequality: Current perspectives on the implementation of school choice policy in Sweden. *Journal of Education Policy* 25: 1–18.
Chubb J. (2013) *A Critique of "The Public School Advantage: Why Public Schools Outperform Private Schools"*. Available at: http://www.nais.org/Independent-Ideas/Lists/Posts/Post.aspx?ID=346.
Coleman J, Campbell E, Hobson C, et al. (1966) *Equality of Educational Opportunity*, Washington, DC: US Government Printing Office.
Coleman JS and Hoffer T. (1987) *Public and Private High Schools: The Impact of Communities*, New York: Basic Books.
Coleman JS, Hoffer T and Kilgore S. (1981) *Public and Private Schools: A Report to the National Center for Education Statistics*, Chicago, IL: National Opinion Research Center.

Collett J. (2016) *How to Save for Your Kids' Education*. Available at: http://www.theage.com.au/money/investing/how-to-save-for-your-kids-education-20160127-gmfmzk.html.

Coulson AJ. (2009) Comparing public, private, and market schools: The international evidence. *Journal of School Choice* 3: 31–54.

Crabb A and Guerrera O. (2004) PM queries values of state schools. *The Age*. Melbourne: Fairfax Digital.

Donnelly K. (2004) *Why Our Schools Are Failing*, Sydney: Duffy & Snellgrove.

Dowling A. (2008) 'Unhelpfully complex and exceedingly opaque': Australia's school funding system. *Australian Council for Educational Research* 52: 129–150.

Field S, Kuczera M and Pont B. (2007) *No More Failures: Ten Steps to Equity in Education*, Paris, France: OECD.

Gonski D, Boston K, Greiner K, et al. (2011) Australian government review of funding for schooling: Final report December 2011. In: Department of Education EaWR (ed). Canberra City, ACT: Department of Education, Employment and Workplace Relations.

Green F, Machin S, Murphy R, et al. (2010) The changing economic advantage from private school London: London School of Economics, Centre for the Economics of Education.

Hattie J. (2003) Distinguishing expert teachers from novice and experienced teachers. Teachers make a difference: What is the research evidence? *Australian Council for Educational Research Annual Conference: Building Teacher Quality*. Carlton Crest Hotel, Melbourne: Australian Council for Educational Research.

Ho C. (2011) Respecting the presence of others: School micropublics and everyday multiculturalism. *Journal of Intercultural Studies* 32: 603–619.

Jamal Al-deen T and Rowe EE. (2016) Muslim mothers and school choice: Racism and critical identity junctures in choosing religious and secular schools. Conference paper presented at Interrogating Belonging in Education, June 31st, Deakin University, Melbourne.

Keating J. (2009) *A new federalism in Australian Education: A Proposal for a National Reform Agenda*, Melbourne: Education Foundation.

Kenway J. (1987) Left right out: Australian education and the politics of signification. *Journal of Education Policy* 2: 189–203.

Kenway J. (1990) Education and the right's discursive politics. In: Ball S (ed) *Foucault and Education*, London: Routledge, 167–206.

Kimmorley S. (2015) *Cheat Sheet: The Top 10 Private Schools for Boys in Sydney*. Available at: http://www.businessinsider.com.au/cheat-sheet-the-top-10-private-schools-for-boys-in-sydney-2015–6#1.

Kingdon G. (1996) The quality and efficiency of private and public education: A case-study of urban India. *Oxford Bulletin of Economics and Statistics* 58: 57–82.

Lamb S. (2007) School reform and inequality in urban Australia: A case of residualising the poor. In: Daru-Bellat S, Lamb S and Teese R (eds) *International Studies in Educational Inequality, Theory and Policy*, Dordrecht, The Netherlands: Springer, 672–709.

Lamb S, Jackson J, Walstab A, et al. (2015) *Educational Opportunity in Australia 2015: Who Succeeds and Who Misses Out*. Centre for International Research on Education Systems, Victoria University, for the Mitchell Institute, Melbourne: Mitchell Institute.

Lubienski CA and Lubienski ST. (2013) *The Public School Advantage: Why Public Schools Outperform Private Schools*, Chicago: The University of Chicago Press.

Lubienski ST and Lubienski C. (2006) School sector and academic achievement: A multilevel analysis of NAEP mathematics data. *American Educational Research Journal* 43: 651–698.

Lubienski ST and Lubienski CA. (2005) A new look at public and private schools: Student background and mathematics achievement. *The Phi Delta Kappan* 86: 696–699.

Marks GN. (2015) Do catholic and independent schools "add-value" to students' tertiary entrance performance? Evidence from longitudinal population data. *Australian Journal of Education* 59: 133–157.

McConney A and Perry LB. (2010) Science and mathematics achievement in Australia: The role of school socioeconomic composition in educational equity and effectiveness. *International Perspectives on Successes and Challenges: Research and Policy Directions* 8: 429–452.

OECD. (2011) *Private Schools: Who Benefits?* Available at: http://www.oecd.org/pisa/pisaproducts/pisainfocus/48482894.pdf.

OECD. (2012) *Equity and Quality in Education: Supporting Disadvantaged Students and Schools*, Paris: OECD Publishing.

OECD. (2013) *PISA 2012 Results: Excellence through Equity. Giving Every Student the Chance to Succeed (Volume II)*, Paris, France: OECD Publishing.

OECD. (2014) *PISA 2012 Results: What Students Know and Can Do (Volume I, Revised Edition, February 2014): Student Performance in Mathematics, Reading and Science*. Available at: http://www.keepeek.com/Digital-Asset-Management/oecd/education/pisa-2012-results-what-students-know-and-can-do-volume-i-revised-edition-february-2014/a-profile-of-student-performance-in-reading_9789264208780-8-en#page1.

OECD. (2015) *Education at a Glance 2015: OECD Indicators*. Available at: http://www.oecd-ilibrary.org/education/education-at-a-glance_19991487.

Perie M, Moran R and Lutkus AD. (2005) NAEP 2004 trends in academic progress: Three decades of student performance in reading and mathematics. In: Education UDo (ed). Washington, DC.

Perry LB and McConney A. (2010) School socio-economic composition and student outcomes in Australia: Implications for education policy. *Australian Journal of Education* 54: 72–85.

Perry, L. B., & McConney, A. (2011, November). *Achievement gaps by student and school socioeconomicstatus: A comparison of Australia and Canada*. Paper presented at the annual conference of the Australian Association for Research in Education, Hobart, Australia.

Perry LB and McConney A. (2013) School socioeconomic status and student outcomes in reading and mathematics: A comparison of Australia and Canada. *Australian Journal of Education* 57: 124–140.

Perry LB and Southwell L. (2014) Access to academic curriculum in Australian secondary schools: A case study of a highly marketised education system. *Journal of Education Policy* 29: 467–485.

Posey-Maddox L. (2016) Beyond the consumer: Parents, privatization, and fundraising in US urban public schooling. *Journal of Education Policy* 31: 178–197.

Ravitch D. (2011) *The Death and Life of the Great American School System: How Testing and Choice Are Undermining Education*, New York: Basic Books.

Renzulli JS and Park S. (2000) Gifted dropouts: The who and the why. *Gifted Child Quarterly* 44: 261–271.

Rouse CE. (1998) Private school vouchers and student achievement: An evaluation of the Milwaukee Parental Choice Program. *The Quarterly Journal of Economics* 113: 553–602.

Rutkowski L, Rutkowski D and Plucker J. (2012) International determinants of private school attendance. *Educational Research & Evaluation* 18: 375.

Ryan J. (2013) *Are Private Schools Worth It?* Available at: http://www.theatlantic.com/education/archive/2013/10/are-private-schools-worth-it/280693/.

Schmidt WH, Burroughs NA, Zoido P, et al. (2015) The role of schooling in perpetuating educational inequality: An international perspective. *Educational Researcher* 44: 371–386.

Seppánen P. (2003) Patterns of 'public-school markets' in the Finnish comprehensive school from a comparative perspective. *Journal of Education Policy* 18: 513–531.

Skourdoumbis A. (2013) The (mis)identification of ineffective classroom teaching practice: Critical interrogations of classroom teacher effectiveness research. *Asia-Pacific Journal of Teacher Education* 41: 350–362.

Strauss V. (2013) *Are Private Schools Better than Public Schools? New Book Says 'No'*. Available at: https://www.washingtonpost.com/news/answer-sheet/wp/2013/11/05/are-private-schools-better-than-public-schools-new-book-says-no/.

Tooley J, Bao Y, Dixon P, et al. (2011) School choice and academic performance: Some evidence from developing countries. *Journal of School Choice* 5: 1–39.

Vickers M. (2005) In the common good: The need for a new approach to funding Australia's schools. *Australian Journal of Education* 49: 264–277.

Watson L and Ryan C. (2010) Choosers and losers: The impact of government subsidies on Australian secondary schools. *Australian Journal of Education* 54: 86–107.

Win R and Miller PW. (2005) The effects of individual and school factors on university students' academic performance. *Australian Economic Review* 38: 1–18.

Windle J. (2009) The limits of school choice: Some implications for accountability of selective practices and positional competition in Australian education. *Critical Studies in Education* 50: 231–246.

Witte JF. (1992) Private school versus public school achievement: Are there findings that should affect the educational choice debate? *Economics of Education Review* 11: 371–394.

Chapter 6

White flight and repopulating the urban public high school

The en masse departure of white middle-class parents away from the urban public school, or 'white flight', to the more prestigious suburban schools, is a commonly understood (and accepted) concept. The 'flight of middle-class families to the suburbs in search of "better" schools was a common pattern and the subject of much concern' (Cucchiara and Horvat, 2014: 495). However, it is increasingly evident that, in different OECD countries and in the context of changing economic conditions, some sections of the middle class are repopulating the urban public school. Research trends 'suggest that middle-class parents may be a growing constituency in urban public schools' (Posey, 2012: 1). Whilst there are key differences in how middle-class parents are navigating public school choices, from 'seeking a critical mass' (Posey-Maddox et al., 2014) to resisting conventional markers and going 'against the grain' (Reay et al., 2013) or collectively campaigning for a brand-new public school, the urban middle class are demonstrating contemporary methods and movements to challenge the existing ways of conceptualizing middle-class choice.

The campaigners in this study, who are lobbying and pressuring the state government for a brand-new public high school, present a contrary narrative around public school choice, in the face of the ongoing enrolment decline of the public school sector, 'white flight' and decades of funding neglect. Whilst their actions are distinctive, they are not alone in this pursuit. Across the US, UK, Europe and Australia some sections of the middle class are 'turning back' to urban public schools. 'In cities across the US (including Chicago, Boston and New York) and in Europe (including Paris and London), groups of middle-class parents are making similar choices in growing numbers' (Cucchiara and Horvat, 2014: 487). In this instance, the authors are referring to public elementary schools, as opposed to public high schools.

Scholarship has turned to focus on what this may mean for education sociology and policy-making. The renewed interest and commitment to public education amongst certain factions of the middle to upper-middle class, a more affluent population, is frequently upheld as a categorically positive sign for desegregation and public education. For many policy-makers, the middle class are regarded as the gold star for educational improvement and the regeneration of resources (Crozier et al., 2008; Cucchiara, 2013). As the middle to upper-middle class's renewed commitment to public education is celebrated, what does this mean for those core ideals around democracy, social justice and equity? Is the middle-class uptake of public schooling benefiting all, or only a select few?

Australian landscapes: Urban, rural, remote

In the context of this study, the Australian educational landscape offers parallels with the US and the UK, but also contrasts that I briefly touch on here. Australia's landscape is vast, and the land mass itself is comparable to the US, however the way it is populated immensely differs. Two-thirds of the entire population is clustered within the capital cities and coastal areas surrounding the city (ABS, 2014). Some Australian capital cities are more spread out (e.g., Perth) and therefore less concentrated within an urban centre, and others maintain higher density (e.g., Melbourne and Sydney). Australian schooling environments tend to be captured between these vast juxtapositions of rural and remote, regional and city centres. The population distances also tend to capture the differences in wealth – coastal city areas are wealthier on average, with the rural and remote landscape tending to serve more of the disenfranchised population. In this context of vast distances between rural and remote, in comparison to urban spaces, there are stark distinctions in how middle-class choosers take up choice, depending on their location. This is well captured by Doherty, Rissman and Browning (2013) in their study of middle-class professionals in regional and outback Australia. The authors refer to the *My School* website, which 'nominates "local" schools as those "within 80 kilometres" (approximately 50 miles, in stark contrast to the two mile condition on Bell's notion of the geographic set), which might seem excessive for urban dwellers' (124).

In a similar way to how it is captured within the international literature, with a high influx of migrants to the city centres in the inter-war and post-war years, affluent families were likely to move to the outer-ring suburbs for more prestigious schools. However, inner urban locales have gentrified at separate paces, and have gradually grown to symbolize city life, cosmopolitanism and diversity. By urban schools, I am referring to schools located in high-density locales, which were once regarded poorly through a lens of race and poverty, and yet have substantially changed via demographic shifts (Ho et al., 2015).

Indeed, it is questionable whether the parents are 'turning back' to public schooling as suggested within the international literature. The parents are not organizing around an existing public school, in order to 'improve' and gentrify the existing public school (Cucchiara, 2013; Posey-Maddox et al., 2014; Posey-Maddox, 2014), but rather, the parents are pushing and lobbying core decision-makers for a brand-new public high school. This is in spite of the relative accessibility of surrounding public high schools.[1] However, the parents' activities, choices and behaviours evoke parallels with urban school choice studies, both in *who* the campaigners are, and *what* they want – a high-quality and local public school. Participant Matthew from 'New School for Lawson' captures this:

> And there is a difference in this area, I mean, the outer neighbourhoods around us, they're not making these demands for better and more

infrastructure. I mean, you see it in the local papers, someone will raise an issue and . . . we're pushing for a local high school and other people say, they say, from Charles neighbourhood, well you're not that far away from Charles High and why don't you make do, it's not far and your kids are old enough to travel and there are a number of arguments that are presented and basically it's just put yourself back in place and make do with what you've got, um, yeah . . .

Crozier (1997) utilizes the broad categories of working-class and middle-class parents to argue that the more affluent and educated parent is more likely to exert influence within a school, and be involved in their child's schooling, arguably due to greater levels of social capital and confidence. The educated parent may feel on professionally equal ground in the school setting and therefore, feels able to make demands on the school. Hirschman (1970) refers to this as 'voice' and 'exit', and scholarship suggests that the middle-class school chooser is more likely to utilize 'voice' rather than the working-class or lower-income chooser. Voice is defined as 'any attempt at all to change, rather than escape from, an objectionable state of affairs, whether through individual or collective petition' (Hirschman, 1970: 30). Across all OECD nations, there is commonality in terms of which class subsets are exercising voice, 'especially in the more fundamental issues concerning educational policy . . . There are issues about the gap between activists and the rest' (OECD, 2006: 90).

It is worthwhile to insert that a renewed interest in public services was predicated many years ago by policy-making think tanks, primarily at the same time that many of these lobby groups emerged, and scholars began to see a cultural 'turn-back' to public schooling for particular factions of the middle class. Peters (2004) describes the 'citizen-consumer' as the perfect 'market-democracy hybrid', an emerging construction from a hyper-globalist and consumerist population:

> Pressures on existing [public] services will increase . . . Not only will expectations of quality public services rise as public services users expect higher standards, but the public will also become less afraid to express dissatisfaction. . . . Rather than explicit political power, the spread of power to lobby groups and the willingness of the public to express political views through customer choice will weaken the national government . . . In an age of consumerism, the fundamental question is to what extent, if at all, 'citizen-consumers' – the market-democracy hybrid – can shape privately funded public services in ways other than through their acts of consumption, and whether acts of consumption can genuinely enhance the social dimensions of the market.
>
> (621)

I draw on this extended quote from Peters (2004) to explicate the usefulness of the 'market-democracy hybrid' in thinking about the middle class and their renewed interest in public schooling. Is this chooser enhancing schooling for all users, or are they only furthering their own positional advantage? Moreover, within a market-based system that promotes choice, individualism and competition, is it possible for acts of consumption to 'genuinely enhance the social dimensions of the market'?

White flight

Historically speaking, the concept of 'white flight' was widely commercialized following the landmark *Brown v. Board of Education* case. In 1954, the US Supreme Court ordered that high levels of racial segregation within public schooling was unconstitutional, which clearly impacted matters around inclusion and fairness, educational access and opportunity to learn. Decades later, James Coleman and his colleagues argued that court-ordered busing and desegregation of urban public schools had provoked and accelerated 'white flight' (Coleman et al., 1975). The authors claimed that these court-ordered interventions—whilst endeavouring to promote integration and decrease within-system segregation—were effectively achieving the opposite, with a mass exodus of white parents to either the suburbs or the more prestigious private schools. Thus, the concept of 'white flight' refers to the large-scale migration of white parents from urban public schools, to the further afield suburban schools, dominated by white parents and children.

'White flight' rapidly became popularized by the mass media, and James Coleman participated as an outspoken policy advocate against desegregation. He supported a series of affidavits for anti-busing lobbying groups (Pettigrew and Green, 1976). Following the rather vague original contentions, Coleman and his colleagues later put forth that court-ordered busing and desegregation in the period 1968–1970 led to lower percentages of white enrolment in urban public schools from 1970–1973 (see Coleman et al., 1975; Pettigrew and Green, 1976). The research and their claims were widely and veritably discredited by a range of scholars, on the basis of methodology. Whilst racial segregation was evident within schooling composition (Coleman et al., 1966), studies did not substantiate the direct correlation with the desegregation laws (see Green and Pettigrew, 1976; Pettigrew and Green, 1976; Rossell, 1975).

A wide range of contemporary studies have taken up the concept of 'white flight', outside of the context of court-ordered desegregation. More recent studies tend to adopt the concept in order to explore the movement of white middle-class parents away from the public sector (Fairlie and Resch, 2002) and how white flight coalesces with gentrification (Butler, 2003; Butler and Robson, 2003). In *Marketing Schools, Marketing Cities*, a study of urban renewal and the marketing and gentrification of public schools in Philadelphia, Cucchiara's (2013) participants speak about 'middle-class flight' as opposed to white flight, with the former being far more palatable than the racist undertones of the latter, as Cucchiara suggests.

There are programs across the US working to attract high-income parents back to city or urban public schools on the premise that higher-income parents will promote urban renewal via the growth of city tax revenue and have a flow-on effect for combatting crime and poverty (see Cucchiara, 2013; Cucchiara and Horvat, 2014; Posey-Maddox, 2014, 2016; Posey-Maddox et al., 2014). However, in looking to attract and increase high-income parents within urban public schools, lower-income parents are only being pushed further out, and segregation is carved into fixed spatial boundaries, with high-achieving public schools versus stigmatized and residualized schools.

In *Marketing Schools, Marketing Cities*, Cucchiara (2013) describes the many activities that middle to upper-middle-class parents engage in, to 'rebrand' their selected urban public school – a school previously ill-regarded by white middle-class choosers – and promote the school to a certain social and cultural market. The 'neighbourhood parents', dominated by white and affluent middle-class parents, as opposed to the 'transfer parents' constituted mainly by African American lower-income parents, are involved in an extensive list of activities to promote and 'rebrand' the school to other neighbourhood parents. Based in the city of Philadelphia in the US, the parents are instrumental in generating new resources and fundraising for the school through their influential networks and contacts, including a new playground for the younger children, a library and library services. The neighbourhood parents are overly concerned with the image and marketability of the school, and on occasion, even answer the phone at reception to avoid potential customers forming negative first impressions of the school. The neighbourhood parents also play a role in the school's educational policy-making and decision-making. For example, they are involved in staffing issues such as removing an unpopular principal and recruiting a new principal; raising funds and revenue for the school through events (e.g., an opera performance); organizing and leading school tours; meeting regularly as a parent group to consider future marketing and fundraising plans for the school.

The 'neighbourhood parents' are also aware of the value they bring into the school, and at times, utilize this value at the expense of access for lower-income students. There is opposition to the No Child Left Behind transfer policies, which allow 'transfer students' from lower-income areas to enrol in the school. Some of the neighbourhood parents threaten to leave the school if they are unhappy with certain decisions, a threat that is routinely made to policy- and decision-makers. For example, one parent was unhappy with the ratio of teacher to pupil within her daughter's classroom and, drawing on a well-developed and affluent network, made a direct phone call to administrators and head decision-makers. The classroom size was quickly modified, with a lower teacher to pupil ratio.

Whilst this is positive in that the school is able to generate greater revenue and resources for their students, and even lower class sizes, Cucchiara (2013) also shows how it increases segregation between schools within the public sector, as based on family income and race. The unequal and favoured treatment of certain parents and students, as based on income and race, undermines the democracy of public education. Moreover, lower-income parents are pushed into schools struggling with lesser resources. Schools that serve a more affluent population benefit from higher levels of funding and attention from key decision-makers.

From the UK, Crozier et al. (2008) ask whether this renewed commitment to public schooling is a positive signal for engaged citizenry:

> At a time when the public sector and state education (in the United Kingdom) is under threat from the encroaching marketisation policy and private finance initiatives, our research reveals that white middle-class parents are choosing to assert their commitment to the urban state-run comprehensive school.
>
> (261)

The authors expand upon these arguments in their later work, positing 'against-the-grain' school choice, as well-resourced choosers dismiss 'conventional indicators and comparisons' that would typically portray their choice as a 'bad' one (viii). The public school is typically situated as inferior to the private school, or as these authors argue, there is a 'prevalent middle-class fear that state comprehensives are in some way inferior' (Reay et al., 2013: 111). This is substantiated by Campbell et al. (2009) in their study of Australian middle-class school choice. The authors write that the ordinary government comprehensive merely acts as 'safety net' (5). In the context of market framings of public schooling, those electing to 'turn back' are potentially disruptive and problematic for market theory, defying the postulation that consumers with the resources will automatically defer to more exclusive schools, those which charge higher tuition fees.

For some choosers, the public school is regarded as the more ethical and inclusive decision, with 'clear reference points in the political and moral landscape' (Reay et al., 2013: 71). At the same time, many of the parents in Reay et al.'s (2013) study were involved in a complex duality between surveillance and support for the school. By choosing the urban public secondary school, parents felt they had more privileged access to the school, with their voice and ideas given greater weight in decision-making and their children well looked after – the school felt the need to retain the students and their affluent families.

This is a theme that is evident across the literature. As middle-class constituents grow in urban public schools, collective strategies have also grown far more sophisticated, particularly around marketing of the school and improving the 'image'. This very much highlights the tensions in arguing for the public school as a site of resistance against class- and race-based segregation, especially for white middle-class campaigners. Although many middle-class parents claim a commitment to diversity and 'public' schooling, their educational work succeeds in further privatizing the school intake (Kimelberg and Billingham, 2013; Posey-Maddox, 2016). This echoes Reay et al.'s (2013) earlier work from the UK arguing that comprehensive schools are 'caught up in processes that reproduce social class relations' (81) and whilst these choices may seem to resist status-driven and neoliberal individualistic frameworks, the public school offers social and economic leverage, or as these authors put it, 'specific social, cultural and ideological returns' (80). In order to tease out these frictions, and the intensification of segregation, I draw on an extended narrative from a 'New School for Lawson' general meeting (Field notes – August 26, 2012).

Community orientations

As per usual, I arrive early at the monthly 'New School for Lawson' general meeting, held in the local pub. I sit in the lobby with a few other regulars. A man in a dark suit, who I have not met before, arrives and moves around the small group shaking people's hands. He's rather overdressed in my opinion. He politely and warmly shakes my hand and, as we stand at the bar, he insists on buying my drink. As we walk into the meeting room, he tells me that he is a political member in the area of Lawson – a local councillor bidding for election.

The group settles at the meeting table. More and more people arrive and I count twenty-five people in attendance. It is the largest meeting I've attended since beginning observation almost one year ago. Actually, there are many people whom I have never met before – which is very unusual at this stage of my observation. The meeting also coincides with the local council election.

Another person walks in – another face I've never seen before – and before she sits down, she clears her throat and announces to the entire group: '*Look* I just have something to say up front'. Everyone turns and the group goes quiet. 'I am here to represent the parents from Charles High School. We have some concerns about this group. My kid goes to Charles High'. She doesn't sit down but continues to stand. Karen, the working party member who is leading the meeting, nods and enthusiastically replies, 'Great, great. It is really good to have you here'.

The 'unknown speaker' (let's call her Janis) continues to address the large group.

'Yes, we live over in [neighbouring suburb] and she goes to Charles High and we really like it'.

Karen responds, 'How far is that [to travel]? It must be a bit of a trek'.

'*Oh no, it's not far at all*'. Janis says emphatically. 'Only five k's [kilometres] or so, really no big deal'.

She finally sits down. There is a marked alteration in the atmosphere. Karen welcomes her warmly, but there is a tension that settles over the group. I feel less inclined to reach for my pen.

Janis is 'different' to other attendees – not only is she dressed differently, in her casual attire – but she announces herself as a representative of (an)other geography. She lives elsewhere. She doesn't share the same concerns as the campaigners and immediately (and rather confidently) disregards Karen's concern of travel distance, from home to school.

I overhear a campaigner ask, 'How did your child go? . . . With changing schools I mean . . . and making new friends?'

'Oh she was fine!' Janis responds enthusiastically. 'They complain about it at first, but they'll be fine!'

The conversation stops and the meeting begins. Karen welcomes everyone and pays 'recognition to the traditional Indigenous land-owners who are the custodians of this land' before clearly stating the values of 'New School for Lawson'. Karen says, 'We are a community group working towards an all-inclusive community, public secondary school and we want to form collegial relationships with all schools in the [region]'.

Karen announces that 'New School for Lawson' has recently received a negative response from the Department of Education in regards to the provision of a new high school. She tells the group that 'we're moving beyond the numbers now', before discussing the need to 'mount pressure' on the current political party and develop core strategies to do so. Karen's remark about the 'numbers' is in reference to the figure of 1,100 students that the 'New School for Lawson' group must reportedly prove to the current state government in order to acquire a brand-new public high school in their neighbourhood. This is a hot topic at every meeting I've attended and it is repeatedly referred to as the 'magic number'—although, at an earlier meeting campaigner Mark asked the group, 'Isn't this a politically decided number?'

The need to mount pressure and build a political campaign evokes a heated debate during this particular meeting and Janis is the first to intervene. 'Look,' Janis says firmly, 'I will tell you our main concerns about this campaign. What I hear is that people are scared that we will lose students to this new school – you know, once it's established and everything – and that means we will lose funding. We're worried that the campaign will stop parents from sending their kids to Charles High, that they'll think Charles High is no good . . . and when Lawson High is established, people will think it is better so they won't send their kids to Charles . . . '. She pauses for a moment. 'The bottom line is *we'll lose funding* . . . Charles High has space for 200 to 300 kids more, that's what our principal says. And there's even talk of another campus, maybe . . . it's not zoned yet, and that's really good, everyone can still go there . . . and neither is Park Secondary. I guess what I'm saying is, you should fill up your local schools, and then ask for another. It makes your case stronger'.

Janis argues that local schools are not full and maintain a very high standard. She expresses eagerness for the Lawson residents to attend Charles High. Janis' promotion of Charles High elicits a strong debate amongst the individuals in attendance. This debate is notable and rare, as throughout observation no one has ever spoken badly about the surrounding schools. There is very much a silence when it comes to the surrounding schools – I haven't even met a campaigner who lives outside the Lawson neighbourhood and it is almost one year into observation. The conversation continues with Sarah, who identifies herself as a 'teacher and a mother'. She has a child at Lawson Primary School.

She says, 'The strong sentiment with the mums in the playground is that schools around [Lawson] are no good, not good enough. You know what I hear is that kids from Charles High smoke bongs on the oval'.

Janis gasps and shakes her head in shock. She vigorously denies the 'bong-smoking' and passionately says what a good school Charles High is.

The teacher continues, 'I'm not saying that's true, but that's the sentiment we hear'.

Another person speaks up. Let's call her Maggie. 'I have to agree with you . . . that's what I hear too. Everyone around here, the strong word I get is that all the schools *around* Lawson are no good. Charles High has a bad rep. I hear bad things about it'.

The members of the working party are quiet as this conversation ensues and, at different moments, Karen leans in, endeavouring to interject.

Maggie continues to speak. 'It's funny you know, when I tell the other mums in my mother's group that I'm going out that night, and I'm heading over to [a restaurant in the Charles neighbourhood], they all gasp with shock! (*Laughs*) I mean, it's odd, it's our closest neighbourhood and it seems to me that no one sets foot in it 'cause it's seen as dodgy or seedy . . . or something like that! We're all on about community you know but we exclude these neighbourhoods and communities that are just outside of Lawson . . . *So how community-orientated are we?*'

The room goes quiet for a moment. Maggie poses an important question, one that probes into the genuine breadth of community. Maggie suggests that notions of community posit imagined borders, shaping and defining territorial boundaries. The neighbourhoods surrounding Lawson are considered apart and socially distant. Nobody answers Maggie's question but Harry does pipe up, 'Maybe Charles . . . I mean Charles High School . . . maybe it should change its name, you know? Anything that has the name "Charles" in it . . . just sounds dodgy'.

Harry is suggesting that a possible solution, and possibly a way to attract the middle- to upper-class campaigners from Lawson, is to make changes to the school's branding. This suggestion stymies the debate around the breadth of community and Karen quickly interjects. She recommends that 'New School for Lawson' maintain a focus on collegiality with the surrounding schools and parents.

She says, 'I think that all of us – our school communities – need to band together to pressure the government [for a new school in Lawson]'.

Janis scoffs loudly from the other side of the room, as does another person (let's call her Helen). Helen tells the group that she is a teacher at Park Secondary School. I've never met her before. Helen speaks forcefully to the group, visibly perturbed by the suggestion. *'Band together? It's so competitive out there! It's extremely competitive . . . and you want people to band together?'*

Janis vigorously nods her head in agreeance. 'It's so competitive that Charles [High] buses kids in each week from [a local primary school] for a free lunch – every Friday! They're trying to get all these kids to come to their school so they're handing out free lunches . . . It's that competitive!'

Helen nods, 'It's all about bums on seats. That's what it's all about. Bums on seats equal money. If we don't get the kids, that's it, we're done and dusted. It's so hard. *And you're talking about getting these schools banding together!*' Helen laughs, but not in a happy way.

This is definitely the most conflict or tension I have experienced before at a general meeting. It is contrary to my usual experience of adamant agreeability amongst the participants. Helen describes the current funding situation as dire and *'it's a dog-eat-dog world'*. By no means is Helen describing a 'community' environment – rather she depicts a hostile situation, in which schools are permanently teetering on the brink of closure. Karen nods diplomatically, as Helen continues. 'It is a vicious cycle. If we don't get the kids, then we don't get the money. There's no way any schools are going to work together. If they don't get the money, that's our school . . . *done, dusted*'.

There is a pause and Karen hurriedly says, 'Well, yes . . . I'm putting my names down for lots of different schools. I'm hedging my bets'. Karen is referring to private schools which require parents to list their child's name on a waiting list for future potential enrolment, which can cost parents a wide range between one hundred to five hundred dollars. Helen and Janis do not respond to this, and the room is quiet again, for a moment.

At this point, the local councillor who warmly shook my hand at the beginning introduces himself to the group. At this meeting, there are four local councillors in attendance, and each is aligned with the politically left-of-centre Labor Party. Each councillor introduces themself by their affiliation or position within a political party. Labor MP 'John' says, 'I'm keen to support a community solution. I think the best outcome is a solution made by a parent-led community'. He looks over at the dissenters such as Helen and Janis. 'You can be assured that I don't want to support anything that the entire community doesn't want. We all have to be together on this'.

His diplomatic speech doesn't stir Janis or Helen to respond. John has publically supported 'New School for Lawson' for many years, as evident on his website. It is one of his major political platforms, as it is too for Labor MP 'Sarah', who also introduces herself. 'I'm here because I have supported 'New School for Lawson' from the very beginning. I care about public education. That's why I got into politics in the first place. I believe in public education and I want to give back to the community'.

Karen quickly interjects, 'But we do invite all local members to attend our meetings . . . it's just that only the Labor reps have supported it so far. *We are not aligned with a political party.* Sarah and John have attended meetings and supported us over the years and we are very grateful . . . but we do invite all the members'.

Twice, Karen stipulates that 'New School for Lawson' invites all political representatives to attend. The group is firmly bipartisan, and consistently stipulates their lack of association or alignment with a political party (as do all other campaigns, e.g., Dodson and Smith). However, it is clear that whilst 'New School for Lawson' does not associate themselves outwardly with a political party, local members associate themselves with the group for political gain, and they *exclusively* represent the left side of politics.

The meeting did not lose its heat that night, although Karen did endeavour to end the meeting in a diplomatic way. John was busy shaking hands and meeting people, but he was competing with Robert and Sarah, also looking to win voters. Janis and Helen spoke for a little while to other participants before leaving, and I never saw them again at another meeting.

This meeting may suggest the circulation of 'hot knowledge' within the Lawson social network towards public high schools in the surrounding neighbourhoods (Ball and Vincent, 1998). Whilst the negativity towards Charles High was clearly expressed in this meeting as a school associated with criminality and drug use, these sentiments were rarely expressed throughout my observation or within the interviews. But after this meeting, this evasive silence stood out as far more revealing than I had previously considered. This is reiterated by Robert during his interview:

> You can say what you like you know and beat at the table and say oh no, Charles High is a great school and you should send your kids there but what happens is . . . in my experience, parents would just go quiet – particularly mothers – *not say anything* . . . and send their kids off, the very next year, to private schools [lists elite private schools] . . . and so it went . . . *legions of them*. You know, *legions of them*. I don't look left, I don't look right, I just watch what these people are doing.

Parents may be hesitant to criticize this school in open meetings such as this one in the fear of casting themselves in a negative light – and there are moral implications for this – in the fear of being seen as judgemental, pretentious or classist. This presents a paradox around school choice and in particular, these parent's activities; whilst the parents proclaim the virtues of public schooling, they are aware that their level of inclusion and accessibility only extends so far – and clearly, not beyond the boundaries of their neighbourhood.

Autobiographical and passionate prescriptions of public: God, politics and morality

Matthew: I find the public system really refreshing, I find, um, it also has a very strong, um, set of core values of tolerance and . . . it creates well-rounded children . . . much to – I know the criticism that is levelled at the public system is that there aren't any values, that the kids are taught . . . just, anything, no values. . . *but it's not true*, I mean my kids are growing up through the public school . . .

When asked about their involvement or motivation for campaigning, 'New School for Lawson' campaigners cite their passionate commitment to public schooling and frequently reiterate their belief that public schooling inculcates superior moral values. This ideological commitment to public education is underscored by a number of autobiographical accounts, including childhood memories of schooling; parental professions; religion, politics and morality. The memories of their own public schooling, coupled with ideological and political associations with public schooling, are frequently used as a touchstone for their identity.

Stay-at-home dad Matthew points to these ideals throughout his interview. Matthew used to be employed in the financial sector, but has since stayed home to care for his young children full-time whilst his partner, who has a doctoral degree, is employed full-time at a university. I see Matthew regularly at meetings and events over the course of my observation, as he is part of the working party. When I arrived at his home one day for the interview, his children greeted me happily at the door, and I stepped over mountains of books in their hallway, his older boy playing on the piano as we talk. When I ask him about his motivation for campaigning, he reflects on his own childhood, common for all participants.

> I went through the whole Catholic education system, from primary to secondary, secondary I went to an all-boys school . . . St Mark's Catholic School for boys . . . it was like a holding pen for wild boys . . . I suppose the dominant profile was working-class boys and ah, um, it seemed like, um, it seemed . . . there was a big sports focus and it seemed like this was perhaps the most important thing . . . I mean they'd educate them a little bit but sport was the big thing . . .

Matthew describes himself as 'anti-sport' and interested in a rigorous mathematics and science curriculum for his children. His short extract points to important choice markers, for his involvement in the campaign, and his pursuit of public schooling. Matthew is passionate in his objection to Catholicism and Catholic schools. He discusses, at length, his own Catholic upbringing and the disdain he feels as an adult towards particular Catholic Church leaders (for example, George Pell), the epidemic of sexual abuse within the Church, and even politicians who connect themselves with Catholicism and the Church. Matthew says, 'I hate the hierarchy, it's so conservative, homophobic' and he describes himself as a 'Catholic atheist':

> My partner is agnostic . . . she's sort of, a bit unsure . . . but I would consider myself as an atheist . . . but not as a dogged atheist . . . I consider myself a Catholic atheist . . . I think when you're brought up as a Catholic, it still permeates a lot of things, I still have a lot of interest in religion, I'm not doggedly atheist, I see that religion brings comfort to people and a lot of support, and I respect that . . . but I'm very happy to have a safe distance from religion.

Matthews procures this 'safe distance' in his social life, refusing to attend Church or Catholic-affiliated events, but he also wants to establish a firm sense of distance from Catholic schools for his children, emphasizing this as a 'conscious' decision:

> It's a very *conscious* decision, to send our kids to the public school rather than the Catholic primary school, because we're actually closer to the Catholic primary school, it's just down the road, St Michaels, we actually walk past it,

or cycle past it every day to get to the public school, so it's a very *conscious* decision . . .

The public school offers Matthew a sense of resistance against organized religion, who regards his decision as 'against-the-grain' in terms of consciously resisting the dominant criticism that is aimed at the public school. The public school inculcates values of tolerance and inclusion – a belief that is echoed by Steven, who believes the public school is more inclusive to different religious perspectives and sexualities. Whilst this may not be inherently true in that many public primary schools provide Christian religious classes, and many Catholic schools can stand out for their progressive practices, the positioning of public schooling as secular and liberal may indicate how the public school is valorized within the marketplace. Within a market that tends to under-sell the public school, the lack of organized religion and 'branded' secularism may be the unique selling point for the cosmopolitan, globalized consumer.

Certainly, this is a consumption preference that is indicated for many of the participants, in terms of their explicit choosing around public schooling. Interviewees Mark, Adele and Matthew are the most passionate in expressing their objections to religious schools. For these participants, the public school offers an important counterpoint to God and religion. Adele discusses this at length during her interview:

> Because oh my goodness if I'm ruling out Catholic and then the state schools aren't . . . you know . . . and potentially at capacity, just because they're government, I mean look at our surrounding schools, *we might not have a choice*. If you start to rule out the Catholic – well I have ruled it out, it's just not an option there, so . . . are you forced then into the private system . . . you know, *it's ruling out a lot of schools for me and options for me, but no.*

Busy full-time employee Adele, who I meet during her lunch hour at her place of work, describes herself as a 'committed atheist'. She is aware that her rejection of religious schools is costing her in the way of choices and options. It is in this way that her choice of public schooling acts as a form of rebellion, in that she sees the public school as a necessary counterpoint to religion. However, it is difficult to argue that the public school exclusively acts as a site of resistance for Adele. Rather than feeling empowered, she is feeling pushed into the private system, and this is on account of 'state schools aren't . . . *you know*' (my emphasis). This is a pointed reference to me, the interviewer. Her silence or 'gap' is telling; there is an implication that I will readily understand, as a white middle-class person. Are the surrounding state schools 'not good enough'?

Participants frequently introduce their religious preferences during interviews. Sociologists Savage et al. (2001) describe class as a 'loaded moral signifier' in that when people talk about class, they 'tend to talk about politics . . . people are aware of the politics of class as a label' (889). So too, when the participants discuss their motivation for campaigning and their pursuit of public education, they generate a range of philosophical topics, around politics, God and religion, morality, class and the middle class in particular. Not only is the public school 'a loaded moral signifier', it is a loaded religious signifier – utilized to express progressive values, atheism and disassociation with organized religion. There are participants who identify with an organized religion, such as Harry and Naomi, Karen and Adam, but they immediately endeavour to distance themselves from traditional religious beliefs:

Harry: Yeah I'd *definitely* say my values are heavily influenced by [Christianity] but it's sort of more . . . on the . . . more on the humanist side . . . you know, treat people the way you'd like to be treated, side of things, rather than about everyone who's not a Christian will go to hell sort of thing.

Karen: No, no, I'm not practicing . . . oh well, I talk about [Christianity]. . . but I also talk about that there's lots of other beliefs and I guess . . . if my children want to choose something else, that's fine.

Certain participants, such as Karen and Michelle, are willing to consider schools that are associated with a religion, as long as they are 'hands-off, religion-wise' and do not impose 'any particular dogma' (Michelle, Interview August 23, 2012). However, there is a bilateral preference amongst the participants for a school that is either secular or for a school that educates their children about world faiths. All of the participants connect the public school with secularism, and express a preference for a total lack of religious instruction in school, or the teaching of multiple religions in a philosophical or ethical way. By choosing the public school, the participants are signalling their secularism, progressive values and 'left-leaning, pro-welfare . . . cosmopolitan dispositions' (Reay et al., 2013: 45).

Identity clearly has a major part to play in choosing schools, especially for the more privileged or well-resourced school chooser. For Cucchiara and Horvat (2014), the choosers in their study describe themselves as 'city people', believers in public education and diversity. They are politically aware and politically engaged, and 'not private school people' (500). One mother describes herself as 'more worried about the impact of privilege than poverty' on her son (500). This is a theme that is shared in this data, with many participants worrying about the influence of elite schools and values on their children.

Elitism and unlikeable moralistic dispositions

Matthew draws a direct connection between private schools and elitism, and conversely, public schools and inclusion. I draw on an extended extract from his interview:

> We don't want the elitism of the private system, the private system sells its product on fear and that, um, if you don't send little Johnny

> to our school then they . . . won't reach their full potential and um, they won't access all their wonderful resources they can offer, they won't fare the best, they won't achieve the best (*sarcastic tone*) . . . and, of course, they very carefully cultivate their product in that they will embrace your kids at that early stage, but as, ah, as the kids move into the higher levels of secondary education if they do not perform satisfactorily, they will be expelled from that school. . . so that their performance figures aren't compromised, by your, um, failings of the child . . . so, it is quite a cruel thing, but it is certainly the way they operate. The public system doesn't do that more or less . . . um . . .
>
> *E:* So you see the public as a more inclusive school?
>
> *Matthew:* *Yes. Yes.* Yeah, and to give them a better exposure to the real world, instead of a closeted, materialistic system . . .

It is fair to suggest that many elite, private schools in Australia do celebrate exclusion – after all, that is partially what makes them desirable for so many choosers, and worthy of their exceedingly high price tag. When free schools are available, the costly elite schools enable the consumer to signal their wealth and affluence to other affluent networks. Matthew associates this schooling system with an inferior set of *morals* – a lack of compassion and empathy, dishonesty and even cruelty. There is a 'moral significance to class' in that a sense of morality underpins how we compose our class identity (Sayer, 2005, 2010). Class identity is constructed not by how we produce, but how we consume (Reay, 1998). This tends to be highlighted in how the middle class position their consumption of schooling within social democratic frames, relating their choices to egalitarianism, justice and inclusivity.

By arguing this, I am not suggesting that certain class fractions hold a monopoly on morality, or are more moral than others. I am also not suggesting that these notions of morality are untroubled. Rather, the way in which these choices are presented as 'against-the-grain' (Reay et al., 2013), or making choices despite their class-based resources, suggests there is a credence that public schooling offers for the urban and gentrified middle-class identity. This marker is frequently underlined by critical identity narratives, in association with religion and politics.

Many of the participants in this study express similar ideological sentiments. Husband and wife Harry and Naomi discuss their individual childhoods and their parents in order to explain their involvement and motivation to campaign for public schooling. Harry grew up in the country, in what he describes as a conservative Christian family. His parents were school teachers, 'both passionate about education and access to education for everyone . . . you know, not being elitist'. He feels this has informed his own values, and his wife Naomi agrees, consistently emphasizing their mutual support of public education. I ask,

> And what sort of values do you attach – what do you . . . sort of . . . think of . . .?

Naomi: Fairness.
Harry: Fairness and the egalitarian piece I think . . . and I suppose values wise that the . . . the equality of the rights of human beings . . . you know, a moneyed school where you can afford to assume that everyone else is somehow lesser than you . . .

Harry is the current president of 'New School for Lawson' and I met him early into my observation. Having grown up in the country, he describes his hour-long bus trips to reach school each day, and is adamant that his own children can walk to school. Harry is a regular at the monthly meetings, held in the evenings, and Naomi stays at home with their two young (pre-school-aged) children. I ask Naomi about her involvement in the campaign; whilst she regards herself as more of a silent supporter, I regularly see her at the weekend events.

Harry and Naomi are both university-educated with postgraduate qualifications. Harry is employed full-time as a manager of an IT firm, whilst Naomi works part-time in policy, staying home part-time with their children. Harry and Naomi are keen to emphasize their available school choices from the start of the interview:

Harry: I mean the bottom line is, we could probably afford to put our kids through private school, all the way through, if we wanted to . . .
Naomi: Yes, but the *conscious* decision is if we have a public school option that we're comfortable with, we'd much rather support the public education system.
Harry: It's a conscious thing, the conscious buy . . .
E: The public school?
Harry: Yeah.

In similarity to Matthew, who also draws on this notion of 'conscious' to describe his choice-making, Harry and Naomi emphasize their conscious – or thoughtful, mindful, deliberate – choice to support public schooling. In the marketplace, the consumption of public schooling offers the purchase of particular values. Harry tends to swing back and forth between celebrating egalitarianism and public schooling, simultaneously offering disclaimers for their rejection of Charles High, simply as it is too far away.

For Harry and Naomi, the public school choice is 'against-the-grain' on the basis of their financial abilities to choose private schooling. However, they are keen to disassociate themselves from individuals for whom the public school is a necessity and in this way, the reclamation of public schooling is highly conditional. Additional costs are acceptable, even though these costs may pose hardships for lower-income earners:

Naomi: My view of public education is that . . . the basic education should be free, but I think . . . I think excursions are extra and . . . sadly that

	probably means lower socio-economic groups wind up in a predicament around that and maybe there should be some sort of system to deal with that but . . . But there's a cost in that, to me. So I don't mind . . . we're in a position that we're able too, so therefore I don't mind.
E:	So, you wouldn't mind the extra costs?
Naomi:	Not at all, for me. But I know my sister desperately would mind and it's completely unfair that her children should get a different education to my children because they've chosen different careers to what we have . . .
E:	Does [your sister] choose public schooling?
Naomi:	Oh yeah, but she probably doesn't even have the choice. I don't think private would even be an option for those guys.

It is questionable why excursions should impose extra costs on parents when they are part of the schooling curriculum. Naomi accepts the extra costs of school excursions because her family has the ability to meet these costs, but she also accepts the hardships or 'predicament' that lower-income earners may face due to these extra costs. This reflects work by Skeggs (1997), who argues that class structures and separations tend to be ignored or not accounted for by those who have the privilege to ignore the barriers that class and financial limitations construct. It is important to contrast this acceptance or tolerance of exclusion to previous ideological commitments to public schooling, on the basis of equity, inclusion and elitism. Arguably, the schooling market provokes slippery and contradictory ideological attachments for parents, who find it difficult to reconcile their aspirations for their children with their social democratic visions.

The public school as an ideological proxy for 'leftiness' and social democracy

The public school is symbolic and meaningful for the middle-class school chooser but it is also conditional and constrained. Public schooling may stand as the purchase of a 'brand community', as described by Cucchiara and Horvat (2014),

> . . . the dynamic of the "brand community" suggests the deep sense of connection people can feel with others who make the same consumption choices, while the construction of certain choices as markers of difference suggests the important role it can play in drawing social boundaries.
>
> (490)

The community brand speaks to concepts around religion, shared morality but also politics. The majority of the Lawson neighbourhood, just like Smith and Dodson, vote for the left-of-centre political parties, and it has been this way since the early 2000s. In political speak, they are not regarded as a 'marginal seat', a neighbourhood that is on 'the margin', and positioned between a dominant vote for the Left and Right political party. The neighbourhood of Thompson shifted from an historically strong left-of-centre vote to a marginal seat in 2010. In 2011, the following year, the neighbourhood of Thompson received a brand-new public high school, commissioned and initiated by the right-of-centre state government. Adam approached me early into my observation, regaling the dangers of *not* being a marginal seat, 'It's all bloody politics, you know. We'd have a school yesterday if we were marginal'.

I discuss this subsequently, but perhaps on the basis of their progressive values, it is little surprising that the campaigners – whilst firmly demarcating their institutional bipartisanship – individually pronounce and celebrate their political 'leftiness' or social democratic values. Any alignments with right politics is discursively posited as unethical. Again I draw on Naomi and Harry to explicate this further:

Naomi: Voting for the right-of-centre Liberal Party goes against the basic ethics of why we want a public high school in the first place . . . (*Laughs*) that's why it's not a marginal seat, because the people here want a public high school so . . . I don't think it would come to that [voting for the right-of-centre Liberal Party].
Harry: I do think Naomi is right, I do think . . . that . . . the kind of values that people have here mean that they do sort of . . . um . . . you know tend to vote more in the direction of the parties whose values are also about the . . .
Naomi: *Public education.* (*Harry nodding*)

The public school is positioned in a problematic light in this instance for how it stands as a proxy for a certain social democratic identity – one that is aligned with egalitarianism and collectivism. However, this is limited to the nearby Beakin High School, rather than Charles High or Park Secondary. The campaigners are representative of Third Way politics, as stipulated by Giddens (1999) – endorsing the social democratic values of the welfare state whilst simultaneously accepting inequality and pushing for market provision. I return to this further in the following chapter in discussing the notion of community schooling. Indeed, there is a sense of social democratic collectivism within their consumption choices, but so too, savvy individualism. Steven also believes that 'lefties' are more likely to use political strategies to obtain what they want:

> You're gonna get much more people, much more left people wanting a *public* high school than right-wing you know.
>
> *E:* Do you think that the dominant left-leaning profile [of Lawson] contributes to the fact that people are campaigning strongly?
> *Steven:* *Yeah*, I think they're more likely to campaign you know.

Matthew stipulates that this sense of entitlement and awareness is connected to class, namely the middle class:

Matthew: Ah . . . the profile of the electorate in Lawson, um, most of the parents are well educated, they're middle-class and they are aware that because we are not a marginal seat, we don't do as well as we could [with getting a new high school] . . . and so often, there are conversations around, well, you know, we should vote differently . . .

Matthew questions whether the Lawson residents need to vote strategically in order to acquire their local high school, believing that if the neighbourhood represented a 'marginal' seat, the opposing party would offer them a school. Even though the campaigners assert a fundamental relationship between left-of-centre politics and the 'values' of public schooling, there is very little commitment to any particular political party. Harry cautiously discusses his 'swinging voting' in the past, whereas Matthew believes that 'more educated' voters will strategically vote to demand 'better facilities and more facilities'. Like Peters (2004) put forth in the beginning of this chapter, the 'market-democracy' hybrid, straddling the role of consumer-citizen, is able to utilize their democratic powers but also their rights as a consumer. Herein, the campaigners are drawing on citizen rights and speaking about the nobility of public education, whilst simultaneously utilizing their leverage as consumers and voters. These strategies could be read as a reaction and form of resistance towards the significantly decreased funding and mass-closure of public schools; yet, the strategic avoidance of nearby public schools and agitating for your 'own' could also be argued as class entitlement and class power.

Both the Lawson and Smith High campaigns are ecologically aware and mindful when it comes to their imagined school, routinely emphasizing sustainability and environmentally friendly principles. The Smith High Campaign want worm farms, compost bins, clean energy and sustainable gardening practices in their imagined school (Smith High Campaign Website, 2008). The building would include 'solar panels, water tanks and secure space for 2000 bikes' (Hoffman, 2011). This enthusiasm for environmental sustainability is shared by 'New School for Lawson', arguing that a brand-new school would reduce carbon output, by lowering the number of cars commuting to and from distant schools, and their imagined school would educate teenagers about environmental responsibility. This reflects their uptake of social democratic principles, infused within the territorialized urban school market.

Concluding discussion

In many different countries, in post-welfare policy conditions, sections of the affluent middle class are repopulating the urban public school in the context of economic pressures and a sense of global risk. It is important to caution however, that these groups do not represent the majority, and the previous chapter indicated the persistent decline of public school choice, particularly in Australia.

Whilst they do not represent the majority, this study would suggest how the public school is valorized within the marketplace as a secular and progressive alternative for the affluent, inner-city consumer. It clearly retains economic benefits, but also ideological and cultural benefits. The public school offers a type of 'brand community' (Cucchiara and Horvat, 2014) and fractions of the middle class conceptualize the public school as the purchase of classical social democratic values – around egalitarianism, collectivism and welfare (Giddens, 1999). The campaigners stand opposed to 'private' schools, those facilities that are connected to the upper classes, elitism and right-wing politics. However, they are positioned in an idiosyncratic middle; they are keen to distinguish themselves from the perceived criminality of certain public high schools – the 'working-class' – but also adamant to be distinct from the moral vacuum of the elites. Taking up this notion of the brand community, the following chapter discusses rebranding and the co-opting of the urban public school.

Note

1 See Chapter Three for more details regarding the campaigns and distances of surrounding public schools.

References

ABS. (2014) *3218.0 — Regional Population Growth, Australia, 2012–13.* Available at: http://www.abs.gov.au/ausstats/abs@.nsf/products/AC53A071B4B231A6CA257CAE000ECCE5?OpenDocument.

Ball SJ and Vincent C. (1998) 'I heard it on the grapevine': 'Hot' knowledge and school choice. *British Journal of Sociology of Education* 19: 377–400.

Butler T. (2003) Living in the bubble: Gentrification and its 'others' in North London. *Urban Studies* 40: 2469–2486.

Butler T and Robson G. (2003) Plotting the middle classes: Gentrification and circuits of education in London. *Housing Studies* 18: 5–28.

Campbell C, Proctor H and Sherington G. (2009) *School Choice: How Parents Negotiate the School Market in Australia,* New South Wales: Allen & Unwin.

Coleman J, Campbell E, Hobson C, et al. (1966) *Equality of Educational Opportunity,* Washington, DC: US Government Printing Office.

Coleman JS, Kelly SD and Moore JA. (1975) Recent trends in school integration. *American Educational Research Association.* Washington, DC, 2 April 1975.

Crozier G. (1997) Empowering the powerful: A discussion of the interrelation of government policies and consumerism with social class factors and the impact of this upon parent interventions in their children's schooling. *British Journal of Sociology of Education* 18: 187–200.

Crozier G, Reay D, James D, et al. (2008) White middle-class parents, identities, educational choice and the urban comprehensive school: Dilemmas, ambivalence and moral ambiguity. *British Journal of Sociology of Education* 29: 261–272.

Cucchiara MB. (2013) *Marketing Schools, Marketing Cities: Who Wins and Who Loses When Schools Become Urban Amenities*, Chicago: University of Chicago Press.

Cucchiara MB and Horvat EM. (2014) Choosing selves: The salience of parental identity in the school choice process. *Journal of Education Policy* 29: 486–509.

Doherty C, Rissman B and Browning B. (2013) Educational markets in space: Gamekeeping professionals across Australian communities. *Journal of Education Policy* 28: 121–152.

Fairlie RW and Resch AM. (2002) Is there "white flight" into private schools? Evidence from the National Educational Longitudinal Survey. *Review of Economics & Statistics* 84: 21.

Giddens A. (1999) *The Third Way: The Renewal of Social Democracy*, London: Wiley.

Green RL and Pettigrew TF. (1976) Urban desegregation and white flight: A response to Coleman. *The Phi Delta Kappan* 57: 399–402.

Hirschman A. (1970) *Exit, Voice and Loyalty*, Cambridge, MA: Harvard University Press.

Ho C, Vincent E and Butler R. (2015) Everyday and cosmo-multiculturalisms: Doing diversity in gentrifying school communities. *Journal of Intercultural Studies* 36: 658–675.

Hoffman T. (2011) Budding architect designs a new secondary high. *The Leader*. Melbourne: News Limited.

Kimelberg SM and Billingham CM. (2013) Attitudes toward diversity and the school choice process: Middle-class parents in a segregated urban public school district. *Urban Education* 48: 198–231.

OECD. (2006) *Demand-Sensitive Schooling? Evidence and Issues*, Paris: OECD Publishing.

Peters MA. (2004) Citizen-consumers, social markets and the reform of public services. *Policy Futures in Education* 2: 621–632.

Pettigrew T and Green R. (1976) School desegregation in large cities: A critique of the coleman "white flight" thesis. *Harvard Educational Review* 46: 1–53.

Posey L. (2012) Middle- and upper-middle-class parent action for urban public schools: Promise or paradox? *Teachers College Record* 114: 1–43.

Posey-Maddox L. (2014) *When Middle-Class Parents Choose Urban Schools: Class, Race, and the Challenge of Equity in Public Education*, Chicago, IL: University of Chicago Press.

Posey-Maddox L. (2016) Beyond the consumer: Parents, privatization, and fundraising in US urban public schooling. *Journal of Education Policy* 31: 178–197.

Posey-Maddox L, Kimelberg SM and Cucchiara M. (2014) Seeking a 'critical mass': Middle-class parents' collective engagement in city public schooling. *British Journal of Sociology of Education*: 1–23. Available online.

Reay D. (1998) Rethinking social class: Qualitative perspectives on class and gender. *Sociology* 32: 259–275.

Reay D, Crozier G and James D. (2013) *White Middle-Class Identities and Urban Schooling*, London: Palgrave Macmillan.

Rossell CH. (1975) School desegregation and white flight. *Political Science Quarterly* 90: 675–695.

Savage M, Bagnall G and Longhurst B. (2001) Ordinary, ambivalent and defensive: Class identities in the northwest of England. *Sociology* 35: 875–892.

Sayer A. (2005) *The Moral Significance of Class*, Cambridge: Cambridge University Press.
Sayer A. (2010) Class and morality. In: Hitlin S and Vaisey S (eds) *Handbook of the Sociology of Morality*, New York: Springer, 163–178.
Skeggs B. (1997) *Formations of Class & Gender: Becoming Respectable*, London, California & New Delhi: Sage.
Smith High Campaign Website. (2008) *Home Page*. Available at: www.smithcampaign.org.

Chapter 7

Rebranding and marketing the urban public school

This chapter explores rebranding and marketing of the urban public school, drawing on a case study to explicate this further. Rebranding is a marketing strategy to reposition a product within the market in a new, original and attractive way, revitalizing the customer base. It may involve recreating the imagery that is associated with the product, modifying symbols, logos or captions, even the colours. This is what schools are endeavouring to do when they change their names, renovate their online profile with professionally designed websites, or revamp their uniforms – each endeavouring to change the connotations, subtext and value markers of the school for the consumer, and inherently, attract 'higher-end', higher-income consumers. The rebranding or 'brand management' of the urban public school has been an issue of investigation in education sociology in recent years (Cucchiara, 2008, 2013; Lipman, 2009; DiMartino and Jessen, 2014).

I start this chapter by referring to Thompson High, the new public school that was initiated in neighbourhood Thompson in 2011, after a brief grassroots parents campaign. The case of Thompson High effectively elucidates how a public school may effectively 'change their colours' for the savvy consumer, such as its architecturally designed building, even the uniforms designed to mimic the popular US brand Abercrombie and Fitch.

The case of Thompson High

Michelle: Really, we only got in [to Thompson High] because it was the first year of opening . . . We were so lucky to be accepted. *It is not like a typical public high school* . . . during the open day, we all ate canapés on the veranda, overlooking the ocean.

I met Michelle for the first time at a 'New School for Lawson' general meeting, when she introduced herself to the group as a 'single mother'. Michelle is university-educated and professionally employed with two school-aged children. When I first met her, she had only recently moved to the neighbourhood of Lawson, laughingly describing herself as a 'gypsy'. We met again for an interview at a local café and she talked about the difficulties she had experienced in finding a school for her son, who is on the autism spectrum and receives funding support for a learning disability. Michelle says,

> At this point I can only work part-time because I'm on a care package to support my son and so it may be that we're kind of. . . lower-income bracket for the next ten years. Cost is prohibitive and . . . a huge access issue, really.

Michelle was renting in an adjacent neighbourhood to Thompson, when the school first opened in 2011. She describes in great detail the day she received the letter from the Department of Education with an offer of enrolment for her son at the nearby Thompson High. She stresses the feeling of 'luck':

> When I opened the letter, I couldn't believe my luck . . . I felt really lucky to get into Thompson High because of the sense of prestige of that area and it had me feel that um . . . my son might be more catered to academically. That there would be an emphasis on art and culture and . . . some of those things that I value um, so it's sort of a hybrid school. *It's not quite public-public (laughs).*

Michelle describes Thompson High as a 'hybrid' school, not like a typical public high school – the low-performing ones I assume. Michelle's description of the 'hybrid' school captures the scope of this chapter – the hybridity of the contemporary public high school amongst the confluence of rebranding and marketization. Her description of Lawson High, and the feeling of 'luck' that she expresses in gaining enrolment, accentuates the paradox of public schooling and the complications that market rebranding poses for equity. The canapés on the veranda add to the sense of exclusivity and prestige, which is clearly quite effective in disassociating the school from its public counterparts.

The new Thompson High School was designed by 'Daly and Sons', high-status and 'award-winning architects', to create a contemporary 'cutting-edge' look. The principal was reportedly concerned with how the colour scheme, of both the school buildings and uniforms, reflects the environment: 'The soft colours [of the school building] pick up on the location; the liquid blue green of the sea and the yellow of the beach' (Topsfield, 2011; THS, 2013). It is not only the 'liquid blue green' aesthetics of the school building – perfectly blending into the landscape – but parents also want a uniform that 'stands out in the crowd'. Professional designers were brought in, reportedly costing between $50,000-$100,000, to design a 'tailored ensemble' inspired by classic styles from the 1950s and the 'funky American fashion label Abercrombie and Fitch' (Milburn, 2011b).

The school markets itself on relationships with professional bodies, ranging from a nearby Arts Centre, iconic for its contemporary and classical art; an elite sporting team; sailing and skiing trips, but also the best-of-the best in technology, including iPads for every student and fast Wi-Fi across the campus. The school runs a competitive and select-entry academic stream for accelerated studies, a program that is reportedly very popular to potential parents (Topsfield, 2011, 2012a; THS, 2013). According to media reports, facilities are 'similar to the standard of private schools' and the school is experiencing rapid over-subscription. Parents have 'rushed to enrol their children' (Milburn, 2011a). A parent with an enrolled child at Thompson High says to the media,

> At Thompson High there's a real dynamism about the place and it's like a private school. We're very happy with it. So why would you pay $25,000? That's the equivalent of an overseas trip to Paris every year.
> (Milburn, 2011a)

In 2012, more than 300 students applied for 150 places, twice the number of students who applied at the start of 2011. As a result, after only one year, Thompson High made a request to the Department of Education that the school be rezoned due to the exceedingly high demand for a limited number of places. Subsequently, the school confirmed that the zone of the school would be altered for the 2013 intake, and future catchment reviews were imminent. The following map illustrates the confirmed change, marked as 'new boundary' (see Figure 7.1).

The third line is a boundary that Thompson High indicated as a potential school enrolment zone in the near future (Thompson High School, April 2012, Issue 3). This potential boundary would exclude neighbours who reside in public housing less than two kilometres from the school. The press labelled this as 'education apartheid' (Topsfield, 2012a) and protesting parents from surrounding neighbourhoods quickly emerged in response (Spalding, 2012; Topsfield, 2012b). Albeit, the protesting parents include many who reside closer to Clarke Secondary School.

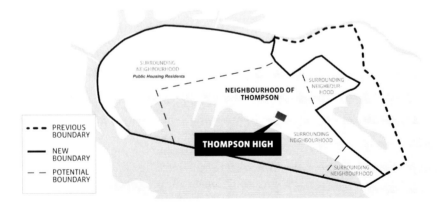

Figure 7.1 The changing school enrolment zone for the public Thompson High, one year following its opening.

However, the future regarding their enrolment zone was more exclusive than the school (or the Department) predicted. Just four years later, in 2016, the enrolment zone encompasses only 1.2 square miles, as indicated by the small black square around the school (see Figure 7.2).

On their website, Thompson High issues this warning to parents: '*even if you reside in the school zone, this does not guarantee you school enrolment.* The zone is reviewed every six to twelve months'. This could potentially mean that families who may purposely buy residential property in this small patch of designated urban space still do not acquire enrolment, or the enrolment zone may be modified after their purchase. Thompson High stresses their right to request previous academic transcripts for students seeking enrolment, in addition to reports on behaviour and extra-curricular activities.

Reportedly, there has been a scramble to buy into the zone, and real estate agents tend to utilize the school as their unique selling point in the property market: '*Inside the Thompson High School zone*' or even in short form, '*Inside the coveted THS zone*' (no need for further explanation). Since 2011, the neighbourhood of Thompson has experienced unprecedented price growth in the property market, and in 2014, recorded the highest growth in all of Australia, increasing 48.7% in one year alone.[1] Barriers to enrolment only amplify the sense of prestige and exclusivity of the school – which clearly helps for brand management.

This modification of enrolment perimeters on the basis of demand complicates theoretical propositions of demand-sensitive schooling, intended to respond to customer demand, first and foremost (OECD, 2006). Rather than expanding the enrolment zone due to increased consumer demand, Thompson High and the associated funding governance of the school is opting to increase restrictions to access. Clearly, the geographical boundaries of the school are significant for intensifying markers of social exclusion (Madanipour et al., 1998; Thomson, 2007). In

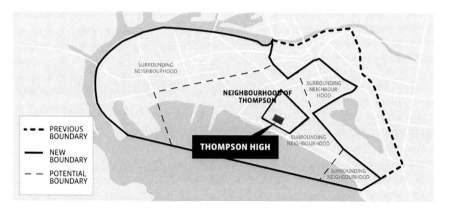

Figure 7.2 The 2016 enrolment zone for public Thompson High (the square around the school).

this case, the school boundaries are instrumental for defining fixed access points, set boundaries and spaces of inclusion and exclusion, but the boundaries alone are insecure and ever-shifting, offering very little guarantee for the consumer. As the school reinforces on their enrolment page, residential address within the defined boundaries does not secure enrolment and is open to further select-entry processes.

At times, the public school can be imagined as a space that brings together a type of idealistic gentrification, in that people of different races and ethnicities, incomes and social backgrounds come together and create cosmopolitanism, rejecting homogeneity and dissolving the 'bounded community' (Turner et al., 2014). But the construction of the public Thompson High, because 'we all have the right to public education' (as one parent commented to the press), has facilitated a type of bounded community that is far from fluid or flexible. As Harvey (1973) originally proposed in his work around space and the city, urban space can bestride the absolute and the relative – absolute in the composition of small grids, positioning class status as increasingly spatially oriented – but space itself is subjected to the schooling market, highly relative and commoditized. I draw on Massey's (2005) description of the city to emphasise this:

> 'Cities' may indeed pose the general 'question of our living together' in a manner more intense than many other places. However, the very fact that cities (like all places) are home to the weavings together, mutual indifferences and outright antagonisms of such a myriad of trajectories, and that this itself has a spatial form which will further mould those differentiations and relations, means that, within cities, the nature of that question – of our living together – will be very differentially articulated. *The challenge of the negotiation of place is shockingly unequal.* And the politics, economics and cultures of space – through white flight, through gated communities, through the class-polarising geographies of market relations – are actively used in the production of that inequality.
>
> (169, my emphasis)

The neighbourhood of Thompson is exceedingly white with a high-income population. Indeed, this is similar to all of the neighbourhoods in which a campaign has emerged, but the neighbourhood of Thompson is less integrated than its counterparts (see Appendix, Table A.4). For example, in the Thompson neighbourhood 63% of the residents are Australian-born and 6% are UK-born (the second-highest contingent). This is contrasted to neighbourhood Park (38% Australian-born, 1% UK-born), where a high proportion of residents were born in Vietnam (21%), and neighbourhood Riley (47% Australian-born, 1% UK-born). The median weekly income for Thompson households is $2,063 Australian dollars. This figure is considerably higher when compared to the median weekly income for Victorian households, cited as $1,216 Australian dollars. It is also high if contrasted to the neighbourhoods with rejected public high schools, such as neighbourhood Park, where the median weekly household income is $792, or neighbourhood Riley ($865) (2012 data).[2] The affluence of the neighbourhood offers it a sense of status and security within the urban schooling market, 'canapés on the veranda' and as Michelle says,

> We know that this school has a good name . . . I am swayed by the fact that it's *Thompson*. Everyone knows that to be a well-to-do neighbourhood and therefore the families there are . . . the families are stable, they're educated, so there will be a cultured element . . . there will be quite high expectations of the degree of culture at that school.

Paradox of the public and social equity

During the one-hour interview, Michelle refers to 'luck' or feeling 'lucky' several times (seven times, in fact), stating that she 'is one of the lucky ones' in achieving access to Thompson High. There is a conveyed sense of disempowerment embedded within the notion of luck, accentuating the barriers of exclusion within the urban school market. Yet this axiom of choice simultaneously fails to acknowledge the pro-active choice-making and 'class resources, personal actions and decisions' (Oría et al., 2006: 99). Middle-class school choosers tend to actively welcome and endorse barriers of exclusion, but certainly this is in the context of a hyper-competitive market. Michelle says,

> At Thompson [High], there's not a sense that we're bottom feeders. It's more like wow, aren't we lucky we've got this . . . you know because other kids don't get to have plasma's in the classrooms and iPads and . . .

In a market that legitimizes and enables 'bottom feeders' in the way of residualised, high-poverty schools with very little injection of capital funds, it is understandable that Michelle wishes to escape from schools such as this. In statements like this, class motifs are barely concealed, and Michelle acknowledges during the interview that the school is growing 'more and more tough to get into', feeding into her belief that she accessed the school – only through sheer good fortune. She is involved with 'New School for Lawson' because she does not believe that her daughter will acquire enrolment in Thompson High, despite having an older sibling there. The matter of fairness of accessibility to high-quality education, but also the stark differences and gaps that parents perceive around secondary education, pose questions for equity of access, opportunities to learn, and fair distribution of resources.

Whilst Michelle celebrates her enrolment 'win', the experience is not always inclusive for her son. She narrates the story of a ski-trip, advertised in the school newsletter. Her son wanted to attend because 'he loves skiing, he used to go all the time with his dad'. Whilst a contact person wasn't listed, Michelle immediately got in touch with the school to enquire about it. She says that the school gave her 'the run-around', and she made multiple calls before finally contacting a representative [David] from one of the parent committees. He would get back to her after speaking to the other parents on the committee. Michelle says, 'It was expensive, that's for sure, but I was willing to put it up [the cost] and I even told [David] that I could accompany my son on the trip, if necessary'. This would have required Michelle to take leave from work, and arrange care for her daughter. Unfortunately, she did not hear from the committee until the day before the ski camp, advising that her son was unable to attend due to his 'behaviour problems'. Michelle says,

> And so it did feel to me that there's a little clique who all know each other and because they have a responsibility to inform everyone that it's happening, they'll inform everyone that it's happening but in fact the numbers are decided beforehand.

Inclusion within the trips, which are advertised through the school, is subject to approval by the parent committee, something that Michelle feels is unfair and lacking in transparency. She believes that because her son is on the autism spectrum, he was deemed as 'risky' or unsuitable for the trip, although the reasons were not made overly clear to her. I ask her about the official school camp that the school runs each year,

> [The school camp] was five, six hundred dollars. And we're talking about . . . four days. We're talking about four days in the bush. We're not talking about the Ritz Carlton or whatever you know (*laughs*). It's a lot of money for a public school. And I was very disappointed that they didn't at least have a fundraising drive to assist families who couldn't afford it or subsidize it. Thirty per cent of the kids could not go to the school camp.

Whilst the parents at Thompson High talk about the merits of public education, routinely reported in the press, and that 'we all have the right to public education', costly and exclusive programs are endorsed. From Michelle's account, it is mostly assumed that parents have the resources to meet the high costs. The school's professionally designed uniform cost parents between $800 to $1,000, in addition to the many costly excursions and annual fees, such as the essential $460 school levy and $300 leadership program, all of which are mandatory. Each parent is expected to buy their own books and specially designed 'apps' for the student's personal iPad. If parents are unable to pay the fees, their child risks exclusion from social activities, or perhaps those activities that are regarded as 'optional extras' such as school camps. Michelle has difficulty in paying for her son to attend a sailing program that Thompson High offers, 'a program not offered by any other school around here', and she says,

> I have found [the elitism] frustrating and I suppose that's the double-edged sword of having a school in that kind of area . . . There's a lot of school pride,

there's no graffiti . . . um kids are getting around with blazers . . . it's quite nice.

Elitism stands as irreconcilable for Michelle. She welcomes the prestige that the school enables yet struggles to access the resources within the school itself. Windle (2008) discusses the production of inequalities internally within a school as an intensification of exclusion (158), drawing on Bourdieu and Champagne (1992) to describe it as, 'the excluded from within'.

Working the zones

In the case of Thompson High, a public secondary school initiated in a high-income neighbourhood, it has led to a school that is arguably more private than public. Of course, this begs the question around what constitutes public schooling within a market context, yet it is evident that Thompson High maintains quite difficult points of access, particularly for low- and even middle-income earners. This is further substantiated by the student cohort within the school, with the socio-economic composition reflecting that of elite private schools (see Chapter Four).

This does pose important questions for whether campaigns situated in neighbourhoods Lawson and Smith also envision schools such as this. Even though the campaigners push the importance of inclusion, and certainly, have firm beliefs in these tenets, it is questionable to what degree they are 'working the zones'. As savvy and educated school choosers who meet regularly with the Department, the campaigners routinely discuss school zoning and enrolment perimeters. They each know the rules and finer points around the school zones in their local area, and even beyond. For example, Harry says,

> Beakin High has different zones for girls and guys because they have a larger female intake. Because they've got a girls-only stream . . . The zone for girls extends all the way to Smithers Rd, but not for boys. And you have to show a rates notice to say you're in the zone . . . *(shakes his head)* so it's actually one of the really bad things for us [because we've got two boys] . . . from a schooling perspective, because Beakin High is one of the good options in the local area.

Harry and his wife Naomi's children are both pre-school-aged, not even enrolled in primary school yet, but they are both well-informed and educated in regards to future school intake zones. This is strongly reflected across the data, with many of the participants' children not yet enrolled in primary schools. Adam admits to me during his interview that he is prepared and already planning to lie about his residential address in order to gain access to Beakin High if the campaign is unsuccessful. He also tells me about business contacts that he will draw upon to work the zones.

Mathematician Karen, who later takes the reins from Harry as the president of the working party, and who I meet regularly throughout my observation, talks about her preference for Beakin High, Matheson High and Klein High School. Karen has two children – one in primary school, and the other pre-school-aged – and she has personally visited each of these schools. She has not visited the surrounding non-zoned schools, such as Park, Charles or Hill High. Like fellow campaigner Robert, Karen attended the open day for Klein High School (also referred to as Klein Girls), a high-performing and single-sex public high school. Karen and Robert are planning for their children to sit an academic examination to gain entry, despite the school's distance from their neighbourhood (15.1 kilometres or 9.3 miles). Karen talks about how competitive Klein Girls is, and she knows of other people in her peer group who are aiming for the school:

> The process pits *families against each other* . . . I've heard stories this year of where kids . . . you know they want them to get into Klein Girls school for example and families are turning up at the open days, going, oh I didn't know *you* were applying here . . . I didn't know *you* and *you* . . . and their friends were counting off their chances and who they think is more likely to get in um . . . so there's a case where three good friends, last week . . . *two of them got in* to Klein Girls and *one of them didn't*. And the little girl found out that she didn't . . . well obviously found out on that day, so she had to deal with that on the day . . . so she'll be split up from those friends, and those two will be together . . .

Karen says the more popular schools become, the tighter their zones become, thereby taking only the kids 'outside of the zone' that will 'boost their results'. It has a flow-on effect in boosting particular schools and stigmatizing others. Clearly then, as savvy middle-class school choosers, it is feasible to suggest that the campaigners are aware that their initiated school, which would also be located in a relatively high-income neighbourhood, would attract other affluent clientele and quickly establish strict, well-observed enrolment zones. Evidently, neighbours in surrounding neighbourhoods are also aware of this potential risk (such as Janis, see Chapter Six).

Pragmatically speaking, schools need enrolment ceilings, and it would not always be cost-effective to build on new school buildings to accommodate a growing demand. But there are clearly significant degrees of differences between secondary schools, and it must be questioned whether it is fair and equitable for policy to maintain and reinforce such considerable differences and gaps. Whilst Klein and Thompson offer rowing and sailing programs and cutting-edge technology, schools such as Park Secondary urge students to 'Bring their own technology device' from home (rather than compelling parents to pay for one).

This is not to suggest that these schools do not strive for excellence, nor for that matter, achieve excellence. Schools such as Park, Axis and Apple run debating competitions, environmental sustainability programs and achieve quite similar results on standardized tests. They are also working to rebrand themselves in a competitive market environment. It was reported in the media that Riley Secondary School, which predominantly serves a lower-income clientele, changed the name of their school (to Matthew Riley College) and 'banned hoodies' as part of their revolutionary makeover. The new school spent $100,000 of the school budget to give every student a new summer and winter uniform, complete with school ties and blazers. The College took on a 'business mentor' (a major law firm) to rejuvenate their dwindling customer-base. The law firm runs many different 'aspirational programs' within the school.

Co-opting public schooling and community

Co-opting refers to adopting an idea or practice and then using it for your own benefit or advantage. To this end, the middle-class school choosers co-opt public schooling and the ideas behind it to their own advantage. Progressive values are endorsed (see Chapter Six), alongside principles of inclusion and equity, and the merits of public schooling, and the campaigners celebrate strong discourses around community and community schooling, to the point that the 'community high school' encapsulates their core ideal.

Nikolas Rose's (1996) analysis around community is valuable in orientating this discussion. I draw on quite an extended citation from his paper entitled, '*The death of the social? Refiguring the territory of government*', to utilize his idea of community as pre-existing and mobilizing:

> One's communities are nothing more – or less – than those networks of allegiance with which one identifies existentially, traditionally, emotionally or spontaneously, seemingly beyond and above any calculated assessment of self-interest . . . Each assertion of community refers itself to something that already exists and has a claim on us: . . . as residents in a village or a suburb . . . Yet our allegiance . . . is something that we have to be made aware of, requiring the work of educators, campaigns, activists, manipulators of symbols, narratives and identifications. Within such a style of thought, community exists and is to be achieved, yet the achievement is nothing more than the birth-to-presence of a form of being which pre-exists.
>
> (334)

Moreover, Rose puts forth that this modality of collective allegiance, this pre-existing community, is mobilized as a new sector of government, another legitimate arm of government, or as he puts it, '*government through community*' (332, emphasis in original). The community is yet another instrument of decentralization, as the government endeavours to detach from its responsibility for schooling and place this responsibility onto the consumer. In this case, 'community is not simply the territory of government, but a *means* of government' (Rose, 1996: 335, emphasis in original).

These are themes that are accentuated by the collective actions. Robert, a long-standing campaigner for 'New School for Lawson', discusses the importance of community ownership,

> *We want a school that we can call our own.* And when I say, call it our own, it's not just a case of its physically local, from an inputs perspective . . . it has *very very clear* . . . contributions by parents and friends who come from *a community of commonality, a community of interest* . . . that will have an input into the secondary school and again . . . the tone and tenor, the culture, the direction, the strategic direction . . .

Bourdieu (1984) argues that geographical proximity to certain assets or goods is of vital significance for matters of class, because the geographical proximity affects the ability for groups of people to influence and appropriate the 'assets in question' (124). For the campaigners, proximity to the school matters for how it affects the level of participation, feelings of belonging, and connection to social capital. But it also concerns this sense of ownership of the school and construction of class-status.

In their agitations for a community school, the campaigners 'reveal painful contradictions' like those participants in Reay et al.'s (2013) study. The authors describe the parents as 'caught within impossible tensions between being good neoliberal individualists and their communitarian impulses' (161). Their desire to own or be involved in the school is a 'means of surveillance as well as a means of [support]' (156). Even though the campaigners celebrate a self-governing community, it is uniformly welcomed and rejected, as indicated by Matthew:

> As a group, we've done some work on identifying potential sites, um, again, with the Department [of Education] . . . as a pressure group we've led the process with the Department, and again we're leading the process with identifying sites . . . work they should have done, but they haven't so we've led the process . . . we actually have a document identifying about twenty-five sites . . . of those about five to seven are probably, um, good options for a site . . .

Identifying sites for a new public high school would have traditionally been the role of the overseeing government. Albeit, the campaigners' vision is currently unfulfilled, but it does point to the growing and intensified role that the parent is increasingly taking up, an argument that is reflected in urban studies around middle-class choice. In Posey-Maddox's (2016) US-based study, the author describes the parents as 'economic brokers' (178), taking a significant lead in generating school resources and attracting customers. One parent describes this as stuck 'between a rock and hard place' (178). Matthew shares this sense of inevitability, about something 'they should have done', a cross-national phenomenon in a global landscape of ongoing budgetary cuts of public schooling.

This is a contradiction that campaigners find themselves within, and is the inevitable paradox of the reinforced individualistic and competitive tenets of post-neoliberal economics; whilst wanting the 'public' school, one that is essentially part of the governmental system, the campaigners dually aspire for a school that is local and to some extent 'owned' by the community. This inconsistency between agitations for a public school and forms of quasi-privatization is perhaps most sharply demonstrated by proposed funding mechanisms:

Matthew: It's just unfortunate that the public system can't actually, somehow . . . leverage off that and maybe, perhaps, create their own trusts through parental donations to start that off, um . . .
E: So private trusts . . . set up through the community, or . . .?
Matthew: Through the Education Department, so, um . . . past parents and students could, perhaps, donate to their old school to improve the facilities, like the private system does . . . there has been some initiative, some movement . . . to move the public system to where . . . to grab aspects of the private system that actually feed into these amazing facilities and try to replicate it at the public system . . .

Matthew's proposed funding arrangement is parallel to how a private school operates, with the only difference that it is stipulated as optional. Matthew talks very little about wanting the government to contribute more money to public schooling, even though he demonstrates a knowledgeable and engaged view of politics in general. Rather, the 'community' has taken up this role.

All of the campaigns generate sizeable donations and funding from professional and institutional bodies. As I discussed in Chapter Three, the campaigns generate donations from banks, property developers, local businesses and real estate agents. Members from the Smith High Campaign personally donated $1,000 towards their proposed school (Smith High Campaign Website, 2008). The purpose of funding their own school, as stipulated by SHC, is to increase the 'sense of community ownership', thus leading to greater 'community partnerships with the school', and to raise the profile of the proposed school (Smith High Campaign Website, 2008). Effectively, they are taking on part-responsibility for their school, to the point of self-funding and marketing.

Decentralization shifts the responsibility of the government-owned school onto the consumer (Whitty and Power, 2000). This discourse celebrates parental involvement and parental control, but it begs the question: which 'type' of community is imagined within this discourse? Clearly, the imagined and more desirable community is one that has the resources (for example, time and money) to participate in their secondary school.

However, it is far more advanced than simply participating, and 'community' members are expected to do more than simply participate as *supporters* within their school – supporting teachers to educate and principals to lead – but rather are expected to rejuvenate, improve and remodel the urban school, with many feeling compelled to take up more professionalized responsibilities (Cucchiara, 2013; Posey-Maddox, 2016). This can aggravate levels of access and inclusion for members of the community with lesser resources, but it is not entirely harmonious for the participants either.

I've really stuck my head in the sand

Adele is a full-time employee and mother of two who expresses a constant feeling of pressure on her time throughout her interview. Adele berates herself repeatedly for 'sticking her head in the sand' and 'cutting it really fine' in regards to finding a secondary school. Her eldest is only in grade one at the time:

> *I've really stuck my head in the sand*, until like, probably last year . . . of whether we will have a school but I think for my eldest who is in grade one this year that potentially we're going to be cutting it really fine, so I don't know . . . I always thought the government [school], but . . .

Even though Adele scolds herself for her inactivity, it evidently consumes much of her time. She is a member of the working party and always involved at campaign events. She tells me about her meetings with the state and Shadow Minister of Education, media releases she regularly writes and distributes for the campaign, interviews with journalists, meetings with school principals and concerned local parents, and 'doing drive-bys' to check out local schools, such as Park Secondary. She is the only one who mentions that she has visited the surrounding schools, such as Park Secondary.

Adele is reflective in her interview, feeling that she did not previously grasp how competitive schooling and enrolment is, for particular schools. She grew up in the country, like Harry, and moved into the city with her husband only recently. As soon as her first child was born, her neighbour quickly advised her to 'get onto the schools' and put the name on a waiting list. Her child attends a local primary school in neighbourhood Lawson and part of the time pressure that she experiences clearly comes from this school. I draw on an extended quote from Adele in order to convey a sense of her emotional labour and anxiety:

> Someone turned around to me this year, and said hey maybe we should be going to a private school (*laughs*) 'cause I tell you what, the first two terms being *hit up* with fundraising *like there's no tomorrow* from everywhere! (*Laughs*) If it's *not doughnuts and pies from here and then someone from here and I need something here and I have to make something and I need money for this and that!* And I'm like, I'd be more than happy just to give them a set fee not to ask me to do any of this and then they turn around and say, *maybe you should go to a private school* and in my head I'm thinking hmmm maybe . . . *Don't get me wrong* – I'd love to help and participate but working full time, it's such a challenge and when you get three or four notes home you know,

I need to do this, I need to do that, they need money for this and that it's like (*laughs*) okay!

(Throws her hands up in exasperation).

Adele's narrative reflects the funding pressures and policies that I discussed in Chapter Five, yet in personalized ways. Whilst choice policies may seek to create a more enjoyable or satisfying experience for the consumer, the participants tend to convey an overriding sense of anxiety and pressure. Lane (1991) writes that the market 'stimulates arousal and is saturated with emotion: pride and shame and guilt (the three emotions that are identity-related); anger and aggression; self-love' (58). Adele feels constant pressure to devote time, money and resources to her child's primary school. She explains that she would prefer to pay one-off direct fees rather than be relentlessly compelled to use her very scarce amount of time – although this explanation is echoed with guilt that she is unable to meet the school's request, and arguably, meet the expectations of the parent community.

Adele is rational in her consumption choices around schooling. She is open to private schooling, yet feels squeezed out – not on the basis of economics, but more so, religion. She says, 'If you look at the good public schools and the house prices in that area, *well I mean you're paying for your kids' education anyway, aren't you!* (*Laughs*) I mean we may as well look at private schools!' Hardly shying away or 'sticking her head in the sand', Adele has investigated private school options, particularly the secular private schools. She tells me early into the interview – in a confessional like tone – that she completed a school tour of Kennedy College, a private (fee-paying) school located in Melbourne's central business district, only two train stops from her neighbourhood. Adele told her fellow campaigners that she only completed the tour for the benefit of the campaign, to 'check out the competition'. However, this was not entirely accurate, as Adele admits to me during the interview, and she is seriously considering sending her children to the school. She says, 'It has a marketing manager, a sales team . . . and it's a great choice because it's secular and academic with really good facilities'. Her children travelling to the city on their own is a fear factor for Adele, just like it is for her fellow campaigners, something which they all individually discuss during their interviews, but certainly – not as alarming as Charles High or Hills High.

Adele is also considering relocating for a public high school, a rather prestigious school located thirty kilometres from the neighbourhood of Lawson. She says that, as the school is high-demand, she and her husband would need to buy into the catchment area or enrolment zone. I ask,

Are you prepared to do that? I mean, relocate for this school?

Adele: That thought has only just entered my head . . . but I mean yes we have definitely considered it. But it could be . . . I don't know . . . it could be an option, I don't know at this point.

Arguably, it is far more difficult to change residential locations, buy and sell property, than it is to travel the relative distance to Charles High School. This substantiates the weight of choice and the amount of fear that these choosers have in regard to the 'unknown' public high school. For the majority of choosers, this is constructed through 'hot knowledge' (Ball and Vincent, 1998) within a shared social network, rather than 'cold knowledge', such as standardized test results, pedagogy and curriculum, or actually visiting and learning about the school, first-hand.

The good school and defensive choice-making

Naomi: I think [school choice] is a right. If that's what parents choose to do . . . it *should* be a choice though . . . they shouldn't feel that's the *only* way their child can get a good education, that's what we're scared of.

Harry: If there was a good local school, um, and if they didn't have to travel then you wouldn't have to make a decision. You know that's the issue . . . Rather than having looked around and been unhappy with the . . . the next ring of schools . . . you know there's *not* a local high school. So it's not specifically because I would choose to *not* go to some of the other ones . . .

Many of the participants regard the local school as an abdication from active choice-making, and see their campaign goals as indicative of their democratic rights for community, accessible schooling. If participants are forced to 'travel' to surrounding neighbourhood schools and 'make a decision', many consider this as *active* choice-making, whereas the local school is the non-choice. I conceptualize this as defensive choice-making, in that the participants justify their appeal through a lens of social justice and citizenship. In some ways they are accurate – a new public school would potentially alleviate any enrolment stresses on surrounding schools, such as Beakin or Hampton – and serve a great deal more students. However, in another way, their rejection of surrounding schools on the basis of distance is questionable, and if funding is limited, a new school may divert funds and resources from neighbouring schools serving lower-income students and families.

Detaching from active choice-making enables school choosers to distance themselves from acknowledging social divides and how their choices potentially contribute to reproducing social inequalities. Reay (1998) contends that 'discourses of classlessness are in effect class discourses in so far as they operate in class interests' (261). Judging from the long-term planning and commitment that campaigners bring to school choice, it is reasonable to suggest that they perceive significant differences between secondary schools. They also have firm preferences and are willing to go to considerable lengths to acquire their preference. However, when it comes to articulating this preference or the reasons for it, schools are simply communicated as *'good'*. This is so repetitive and routine during the general meetings, discussions and interviews around desirable schools and choices, that at times, I hardly notice it until reading back over transcripts and notes. There is a space of silence and evasiveness when it comes to precisely articulating what makes a *'good'* school, even though it carries a great amount of weight and import within the social network. When campaigners are discussing surrounding schools, such as Beakin High, these preferences are simply coded as 'a good school', typically received by a nodding affirmation. If campaigners do mention specific qualities of a good school, as some have done in the interviews, it tends to be done in discursive, vague ways, referring to uniforms, an academic focus, or an inclusion of arts and culture. Sports is far less preferable, unless it is rowing or sailing. Only once does a campaigner seem to stop themself when discussing the 'good' school, during a 'New School for Lawson' general meeting:

> Karen is speaking about a phone-call she received from a friend, who lives in the Lawson neighbourhood. 'A friend called me this week – I met her in my yoga class a while ago – and we started chatting about schools . . . her child is in year five and she has started to look for a high school . . . she said to me that she has spent so long, so many hours, going from school to school and she can't find a good sch – [*stopped herself abruptly here*] – good fit for her daughter . . . and they're so far away and she feels so anxious about the whole thing . . . where is she going to send her daughter?'

The notion of a 'good' school is discursively constructed within a certain social network (Holme, 2002) and it is in this network that 'hot knowledge' is shared in simplified, coded ways (Ball and Vincent, 1998). Parents rely on abbreviated communication devices, but clearly, these abbreviated communication devices must be received by an individual knowing and understanding of the currency in order for the constructed code of representation to make meaning (Hall, 1997). This highlights how class is operationalized as a 'structure of relations' in school choice (Bourdieu, 1984). In alignment with how Bourdieu renders forms of capital, as items of value that can be transferred or cashed in for items of greater value, the contemporary consumption of schooling then, and the abbreviated markers that are utilized within specific social networks to guide these consumption choices is a mode of *class currency*. Knowing the code and the more unspoken (or implicit) meanings and values enables the consumer to align their consumption choices with their class network. It is a means of class symbolism – in other words, symbolizing and signalling membership within this class collective.

In the extract above, Karen seems to suddenly stop herself before deeming the neighbouring schools as the opposite of 'good' and relies instead on the notion of 'child-matching', arguing that the neighbourhood schools are not a good fit (Ball et al., 1996). What comes through quite strikingly in Karen's narrative is that, despite their relative proximity to the neighbourhood of Lawson, Karen's friend reportedly feels they are 'so far away'. These feelings of physical and cultural distance in the urban centre characterize this subset of middle-class choosers. This is further illustrated by Karen:

> The Department thinks [Charles High] should be a choice for us . . . It should be . . . well . . . Charles High is deemed to be our local secondary college . . . Other options . . . or even options have been said that we should go to Park Secondary or Box College . . . and that's just the wrong direction again, *totally the wrong direction, not even close.*

As the public school is commercialized and rebranded within the market, the urban space is heightened, with relatively minor distances amplified and distended. Space becomes a marker for many important gains and acquisitions – high-quality affordable schooling, although as the case of Thompson High demonstrates, this is highly insecure and unguaranteed for the consumer – and the local education market is utilized as a credible substitute for class networking and status. The 'hybrid' school, as discussed earlier by Michelle, is afforded a sense of prestige by its location and the degree of distance that it offers from the lower-performing 'bottom feeders'.

Talking strategies

Apart from their collective long-term strategy around schooling, the participants are well aware of a wide multitude of various strategies employed by individual families within their social network. As previously discussed by Adele, one of the most popular strategies discussed is to relocate for a new public high school, or lie about residential address, and these strategies are routinely mentioned. Real estate agents in the Lawson and Smith neighbourhoods regularly promote the campaigns, arguing that a new public high school in the community will drive up house values and curb the 'white flight' from the locale.

Religious strategies are also discussed, and many participants have heard of friends or acquaintances engaging in religious ceremonies to access Catholic schools. Certain participants speak of long-term partnered couples who have only married for the exclusive reason of accessing a Catholic school for their child. Harry discusses his brother's family who – despite identifying as Anglicans – recently baptized their son, principally to enrol him in a low-fee Catholic school. Naomi emphatically says, 'These guys *don't* practice *at all*, they're so *not* religious, so this is just *absolutely crazy* . . . and we just thought that was *really really strange* . . .'. In many ways, certain participants find it difficult to reconcile the strategies of other socially mobile parents. So too, Adele expresses a sense of horror when she hears of a religious ceremony to access a private Catholic school:

> Someone else I was talking to, I've had a few conversations about this and they've said like, I've *only* christened my children to get them into school.

It *absolutely gobsmacks me* and I'm like it's not me, it's not what I'm for and I wouldn't put on a front and pretend to be something I'm not.

Many other participants speak of similar strategies within their social network. Naomi, Harry and Adele find these strategies as unbelievable in their scope. However, the people involved in these strategies may regard long-term pressure groups as far more demanding, in comparison to a one-off ritual.

Karen and Robert are considering private (fee-paying) schools as a back-up option, in case they do not achieve their local public high school. For these campaigners, expensive waiting lists are deemed necessary, as discussed by Karen:

I've basically put their names down *everywhere*! (*Laughs*) . . . Which has been expensive in itself! When they were really little I put them down at [lists elite, Independent schools].

E: And did you have to pay to put their names on the lists?
Karen: *Yeah, yeah*. Fifty dollars for some of them, hundred dollars for others . . . and [elite Independent school] is making a *packet* – it is $250 to put the name on their list. And it's only a waiting list; it doesn't mean my kid will get in.

As iterated earlier, Karen's first child is school-aged, but her second child is still pre-school-aged, and therefore when she expresses that she put their names down on the waiting lists when they were 'really little', this indicates the hastiness of this strategy. This is an expensive second-tier or 'back-up' strategy and indeed surpasses many individuals' financial abilities. Certain schools retain the power and authority to ask parents to compensate the school simply for adding their name to a 'waiting list', which offers little in the way of economic return. This highlights the sense of power or lack of power the consumer may experience in conditions such as these.

Conclusion

The demand for high-quality yet affordable schooling is clearly prescient for urban middle to upper-middle-class school choosers, and the savvy consumer-citizen is consistently looking for strategies to circumvent the severe costs of schooling. In post-welfare policy conditions, the children of lower-income families are positioned as the undesirables, the unwanted and the risk factors. In commodifying schools and education, we are effectively commodifying the students and constructing them as products to be traded for higher value (Gillborn and Youdell, 2000). In the final chapter I will bring these themes together by exploring future possibilities for the public school and the dilemmas of the corporate economy, as characterized by post-neoliberalism and market fundamentalism. This chapter considers the complex struggle between the individual and the collective, and how this is fought out within the educational market, a market that transposes between the political, economic and social purview.

Notes

1 Neighbourhood Thompson recorded the highest growth in median property prices of units, compared to all suburbs in Australia in 2014 (see Allen, 2014).
2 These differences are also reflected in the composition of the student cohort, with Thompson High reflecting an advantaged student composition (see Chapter Four).

References

Allen L. (2014) Units in Melbourne's Thompson neighbourhood show best growth in median value. *The Australian*. Sydney: News Limited.

Ball SJ, Bowe R and Gewirtz S. (1996) School choice, social class and distinction: The realization of social advantage in education. *Journal of Education Policy* 11: 89–112.

Ball SJ and Vincent C. (1998) 'I heard it on the grapevine': 'Hot' knowledge and school choice. *British Journal of Sociology of Education* 19: 377–400.

Bourdieu P. (1984) *Distinction: A Social Critique of the Judgement of Taste*, London, Melbourne and Henley: Routledge & Kegan Paul.

Bourdieu P and Champagne P. (1992) Les exclus de l'intérieur. *Actes de la Recherche en Sciences Sociale* 91–92: 71–75.

Cucchiara MB. (2008) Re-branding urban schools: Urban revitalization, social status, and marketing public schools to the upper middle class. *Journal of Education Policy* 23: 165–179.

Cucchiara MB. (2013) *Marketing Schools, Marketing Cities: Who Wins and Who Loses When Schools Become Urban Amenities*, Chicago: University of Chicago Press.

DiMartino C and Jessen SB. (2014) School brand management: The policies, practices, and perceptions of branding and marketing in New York City's public high schools. *Urban Education* 51: 447–475.

Gillborn D and Youdell D. (2000) *Rationing Education: Policy, Practice, Reform and Equity*, Buckingham: Open University Press.

Hall S. (1997) The work of representation. In: Hall S (ed) *Representation: Cultural Representations and Signifying Practices*, London & California & New Delhi: The Open University/Sage Publications Ltd, 13–75.

Harvey D. (1973) *Social Justice and the City*, London: Edward Arnold Ltd.

Holme JJ. (2002) Buying homes, buying schools: School choice and the social construction of school quality. *Harvard Educational Review* 72: 177–205.

Lane RE. (1991) *The Market Experience*, Cambridge: Cambridge University Press.

Lipman P. (2009) Making sense of Renaissance 2010 school policy in Chicago: Race, class, and the cultural politics of neoliberal urban restructuring. *Great Cities Institute Publication Number: GCP-09-02*.

Madanipour A, Cars G and Allen J. (1998) *Social Exclusion in European Cities*, London: Jessica Kingsley.

Massey D. (2005) *For Space*, London: Sage Publications.

Milburn C. (2011a) Closing and opening schools. *The Age*. Melbourne: Fairfax Digital.

Milburn C. (2011b) Public schools and uniforms. *The Age*. Melbourne: Fairfax Digital.
OECD. (2006) *Demand-Sensitive Schooling? Evidence and Issues*, Paris: OECD Publishing.
Oría A, Cardini A, Ball S, et al. (2006) Urban education, the middle classes and their dilemmas of school choice. *Journal of Education Policy* 22: 91–105.
Posey-Maddox L. (2016) Beyond the consumer: Parents, privatization, and fundraising in US urban public schooling. *Journal of Education Policy* 31: 178–197.
Reay D. (1998) Rethinking social class: Qualitative perspectives on class and gender. *Sociology* 32: 259–275.
Reay D, Crozier G and James D. (2013) *White Middle-Class Identities and Urban Schooling*, London: Palgrave Macmillan.
Rose N. (1996) The death of the social? Re-figuring the territory of government. *Economy and Society* 25: 327–356.
Smith High Campaign Website. (2008) *Home Page*. Available at: www.smithcampaign.org.
Spalding S. (2012) Tell us: Parents unhappy about Thompson High changing zone. *The Leader*. Melbourne: News Limited.
Thompson High School. (April 2012, Issue 3), *Thompson High School News*.
Thomson P. (2007) Working the in/visible geographies of school exclusion. In: Gulson KN and Symes C (eds) *Spatial Theories of Education: Policy and Geography Matters*, New York & Oxon: Routledge, 111–129.
THS. (2013) *'Thompson high school' Website: About Us*.
Topsfield J. (2011) Thompson high. *The Age*. Melbourne: Fairfax Digital.
Topsfield J. (2012a) Thompson high intake. *The Age*. Melbourne: Fairfax Digital.
Topsfield J. (2012b) Zone of a school. *The Age*. Melbourne: Fairfax Digital.
Turner BS, Halse C and Sriprakash A. (2014) Cosmopolitanism: Religion and kinship among young people in south-western Sydney. *Journal of Sociology* 50: 83–98.
Whitty G and Power S. (2000) Marketization and privatization in mass education systems. *International Journal of Educational Development* 20: 93–107.
Windle J. (2008) The management and legitimisation of educational inequalities in Australia: Some implications for school experience. *International Studies in Sociology of Education* 18: 157–171.

Chapter 8

After neoliberalism
Social democracy within the corporate economy

In this final chapter I consider future directions for public education within the globalized market. As I have endeavoured to highlight in this book, the concept of public education is a site of struggle and contestation, and this struggle is entangled with debates across political, economic and cultural lines. In this respect, analyzing and critiquing the role of public schooling in contemporary times is critical for policy-makers and scholars, but also the public who access and utilize this institution. Clearly, many consumer-citizens continue to access traditional or historical concepts of public schooling – drawing on a social democratic lens – as an essential constituent of the social welfare state. In this chapter I seek to problematize and reify this position. I explore the limitations of public schooling in the traditional or historical sense, and particularly within the globalized and urbanized 'ethnoscape' (Appadurai, 1990), dominated by large-scale migration, economic and ecological instability. Traditional concepts of public schooling are limited in the context of market fundamentalism. On the other hand, this chapter proposes the hopeful potential of public schooling and how this institution may be recast within the post-social welfare context.

After neoliberalism

In his book, *The End of Public Schools*, Hursh (2015) suggests that *market fundamentalism*, as opposed to neoliberalism, may be more effective in discussing economic reform and rationalism,

> Since the notion of liberal has taken on many contradictory meanings, it might be prudent to drop the term all together. Block and Somers (2014) do not use the term neoliberal but offer what is perhaps a more accurate description of those who support such policies, describing them as *market fundamentalists* for their almost religious faith in markets.
>
> (7, emphasis in original)

Hursh captures the notion of market fundamentalism effectively here, a term that is also discussed by Giddens (1999) in *The Third Way*, in association with the 'new right', Thatcherism or neoliberalism. I have purposefully used the term 'neoliberal' sparingly in this book, at times utilizing the notion of 'post-neoliberal'. In education research, there is a need to progress beyond reductive neoliberal critique. As I explore further in this chapter, the role of education has a pivotal role to play in larger society and in speaking to the inequality debate. However, by endeavouring to encapsulate and respond to questions of inequality and educational reforms via broad brushstrokes or the 'problem of neoliberalism', we miss the opportunity to engage in meaningful analysis and critique, recognizing nuances of economic theory, in addition to the broader social and cultural contexts of education. In many ways, economic policies that are rooted in neoliberal ideology are only one part of the narrative. Rowlands and Rawolle (2013) capture this, writing that neoliberalism tends to be employed in academia as a 'catch-all for something negative', effectively reducing and largely simplifying complex policy movements, routinely without a 'definition or explanation' (260).

As a theoretical or explanatory apparatus, the concept of neoliberalism is often employed in essentialist and unconditional ways to describe uneven and complex economic, social and cultural shifts. Neoliberalism has grown, mutated and adapted to a digitally oriented, globalized economy since it expanded in the way of policy directives in the 1960s and 1970s. In the 1990s, political leaders from the US, UK and Australia celebrated Third Way politics, which sought to locate the political economy as outside or 'beyond' the neoliberal scope, as taking partly from the traditional left, and partly from the traditional right, or '*social capitalist* by nature' (Savage, 2011: 34, emphasis in original).

Neoliberalism is typically attributed to economists Friedrich Hayek or Milton Friedman, although Friedman himself associates 'the doctrine sometimes called neo-liberalism' with University of Chicago economist Henry Simons, who passed away in the late 1940s (Friedman, 1951: 3). In his writings about 'neo-liberalism' (as he writes it), Friedman strongly emphasizes the importance of the individual, and for a radical, fundamental retreat from collectivist principles, writing,

> Even if I am right in my belief that the underlying trend of opinion towards collectivism has passed its peak and been reversed, we may yet be doomed to a long period of collectivism . . . But if these obstacles [of collectivism] can be overcome, neo-liberalism offers a real hope of a better future.
>
> (1951: 4)

Friedman's theory of 'neo-liberalism', as influenced by former economists, advocates for decentralization and a substantial weakening of nationalization, hypothesizing that centralized economic control fundamentally undermines individual freedom, liberty and democracy. On one hand, theories of neoliberalism are plainly evident in global education reform via the introduction of school vouchers, privatization and the dissolution and devolution of public schooling. However, at the same time, the genesis and intellectual roots of neoliberalism are unrealized. For example, in their earlier work, Milton and Rose Friedman argued that primary years of schooling should be provided by the government free-of-charge for the citizen, as this provision would ensure that all individuals retain the necessary skills and abilities to effectively participate and contribute to civil society. This is largely a social democratic view – the 'state has the obligation to provide public goods that markets cannot deliver, or can do so only in a fractured way' (Giddens, 1999: 9). However, the Friedmans changed their stance in later publications, namely *Free to Choose* (Friedman and Friedman, 1990). Whilst they admit that it is a radical view, the authors contend that the government should fundamentally retreat from any form of intervention into schooling, and compulsory attendance laws for schooling should be abolished. Rather, all levels of schooling should be provided by the market, enabling individuals to have the 'freedom' to choose their school and pay for their own schooling. Hypothetically, this would create the ideal 'clean' market, removing the tax burden for individuals. At all costs, there needs to be a radical retreat from collectivism.

Neoliberalism inaccurately defines and characterizes the extent of contemporary education policy and politics. If we are to use government expenditure in education as a metric for analysis, in transnational economies and for the majority of OECD countries, schooling constitutes 'one of the largest single components' of government spending (Jackson et al., 2016: 157). Government subsidies have remained relatively high and stable in the majority of OECD countries since World War Two, albeit fluctuating amidst economic downturns. According to the OECD (2015a) report, primary through tertiary educational expenditure constitutes 3.7% of the Gross Domestic Product on average across OECD countries. Countries such as Australia, the US, Finland and the UK spend higher proportions than the OECD average. Thus, utilizing educational expenditure as a measure, it is reasonable to argue that government intervention, subsidies and centralized control remain – albeit, this occurs in paradoxical and diverse forms. Well-funded central departments work alongside multinational nongovernment organizations, policy actors and bureaucrats, overseeing and intervening in significant educational reforms. For example, nongovernment organizations and corporations such as Intel, Apple and the World Bank are looking for ways to 'leverage private sector involvement in education' (Rutkowski et al., 2012: 375). Businesses are widely instigating for-profit relationships and market-driven initiatives with public schools in order to promote and sell mass-produced products to students, with Apple (2013) writing that students 'are sold as a captive audience to corporations' (63).

Neoliberal polices and the radical retreat from collectivism is mirrored in the pursuit of private capital – and the constitution of schooling as private capital to be purchased and transformed. Simultaneously, neoliberalism struggles to capture the full scope of these movements. It may be more accurate to describe these movements as the post-neoliberal corporate economy, and rather than *defined* by a radical retreat from collectivism, it is dominated by alliances between government and nongovernment – transnational networks, multinationals and corporate sectors. US President Franklin Roosevelt originally described this as an 'unholy alliance' between government and business (Korten, 2015). Clearly this alliance is felt and experienced in a palpable way within the education sector. Many scholars have turned to explore the 'corporate reform agenda' (Hursh, 2015) as philanthropic, non-profit groups and wealthy nongovernment foundations intervene in key decisions around education, encouraged in their bid for public school take-overs via tax rebates and concessions (Lipman, 2013). We are 'witnessing the emergence of whole trade associations dedicated to optimizing opportunities for investors looking to capitalize on the education sector' (Verger et al., 2016a: 3). The Bill and Melinda Gates Foundation, Pearson Affordable Learning Fund and Teach for All are notable examples of influential and wide-reaching nongovernment organizations, successful in reshaping and rearticulating education policy. This occurs in concert with key stakeholders, including the Organisation for Economic Co-operation and Development (OECD), with interventions around school governance, standardized testing, teacher development and pre-service teacher education programs (Kovacs, 2010; Ravitch, 2013; Hogan, 2015; Schneider, 2015; Verger et al., 2016b). The Gates Foundation allocates and gifts sizeable donations to 'thousands of organizations favouring privatization, standardized testing, and Common Core curriculum', intervention into the Common Core Standards Initiative directly benefiting Pearson, now responsible for the provision, grading and administration of the tests (Hursh, 2015: 97). As Gorur (2014) writes, 'with transnational organisations of various kinds importing, exporting and outsourcing goods and services across the globe, standardisation has proliferated and has been greatly scaled up' (59). The proliferation of standardization relates to the measurable, calculable economy, as Gorur articulates in this paper, with the notion of 'equity' as a quantifiable commodity, highly contested and problematic.

Whilst the corporate economy is growing and globalized, it is also stuck within paradoxical dilemmas. The erosion of the nation-state is coupled with the hyper-alert nation-state, erecting and expanding upon costly fences, boundaries and patrolled oceans. It would be lacking not to acknowledge that the year 2014 witnessed unprecedented displacement on a global scale, as millions experienced dislocation and homelessness. A reported 59.5 billion individuals were seeking refuge from war, famine and starvation, a size roughly equal 'to the population of Italy or United Kingdom' and greater in proportion than the post–World War Two era (UNHCR, 2015: 5). Global world leaders have responded markedly differently to this humanitarian crisis. According to the mass media, there are more constructed 'walls' in the world today – to block and impede the migration of the homeless – than during the Cold War, and in the era of the Berlin Wall.[1] Certainly, markers of inequality are greater than ever before in that we have higher levels of global poverty, homelessness, child poverty and starvation in many OECD countries (Atkinson, 2015).

In the after-shocks of World War Two, markers of inequality compressed to an historical low across the US, Britain and France (Piketty, 2014). This was arguably due to the particular injection of policies around collectivism and welfare, in addition to the economic shocks that the World Wars sustained. However, in the contemporary climate, markers of inequality – or the distribution of wealth, and the gap between the highest and lowest incomes – are, according to economists, peaking at an historical high. The question of inequality is a global debate and a global crisis. Since the 1990s, income inequality has risen in the majority of OECD countries (OECD, 2015b). The economic elite, who make up just 1% of the population, are growing richer, faster. Yet, there is also another growing area of inequality, 'namely the declining situation of low-income households':

> In recent decades, as much as 40% of the population at the lower end of the distribution has benefited little from economic growth in many countries. In some cases, low earners have even seen their incomes fall in real terms . . . Just as with the rise of the 1%, the decline of the 40% raises social and political questions. When such a large group in the population gains so little from economic growth, the social fabric frays and trust in institutions is weakened.
> (OECD, 2015b: 20, 21)

The corporate economy is struggling with competing pressures around mass levels of migration, environmental sustainability, inequality and growing levels of social unrest. As Giddens (1999) writes, 'a democratic society that generates large-scale inequality is likely to produce widespread disaffection and conflict' (42). In conditions that are antagonistic to social services, or post-welfare policy conditions, the state-funded or 'public' school is at the heart of these conflicts, as for many people, affordable and quality schooling is a tangible means to escape poverty and achieve economic stability. As inequality has grown within many societies, so too have gaps and disparities in quality educational provision. These structural disparities only intensify wider social levels of inequality, but at a level that is more disturbing for young people and their families.

Individualism within the corporate economy

The individual is at the centre of philosophical debates between social democracy and the 'new right', and political thought has struggled to strike a balance between the rights and responsibilities of the individual within the globalized and modern society. Marxism theorizes the individual firmly as constituent of the collective whole – hence the notion of classes, collectivism and revolutions – as individuals struggled, resisted and revolted together. But the growth of capitalism has resulted in the rise of individualism – celebrating individual choice, lifestyles and diversity – alongside traditional and neoconservative views of moral order (Apple, 2006, 2013). There is a tension at play here, as Giddens (1999) identifies between the 'new right' and views of social order, alongside capitalistic notions of individual and freedom. With the 'proliferation of lifestyles' (34), coupled with high levels of migration and economic instability, the conceptualization of the individual in relation to the market remains in constant tension, caught between comprehensive social democratic welfare systems and capitalistic conceptions of individual freedom, the hyper-mobile and rational consumer.

This is teased out further by focusing on the study which generated this book, and by doing so, I am focusing on the micro rather than the macro; but as I have argued previously, the individual is illuminating for speaking to the 'glocal' and the dilemmas of the corporate economy. Collective behaviours of affluent school choosers within the educational marketplace bring to the fore the importance of the struggle between social democracy and free enterprise – the individual and the collective. In the risk society, and the risk-averse society, in which the 'middle' is experiencing economic pressures, and gaps in wealth are consistently growing, the selection of schooling is a fundamental means for families to evade risk and purchase security, with school choice employed as a highly sophisticated and risk-averse consumption strategy.

First dilemma: The individual consumer-citizen

At the heart of it, the parents in this study highlight the complex and contested work of educational policy – they represent choice actors within the policy agenda, highly involved in fostering state and institutionalized alliances with private interests and policy-makers – in order to influence the allocation of funds for public schooling. But they are also 'reactors', responding and reacting to educational privatization, en masse closure of schools and reduced funding levels.

There are predominant characteristics amongst the campaigners. The majority are left-leaning, university-educated, inner-city residents who cite the value of local 'community schools', walking to school and community networks. All of the participants are Australian-born and speak English as their first language. The majority of participants are incomers to the neighbourhood, purchasing a house with their young family and are paying a mortgage rather than a lease. Many of the participants can be captured as well-educated, progressive and politically engaged, and I met many political representatives during my involvement with the campaign. The majority of the campaigners are employed within professional or managerial positions and draw on these networks for the benefit of their schooling preferences and goals. Most of the interview participants discuss their lack of commitment to a traditional religion, with many citing their commitment to atheism, and firmly want a secular school for their children, or a school that educates their children about multiple faiths. The campaigners routinely express their social democratic commitment to public schooling (see Chapter Six). With these predominant characteristics in mind, it is unsurprising that they are further reflected in the urban neighbourhoods in which they live, with each campaign initiated in a neighbourhood situated less than ten kilometres from the central business district and gentrifying in the early 2000s, with an influx of higher-income earners moving into the neighbourhood. The neighbourhoods share political characteristics, such as Smith and Lawson, with each traditionally representing a strong left-of-centre vote.

The individual and the collective

Spatiality takes on well-defined class dynamics in this study, in terms of how the local education market produces and reifies class. The neighbourhood is frequently imagined and typified as socially homogeneous collectives, via the lens of 'middle-class', and this is important in terms of how it directs parental school choice and consumption. School choice asserts a new modality of class collectivism, garnering traction within the local education market. Many campaigners express a belief in shared class status, values and ideologies, as based on their residential address. This is the one of the drivers for a locale-specific school. The public school stands firmly within the purview of the market, a pragmatic but also paradoxical choice, caught between social democratic aspirations and yet instrumental for constructing boundaries, distances and reproducing privilege.

In this study, parents have formed quite sophisticated and professionalized collectives within their urban neighbourhoods. Their exclusive purpose is to pressure various stakeholders, namely the state government, in order to achieve their local state-funded high school. I provide a short list of their activities here, and I do so to build a larger argument. The groups meet monthly as a working party but also as an open public group; maintain professional websites and are active on social media; produce research, initiate and distribute surveys; generate funding and donations; operate stalls at public community events; establish relationships with businesses and various stakeholders; write and distribute press releases; meet with politicians, journalists and representatives from the Department of Education; and sell merchandise, amongst other time-intensive activities. Clearly the collective is highly engaged and committed to their goal. In this way, the campaigners are 'economic brokers' of their imagined school (Posey-Maddox, 2016), but they are also political agents, with many savvy in developing networks and relationships with policy-makers and politicians. Whilst the participants individually express their commitment to the traditional left or social democratic views, they also indicate a willingness to vote strategically – for the right or the left – as dependent upon which political faction will offer their 'public' service. This is important in terms of thinking about the role of the voting citizen, as increasingly strategic within the post-welfare state, regarding political factions as essentially erroneous.

'New School for Lawson' is unlikely to ever achieve a brand-new public high school in their immediate neighbourhood. They received tentative promises from the state government in 2014, but these were empty promises. After making contact with a high-profile department official in 2016 (who wished to remain anonymous), I was advised that the neighbourhood would *not* be granted a brand-new public high school in the foreseeable future. Thus, the campaigners are yet to realize their vision and it is difficult to assess these campaigns as discursively empowered, privileged and favoured. The neighbourhood of Smith did achieve their primary goal, but arguably this was strongly assisted by the prior existence of a select-entry public high school in their neighbourhood, one that only served the upper years of high school. The new school did not require substantial funds to be initiated. Since the new Smith High School extended its enrolment intake in 2015 and removed the select-entry barrier, the demand for the school has been relatively strong. On one hand then, and for different groups, this collective choice strategy is successful for exerting pressure on the post-welfare state; but on the other, it is unproductive and succeeds only in reproducing bureaucracy in the way of feasibility studies regarding educational provision. In spite of this, the presence of the parental networks and campaigners are ever-growing, and my data indicates that, between the period from 2011–2016, the number of individual parental networks and campaigns pressuring the state government for a brand-new (local) public high school grew by 150%. This may be due to the success of the Smith High Campaign, but also the declining number of public schools, and the increasing tuition costs for private providers.

Through a critical lens, the campaigners' rejection of neighbouring schools, many of which are located in lower-income neighbourhoods serving a more disadvantaged multicultural clientele, are choices that may be read as elitist and further reproducing race-based segregation. Indeed, the majority of interview participants had not even visited these surrounding schools, but rather, rely on 'hot knowledge' regarding the schools as risky and implicated with criminality (Ball and Vincent, 1998). But looking with another lens, the pursuit of a brand-new public high school is to be celebrated in the context of globalized educational reform, in which privatization, large-scale closings of urban public schools, and an ongoing pattern of funding decline are ubiquitous (Lipman, 2010, 2013). Indeed, fighting for a new public high school is momentous and historically pivotal, as parents collectively mobilize to share and generate their resources to combat the neglect of public education. Irrespective of the stance or opinion that you may take in response to these collective actions and choice movements, it is clear that these campaigns do present a significant moment and interjection for contemporary educational reform and the policy agenda. The individual is utilizing their rights as a consumer – arguably, a role that is necessary in order to impart or achieve change in the scope of market fundamentalism – to place pressure on the overseeing government and agitate for new public services.

The degree of commitment for the locale-specific, brand-new public high school demonstrates the weight of school-of-choice but it also demonstrates the *heightened degree of differences* between schools. The choosers in this study are engaged and highly savvy when it comes to choice, aware of the concentrated levels of socio-economic advantage and disadvantage between their school choice options. Schooling in Australia is highly segregated across income and race, and current funding arrangements are lacking in logic and fairness. Data indicate that certain public high schools, which educate a more advantaged student cohort, receive a *lower* per-student level of funding, but *higher* levels of capital funding. In conditions that do not impose caps or regulations onto how school income is generated, the public schools which serve more affluent cohorts consistently generate higher amounts of financial support from parental and private sources. This is clearly indicated in Chapter Five, with the schools considered to be 'popular' within the data set generating almost three times greater funding from private sources, in comparison to the schools serving more disadvantaged cohorts, and in correlation, considered to be 'rejected' within the data set.

Due to the exaggerated differences between schools, such as difference in funding levels and student composition, certain public schools are considerably more attractive for certain choosers than others. The difference in desirability is, in fact, so considerable that parents are willing to engage in longitudinal lobbying and campaigning commitments, which necessitates their time and money. They are also willing to sell their house and relocate. The social composition of the school is a fundamental facet of this equation, arguably more important than curriculum, standardized tests or academic outputs (Holme, 2002). Schools that contain an increased concentration of higher socio-economic students are significantly more preferable for the participants in this study. For the globalized and contemporary school chooser, one with the resources to choose, the public school is valorized by discourses surrounding secularism, cosmopolitanism and progressive values, and yet largely territorialized and evoked within discourses of whiteness.

Empowering school choosers? Anxiety and helplessness in the school choice market

Despite their personal resources, their knowledge of choice strategies, and a sense of confidence in asking for what they want, the campaigners dually express a sense of helplessness when it comes to school choice. Karen encapsulates this feeling, during a general meeting:

> The Department says that all the schools are opened up, the zones are removed and private schools are an option for us . . . Supposedly it's all open and everyone has their choice of school. You can theoretically go wherever you want. But in practice it doesn't exist.

In Pusey's (2003) study of economic reform, he argues that the middle class feel abandoned and let down by the public sector, and experience feelings of helplessness. Rather than an increased sense of freedom and empowerment, the individual may be experiencing feelings of disempowerment, in conditions which tend to favour the upper-elite consumer. Karen expresses that, while school choice exists as theoretically limitless, in practice it translates as limited and constrained. This is well demonstrated by Reay et al. (2013), who write that, 'perceptions of limited choice were commonplace . . . choice was often described as mythical or illusory' (66).

School choice policy theoretically enables freedom – the individual is free to send their child to their school-of-choice. Choice is unfettered by regulations, and taxpayer dollars are provided for religious-orientated or fee-paying private schools in order to support this freedom of choice. Indeed, participants in this study report that policy-makers and representatives from the Department of Education frequently express confusion as to why the campaigners will not simply choose a private school, considering their financial means. However, the participants in this study express dissatisfaction with their potential choices. Within a demand-driven and demand-sensitive environment, one that theoretically promotes and supports freedom of choice, the campaigners represent a consumer demand that is currently not being met.

Second dilemma: High cost, poorer performance

There are mixed results of the success of market-oriented policies within education (Bunar, 2010). The cutting back of public schooling and encouraging parents to choose private schools has not achieved fiscal austerity, nor has it achieved equity. Systems with higher levels of equity are described as 'cost-beneficial' in that an investment in equity is an investment in educational quality and economic growth (OECD, 2012).

Furthermore, studies demonstrate the positive correlation between expenditure and educational outcomes, particularly when utilized to improve teacher-to-student ratio and the quality of schooling resources (Watson and Ryan, 2010; Jackson et al., 2016). However, in countries such as Australia and the US, whilst levels of spending have increased, overall school quality has declined according to the Programme for International Student Assessment (PISA) results. Higher levels of expenditure do not necessarily result in less stratified educational systems, or improved learning outcomes according to standardized tests, particularly if expenditure is not delivered in a fair and equitable way. The matter of how taxpayer dollars are delivered to schools is a vitally important issue here, and in the words of Michael Barber, 'the place you really want to spend the money is as close to the classroom as possible' (Crow, 2009: 16). In countries such as the US and Australia, and despite the devolution of schooling, large portions of funding are allocated to bureaucracy and administration rather than the classroom; and further, convoluted systems of funding favour the more affluent school consumer and affluent schooling collective.

Simultaneously, it is important not to postulate idealistic notions of education; certainly, public education has consistently struggled with segregation across the lines of race, income and gender. In Australia, education is historically rooted in colonialism and racist rhetoric. Thus, these are problems that have cut across the temporal scope and consistently challenged the collectivist underpinnings of education. Gerrard (2015) writes that 'sociological and educational literature is littered with temporal comparisons and references that emphasise the particularity of the neoliberal present' (858). Segregation within education by disability, race and income has persisted – although, it is clear that certain countries, such as Canada and Finland, are more effective in ameliorating gaps between high and low achievers and reducing the relationship between socio-economic status and educational outcomes (Perry and McConney, 2013). Policies can work towards greater equity, inclusion and fairness in education or explicitly undermine equity, thereby promoting exclusion and exclusivity. Transparent and fair funding structures are an essential cornerstone of an equitable education system. Various sources of funding, and for diverse sectors of schooling, coupled with little regulation of private contributions, obfuscate transparency and further intensify quality gaps and revenue differentiations. Government subsidies maintain the ability to mutually incentivize schools and drive consumer behaviour, and this is evident in Australia around private schooling and in the US around charter schools.

Policies can also play a role in facilitating student integration and schooling desegregation. Previous studies identify the importance of regulated choice systems, providing financial incentives for schools to enrol students out of catchment areas, the reduction of academic selection, the regulation of tuition fees and decreasing early student tracking, which tends to track students via socioeconomic status and race (Roda, 2015). The current climate in many OECD countries has created a hostile market for low-income families and students, with concentrated markers of advantage and disadvantage compounded into individual schools.

Future directions

Economist Thomas Piketty (2014) argues that the 'main forces for convergence' – that is, to reduce inequality – 'are the diffusion of knowledge and investment in training and skills' (21). Education remains at the forefront of economic questions around inequality. Thus, the positioning of public schooling as private capital and private accrual deserves continued scrutiny in examining how this may render structural and entrenched social inequality, hindering access to affordable and quality education.

It is unlikely that the corporate economy will decrease its grip on public schooling, however it is also unlikely that collective protestation will decline. Public schooling has the potential to recast itself as an essential pillar of democracy, and as a means for achieving greater social equity, as a public social good. Fiscally speaking, this would require fairer funding and a fundamental shift away from fragmented and multiple tiers and sources of funding. The little-regulated and fragmented sources of funding result in highly complex, ineffective and incoherent practice. Sharpening levels of segregation within and across public schools, and the neglect of capital funding for disadvantaged public schools, warrant social concern. Barriers to access to elite private schools are at odds with notions of equal opportunity to learn and equal access. Clearly the market produces and provokes winners and losers, and there are significant gaps between high-performing schools and stigmatized schools.

The juxtaposition between public and private schools is both problematic, intensifying and yet highly paradoxical. The public school sector is considerably dissolved, with a dizzying array of derivatives and offshoots in many OECD countries, difficult to name and identify – and yet conflict points and attachments around historical conceptions of public schooling only seem to grow stronger. There is scope to further examine public response to global educational reform, firmly situated within the social and cultural context. It is clear that quality gaps, distances and differences between public schools undermine and threaten the democracy of education as a means for individuals to be socially mobile and escape poverty.

Note

1 See reports in *The Daily Mail* and *The Washington Post* (Noack, 2014; Tomlinson, 2015).

References

Appadurai A. (1990) Disjuncture and difference in the global cultural economy. *Theory, Culture & Society* 7: 295–310.

Apple MW. (2006) *Educating the "Right" Way: Markets, Standards, God, and Inequality*, New York and London: Taylor & Francis Group.

Apple MW. (2013) Between neoliberalism and neoconservatism: Education and conservatism in a global context. In: Burbules NC and Torres CA (eds) *Globalization and Education: Critical Perspectives*, New York and London: Routledge, 57–77.

Atkinson AB. (2015) *Inequality: What Can Be Done?* Cambridge and London: Harvard University Press.

Ball SJ and Vincent C. (1998) 'I heard it on the grapevine': 'Hot' knowledge and school choice. *British Journal of Sociology of Education* 19: 377–400.

Block F and Somers MR. (2014) *The Power of Market Fundamentalism: Karl Polanyi's Critique*, Cambridge, MA: Harvard University Press.

Bunar N. (2010) Choosing for quality or inequality: Current perspectives on the implementation of school choice policy in Sweden. *Journal of Education Policy* 25: 1–18.

Crow T. (2009) What works, works everywhere. *Journal of Staff Development* 30: 10.

Friedman M. (1951) Neo-liberalism and its prospects. *Faramand, 17 February 1951*: 89–93.

Friedman M and Friedman R. (1990) *Free to Choose: A Personal Statement*, San Diego: Houghton Mifflin Harcourt.

Gerrard J. (2015) Public education in neoliberal times: Memory and desire. *Journal of Education Policy* 30: 855–868.

Giddens A. (1999) *The Third Way: The Renewal of Social Democracy*, London: Wiley.

Gorur R. (2014) Towards a sociology of measurement in education policy. *European Educational Research Journal* 13: 58.

Hogan A. (2015) Boundary spanners, network capital and the rise of edu-businesses: The case of News Corporation and its emerging education agenda. *Critical Studies in Education* 56: 301–314.

Holme JJ. (2002) Buying homes, buying schools: School choice and the social construction of school quality. *Harvard Educational Review* 72: 177–205.

Hursh DW. (2015) *The End of Public Schools: The Corporate Reform Agenda to Privatize Education*, New York & London: Routledge.

Jackson CK, Johnson RC and Persico C. (2016) The effects of school spending on educational and economic outcomes: Evidence from school finance reforms. *Quarterly Journal of Economics* 131: 157–218.

Korten DC. (2015) *When Corporations Rule the World*, Oakland, CA: Berrett-Koehler Publishers.

Kovacs PE. (2010) *The Gates Foundation and the Future of US "Public" Schools*, London & New York: Routledge.

Lipman P. (2010) Education and the right to the city: The intersection of urban policies, education, and poverty. In: Apple MW, Ball SJ and Gandin LA (eds) *The Routledge International Handbook of the Sociology of Education*, London: Routledge, 241–252.

Lipman P. (2013) Economic crisis, accountability, and the state's coercive assault on public education in the USA. *Journal of Education Policy* 28: 557–573.

Noack R. (2014) *These 14 Walls Continue to Separate the World*. Available at: https://www.washingtonpost.com/news/worldviews/wp/2014/11/11/these-14-walls-continue-to-separate-the-world/.

OECD. (2012) *Equity and Quality in Education: Supporting Disadvantaged Students and Schools*, Paris: OECD Publishing.

OECD. (2015a) *Education at a Glance 2015: OECD Indicators*. Available at: http://www.oecd-ilibrary.org/education/education-at-a-glance_19991487.

OECD. (2015b) *In It Together: Why Less Inequality Benefits All*, Paris: OECD.

Perry LB and McConney A. (2013) School socioeconomic status and student outcomes in reading and mathematics: A comparison of Australia and Canada. *Australian Journal of Education* 57: 124–140.

Piketty T. (2014) *Capital in the Twenty-First Century*, Cambridge and London: Harvard University Press.

Posey-Maddox L. (2016) Beyond the consumer: Parents, privatization, and fundraising in US urban public schooling. *Journal of Education Policy* 31: 178–197.

Pusey M. (2003) *The Experience of Middle Australia: The Dark Side of Economic Reform*, Cambridge: Cambridge University Press.

Ravitch D. (2013) *Reign of Error: The Hoax of the Privatization Movement and the Danger to America's Public Schools*, New York: Alfred A. Knopf.

Reay D, Crozier G and James D. (2013) *White Middle-Class Identities and Urban Schooling*, London: Palgrave Macmillan.

Roda A. (2015) *Inequality in Gifted and Talented Programs: Parental Choices about Status, School Opportunity, and Second-Generation Segregation*, New York: Palgrave Macmillan.

Rowlands J and Rawolle S. (2013) Neoliberalism is not a theory of everything: A Bourdieuian analysis of illusio in educational research. *Critical Studies in Education* 54: 260–272.

Rutkowski L, Rutkowski D and Plucker J. (2012) International determinants of private school attendance. *Educational Research & Evaluation* 18: 375.

Savage GC. (2011) When worlds collide: Excellent and equitable learning communities? Australia's 'social capitalist' paradox? *Journal of Education Policy* 26: 33–59.

Schneider MK. (2015) *Common Core Dilemma: Who Owns Our Schools?* New York & London: Teachers College Press.

Tomlinson S. (2015) *World of Walls: How 65 Countries Have Erected Fences on Their Borders – Four Times as Many as When the Berlin Wall Was Toppled – As*

Governments Try to Hold Back the Tide of Migrants. Available at: http://www.dailymail.co.uk/news/article-3205724/How-65-countries-erected-security-walls-borders.html#ixzz3zGVRedz0.

UNHCR. (2015) *World at War: UNHCR Global Trends,* Geneva, Switzerland: United Nations High Commissioner for Refugees.

Verger A, Lubienski C and Steiner-Khamsi G. (2016a) The emergence and structuring of the global education industry: Towards an analytical framework. In: Verger A, Lubienski C and Steiner-Khamsi G (eds) *World Yearbook of Education 2016: The Global Education Industry*, New York and London: Routledge, 3–24.

Verger A, Lubienski C and Steiner-Khamsi G. (2016b) *World Yearbook of Education 2016: The Global Education Industry*, New York and London: Taylor & Francis.

Watson L and Ryan C. (2010) Choosers and losers: The impact of government subsidies on Australian secondary schools. *Australian Journal of Education* 54: 86–107.

Appendix

Methodology and data sets

Ethnography: Method, epistemology and paradigm

This book draws on a long-term ethnographic and mixed-methods study conducted from 2011 to 2016. This study is influenced by University of Chicago ethnographies, which 'generally used more statistical data, and these data were usually combined with a series of qualitative techniques such as interviews, face-to-face-interactions and life histories' (Deegan, 2001: 12). In a contemporary landscape, ethnography is repeatedly conflated with variant methodological subsidiaries and may rely considerably on one particular source of data collection (Atkinson et al., 2008). A study may be referred to as 'ethnography' even though it exclusively utilizes interviews, participant observation or visual data. For example, the autoethnography seemingly replaces social world interaction with the primary experience and reflection of the researcher (Delamont, 2009). This is a shifting of practices, in terms of the earlier Chicago School ethnographies, which 'studied face-to-face everyday interactions in specific locations'. The descriptive narratives portrayed 'social worlds' experienced in 'everyday life within a modern, often urban, context' (Deegan, 2001: 11). That researching of self remains ethnographic speaks to the fluidity of a bounded field. It also indicates that the field itself is somewhat diluted, in that 'ethnography' denotes a wide range of often unarticulated research methods and techniques (Hammersley and Atkinson, 2007).

The study utilizes qualitative methods, generating data from interviews, participant observation and websites, however it also generates quantitative data in the form of statistics, and carries out comparative geo-coded analyses of the statistics. Multiple data sets and methods were utilized in order to triangulate the data, including statistical triangulation (Denzin, 2009). In utilizing mixed methods, this research simultaneously borrows from positivist and interpretivist paradigms. Indeed, this challenges the incompatibility standpoints (Howe, 1992, 1988). This is 'mixed-methods advocacy' (Creswell and Clark, 2007) and reflects a post-positivist and pragmatic lens (Denzin, 2010).

I utilized a grounded theory approach, in combination with thematic data analysis, to enable a flexible and grounded method for identifying themes and making epistemological contributions (Charmaz and Mitchell, 2001). I explain this approach further in this chapter. The following section documents a comprehensive overview of individual methods and data sets utilized in this study. The large quantity of data precluded the inclusion of the total data corpus within the book. Table A.1 shows the complete list of data sets generated for the study.

Participant observation and field-notes

I recorded field-notes during my observation at all 'New School for Lawson' campaign meetings and events, from September 2011 to March 2013. Field-notes from seven meetings and events are included in this publication, although I attended additional meetings and field-notes were not recorded as I did not have informed consent. I did seek out permission with the Smith High campaign to be a participant observer and record field-notes during their meetings. They initially declined, but months later, following a telephone conversation, the spokesperson granted me verbal consent to attend their working party meetings. Unfortunately, their meetings directly clashed with 'New School for Lawson' meetings and since I had previously committed, I was unable to attend the Smith meetings. For ethical reasons, since I had not obtained written consent from their main spokesperson, I did not pursue interviews with the people from Smith. It is important to acknowledge that participant observation is contentious for how it generates knowledge, and how the researcher is engaged within the research space. I discuss the theoretical influences of participant observation in Chapter Three, and I expand on it further in a subsequent publication (see Rowe, Forthcoming).

The field-notes were written in short-hand and first-person point of view, and coded. I used pseudonyms for individuals, schools and places when recording field-notes. I endeavored to record verbal language as accurately as possible. I always recorded verbal language as accompanied by tone and context, in order to augment and clarify the meaning. Note-taking often subtracted from my actual observation and listening; during particular meetings, when I didn't write down much at all, I was able to listen to more of the conversation, participate actively in conversation, and watch for visual cues to supplement my understanding. Field-notes were rewritten directly following the meeting into a narrative account, less than two hours following the event (Robson, 2002). On the drive home from meetings, I recorded my perceptions and interpretation of events with an audio recorder and listened to these notes, before writing a narrative account. This assisted with the recording of the subtle or more nuanced contents, rather than just the overt.

Pseudonyms have been used extensively within the manuscript to protect the participants and their confidentiality. Cucchiara (2013) writes in her study that the extended usage of pseudonyms disguises the data to a certain extent and forecloses the ability of others to double-check the veracity and accuracy of the data. This was certainly an issue on my mind as I wrote the final manuscript of

Table A.1 Method, data sets and description.

Data	Description	Number	Time period and duration
Participant observation field-notes	Field-notes from seven events and meetings with the 'New School for Lawson' parental group. I attended more meetings (with Smith and Lawson) but these were not included for ethical reasons.	Seven 'New School for Lawson' meetings and events included in the final study.	September 2011 to March 2013.
Interviews (in-depth and face-to-face)	Interviews with ten parents actively involved in the 'New School for Lawson' campaign group, and residing in the Lawson neighbourhood. Four interviews were not included in the final study, due to ethical issues of anonymity.	Nine interviews with ten participants included in the final study.	Generated from November 2011 to March 2013. The interviews lasted between 60 minutes to 120 minutes.
Survey data	Survey data – initiated, generated and distributed by the Lawson and Smith campaign group. The Lawson survey was generated in 2007 (249 responses from 1173 surveys). This survey was posted to residents living in the neighbourhood. The Smith survey was generated in 2012 (267 responses) and this was advertised on social media. It was open to anyone who wanted to participate and respond.	Two surveys: 249 responses (Lawson) and 267 responses (Smith).	The Lawson survey was generated in 2007 and published in 2009. The Smith survey was generated and published in 2013.
Website data: mass-media publications,	Each campaign maintains a professionally developed website (Smith, Lawson). The websites distribute a significant	Two professional websites (Smith and Lawson), and social media (Facebook and	Data collected each week from January 2011– January 2016.

support letters, social media hyper-links	volume of information about the campaigns, e.g., support letters, mass-media publications, social media hyper-links, surveys, etc. Thirty-eight letters by Smith campaigners included within the data corpus (more information- see below).	Twitter) accounts for each campaign (Lawson, Smith).
Emails	Contact with schools determined as 'high-demand' or popular in data to ascertain enrolment levels and rejection rate (2011–2016).	Four schools (Beakin, Hampton, Matheson, Gregory). Enrolment levels/rejection rate (2011–2016).
Thompson High School: website, reports, interview, statistics.	Thompson High School website – comprehensive in regards to curriculum, pedagogy, funding and donation activities; in addition to school newsletters (distributed by their website); an interview with a parent who has a student currently enrolled in the school; ABS data and *My School* data (see below); annual year in review pdf document generated by the school, 2012–2015.	Twelve school newsletters (2012 and 2013); annual year in review pdf document generated by the school (2012–2015); one interview with parent; statistics (see below). Data generated through 2011–2015. The interview generated in 2012.
Australian Bureau of Statistics (ABS) socio-demographic statistical data (median weekly household income, country of birth, religion)	Ten catchment areas with public high schools, and catchment areas without a public high school (Smith and Lawson).	Twelve catchment areas and three variables. ABS data that relates to the year 2012.

Table A.1 (Continued)

Data	Description	Number	Time period and duration
Statistical data – NAPLAN	Standardized test scores (year nine) for five domains.	Fifteen schools and five testing domains (year nine) for each school.	Data that relates to the year 2012.
My School statistical data – Index of Community Socio-Educational Advantage (ICSEA), LBOTE, funding	In-depth school profiles for fifteen different schools within data set.	Statistical data for fifteen public high schools: (1) ICSEA, highest and lowest (2) Funding – ten different sources of data for each school (3) per school LBOTE proportion. (See Chapter Five.)	This differs for each data set (see Chapter Five).
Maps and modifications to photographs	See below for a description of how maps were designed, including the measurement of distances. A graphic designer (Melinda Holme) designed the maps in the study. The graphic designer also modified several photographs (for ethical reasons).	Four maps in total, centring around six neighbourhood and catchment areas. Two images were modified.	The first set of maps was designed in August 2012 and the final maps included in this book were completed in March 2016.
Photographs	A professional photographer took many images of the Lawson and Smith neighbourhood, focusing on the closed spaces in which the public high school used to sit. Many of these photographs were not included in the final text, as they complicated issues of anonymity.	Ten to twenty images (only one image included in the final text).	March to October 2012.

this draft. I have continually strived for researcher integrity and the ethical treatment of data. The extensive use of pseudonyms was necessary for participant confidentiality.

This study received a Human Ethics Certificate of Approval (CF11/2368–2011001353) from Monash University to undertake informed and consensual participant observation and interviews. All data has been anonymized for the purpose of ethical research and will remain with the author for the required duration of time (seven years).

Interviews and recruitment

Interviews consisted of informal conversations during participant observation and formal semi-structured face-to-face interviews. This text includes nine formal and in-depth interviews with ten campaigners that were conducted from November 2011 to March 2013. Four interviews were not included within the final study due to ethical reasons concerning anonymity. Interview requests were limited to those campaigners who had attended at least one public meeting, or signed one petition or completed one survey. After participating with 'New School for Lawson' for two months, I requested interviews from individuals I had met at the meetings or events, via email. Their contact details were included in 'New School for Lawson' group emails that I received. When I asked the individual for an interview, I advised them of interview subjects that may be sensitive, such as religion or political affiliations, how long the interview may take (between 60–120 minutes), and that they were permitted to leave the interview at any point in time. The interview would be audio-recorded and a transcript would be emailed to the participant. Once interview times were established, I travelled to a location of the participant's choice, at a time of their choosing. My interview style aimed to facilitate a level of comfort and ease between myself and the participant through 'attentive listening . . . showing interest, understanding, and respect' (Kvale and Brinkmann, 2008: 128).

Interviews consisted of pre-considered wording of open-ended questions (Minichiello et al., 1990, 1995). The interview questions and topics have been included within this appendix. There were specific questions and also topics, crafted to be flexible and responsive to the interviewee, and they often flowed into lengthy conversations around schooling, politics, religion and childhood. Questions sought to be sensitive to the threat of a 'good participant' or self-censoring, and I did not directly ask participants how they perceived surrounding schools. Rather, participants were asked where they would send their children, if the desired local high school were not yet established. Body language reflected this approach, in that I consciously aimed to be engaged and utilize positive body language, such as eye contact, sitting upright and nodding regularly.

Interviews typically lasted between one and two hours. Directly following the interview, I immediately recorded my impressions and thoughts about the interview into a reflective research journal, as influenced by Kvale and Brinkmann

(2008). I personally transcribed each interview. This process perceptively lessened my inclination to 'disrupt silences' and interrupt the participant during long pauses, at future interviews.

Interview participants

A total of ten individuals participated in the face-to-face interviews. Table A.2 gives a brief description of each interview participant.

Table A.2 A list of the interview participants and brief description.

Interview participants	University-educated	Professional/managerial occupation	Paying a mortgage or leasing their home	Age of children (at time of interview)
Harry and Naomi (a married couple)	Yes, with postgraduate education (both)	Yes (both managerial and professional)	Mortgage	two children pre-school-aged
Adam	No	Yes (manager)	Mortgage (multiple homes)	two children primary school-aged
Steven	No	Yes (professional)	Mortgage	two children primary school-aged
Robert	Yes	Yes (professional)	Mortgage	two children primary school-aged
Adele	Yes	Yes (professional)	Mortgage	one child pre-school-aged and one child in first year of primary school
Mark	Yes, with postgraduate education	Yes (professional)	Mortgage	Two children primary school-aged
Michelle	Yes	Yes (professional)	Lease	One child primary school-aged and one child in secondary school
Karen	Yes, with postgraduate education	Yes (professional)	Mortgage	One child pre-school-aged and one child primary school-aged
Matthew	Yes, with postgraduate education	Yes (professional)	Mortgage	One child pre-school-aged and two children primary school-aged

Interview questions and topics for participants

About the campaign

Please describe, in your own words, what the purpose of your campaign is.

Campaign strategies

- What other goals does the campaign have, if any?
- How does the campaign achieve these goals?
- Are there group decisions on how to achieve set goals?
- Are there are any specific ways in which the campaign achieves goals?
- What kind of relationship does the campaign have with other groups, such as the local council, professional associations, teaching bodies, journalists, primary schools, community members, developers or business groups or other campaigning groups?
- How does the campaign establish these relationships?
- Once the school is established, is that the end of the campaign or are there are other goals?
- What are your other secondary school options if the desired school is not achieved? Do you (and your family) retain specific preferences? How far would you have to travel to these schools, and how would your child travel there? i.e., bus/train/lift in car by parents/walk/ride

About you

Potentially sensitive topics include: employment position, levels of education, religious affiliation and political leanings/engagement with politics.

- How did you become involved in the campaign?
- What are your motivations for being involved?
- Is the campaign meaningful for your family?
- Why is this campaign important to you personally?
- Are there any critical events that led to your involvement?
- Any important or significant ideas that influenced your involvement?
- Did you personally attend a nongovernment or government school?

About your family

- When did you move into the area?
- How old are your children?
- If they have completed primary school, which primary school did they attend?
- If they are currently enrolled in a secondary school, which secondary school are they attending and why? Could you please talk about why you chose this school?

About the desired school

- What is your ideal imaginary of your secondary school?
- What involvement would you like to have in this school? Please be as specific as you like.
- What sort of curriculum do you want?
- Do you have a particular site for the school in mind?
- Would it service everyone, i.e., accessible to everyone? Is it zoned to members of this community/neighbourhood? Would the school offer a SEAL / academic extension program?
- If this school was established in this area – i.e. your 'perfect' school – but you had to pay for it, would you? How much would you be willing to pay?

About public education

- If you were asked to define public education, how would you do so? What words would you use?
- Do you believe that the government should provide secondary education free-of-charge? Is it your 'right' as an Australian citizen? Why/why not?

Visual data (photographs and maps)

The photographs were taken in March to October 2012 by a professional photographer (Elisabeth Devereux). Many of these photographs were not included in the final publication, as they caused ethical issues around anonymity of the spaces.

The maps were designed by a graphic designer (Melinda Holme from Oven Creative). The photographer and the graphic designer were remunerated for their services.

The design of the maps was ongoing throughout this study. The first maps were designed in August 2012 and the maps that were included in the final publication were designed in April 2016 in order to be updated and current. The maps were continually updated in order to be current. The graphic designer modified and adapted several photographs for the purposes of this study. This publication also includes one image (see Chapter Two) that was purchased and sourced from a professional photograph library. The copyright has been purchased, and the author has been accurately cited.

This study utilizes many different visuals for the purpose of contributing a visual ethnography, in being attentive to space and nuances of context. Lemke (2002) argues that visual images can be both 'constraining of the meanings a reader makes or more enabling of the reader as a co-conspirator' (299). A photograph can limit the reader's imagination about place, but it can also extend it. However, the combination of a visual image with text amplifies 'meaning-resource capacity' (303). In selecting the images, I borrowed from Pink (2001), who writes,

> No fixed criteria . . . determine which photographs are ethnographic. Any photograph may have ethnographic interest, significance or meanings at a

particular time or for a particular reason. The meanings of photographs are arbitrary and subjective; they depend on who is looking.

(51)

The images were selected for how they responded to central themes and also reflected the data corpus.

How were distances calculated, as shown on the maps?

All distances are reported in kilometres (1 km is equal to 0.62 miles). Geographical distances or numerical information presented in this study are the findings of the author, and not the findings of the campaigners or participants in the study. Google Maps is used to calculate the actual distance from neighbourhood to school. The starting point is the neighbourhood, a location determined by Google Maps, and the endpoint is the school. All distances are walking distances as opposed to driving distance. Walking distance is typically a shorter distance, as it negates boundary roads that increase travelling distance for motor vehicles. I have sought to reflect the manner in which the Victorian Department of Education (2007) calculates this distance when undertaking enrolment procedures – in a straight-line measurement, front gate to front gate, or 'as the crow flies'.

Travel distances via public transport is calculated by referring to a public transport website (Metlink Melbourne, 2012), the most commonly used public transport method in Melbourne, which includes buses, trains and trams. When using the Metlink Melbourne transport to calculate travel times, these times were calculated by inserting the starting point as the neighbourhood itself and the end point as the school. The website (Metlink Melbourne) determines the start point in Lawson and therefore, this travel time would differ from user to user.

Campaigner material and publications, newspaper reports, support letters

I collected this data weekly from January 2011–January 2016. However, the Smith High campaign was less active in generating data since the initiation of their public high school in January 2015. The Lawson and Smith campaigners were active in generating and distributing material via their professional websites and social media sites (including Facebook and Twitter). The websites generate and distribute surveys, publish working party reports, paraphernalia and advertise their meetings. The websites are crucial for how the collectives organize themselves, and the campaigners elicit followers via their social media pages. The websites also release any mass-media publications in regards to the campaigns, including newspaper reports, radio interviews, television segments or press releases. The websites contain information regarding strategies, relationships, networks, affiliations and goals.

In regards to the Smith High campaign, I collected a total of thirty-eight letters generated in 2011 and 2012, as distributed via their website. These letters were written in support of the campaign, and written by individuals, school leaders (from surrounding schools), businesses, politicians and bureaucrats. The letters are helpful for pointing to the goals of the campaign. Many individuals specified their preferred school choice (the school-of-choice) within the support letters, complaining that the preferred, popular school is over-subscribed and inaccessible.

Survey data were initiated, generated and distributed by the Lawson and Smith campaign groups. The Lawson survey was generated in 2007 (249 responses from 1173 surveys) and published in 2009. This survey was posted to residents living in the neighbourhood. It was published in a working party report and distributed via their website. The Smith survey was generated in 2012 (267 responses) and this was advertised on social media, and therefore open to any participants. The survey asked where respondents lived, whether they would elect to send their children to the new school, and what they wanted in the school. It was not multiple choice and the final question was open to extended responses. The Smith campaign identified predominant and central themes from the questions, mostly relating to notions of community, academic excellence and environmental sustainability. This is discussed further in Chapter Three.

Statistical data

The entire data corpus includes a significant volume of statistical data, which were collected throughout the study, from January 2011 to March 2016 (see Table A.3 to A.10). The sources for statistical data include: *My School* website, Australian Bureau of Statistics, Metlink Melbourne public transport website and Google Maps. I will explain this further in the next section. The metrics are reported in kilometres and Australian dollars, unless stipulated otherwise.

Table A.3 Median Weekly Household Income for twelve school catchment areas, including Lawson and Smith. It is organized from lowest to highest as based on median weekly household income (2012 data).

Rejected, Balanced or Popular School?	Catchment area	Median Weekly Household Income
R	Park	$ 792.00
R	Riley	$ 865.00
R	Apple	$ 954.00
R	Axis	$ 972.00
R	Charles	$ 1,059.00
N/A	Victorian State Median	$ 1,216.00
N/A	Smith	$ 1,325.00
B	Gregory	$ 1,432.00
P	Matheson	$ 1,493.00
N/A	Lawson	$ 1,505.00
P	Hampton	$ 1,564.00
P	Beakin	$ 1,699.00

Table A.4 Country of birth and percentage of residents by school catchment area: includes twelve catchment areas. The table is organized from lowest to highest as based on the proportion of Australian-born residents (2012 data).

Popular, Rejected or Balanced Choice?	Catchment Area	Australia	UK	Vietnam	Born Elsewhere/Country of Birth Not Stated	India	China
R	Park Secondary	38%	1%	21%	20%	5%	3%
R	Charles High	41%	2%	9%	22%	7%	5%
R	Box College	45%	2%	11%	20%	7%	2%
R	Riley Secondary	47.4%	1.0%	1.0%	16.0%	3.0%	1.0%
R	Apple High	54.0%	2.0%	1.0%	14.0%	5.2%	2.0%
R	Axis High	55.9%	2.0%	2.0%	12.0%	4.0%	3.0%
P	Matheson Secondary	57%	4%	1%	12%	1%	6%
N/A	Smith	60.3%	2.0%	1.0%	11.0%	2.0%	2.0%
B	Gregory Secondary	61.0%	3.0%	1.0%	12.0%	2.0%	2.0%
N/A	Lawson	66%	4%	3%	10%	2%	1%
P	Hampton College	68.9%	4.0%	1.0%	8.0%	2.0%	2.0%
P	Beakin High	74%	7%	0%	7%	1%	0%

Table A.5 Religion and levels of religious affiliation according to each catchment area. This is organized from lowest to highest, as based on Christianity affiliation (2012 data). Christianity includes nineteen affiliation religions in the Census, and is not a strong marker of differentiation between rejected and popular schools. 'No Religion' affiliation is a stronger marker for popular public schools, and Islam affiliation is a stronger marker for rejected schools.

Popular, Rejected or Balanced Choice?	Catchment	Christianity	Buddhism	Hinduism	Islam	No Religion
R	Charles High	33%	11%	6%	6%	26%
P	Matheson Secondary	40%	5%	2%	2%	38%
R	Park Secondary	40%	20%	3%	8%	16%
B	Gregory Secondary	40%	3%	2%	5%	39%
P	Hampton College	44%	2%	1%	1%	41%
N/A	Lawson	48%	4%	1%	2%	34%
R	Box College	51%	11%	4%	5%	15%
N/A	Smith	52%	2%	2%	8%	25%
R	Apple High	54%	3%	4%	16%	12%
P	Beakin High	60%	1%	1%	1%	28%
R	Axis High	61%	3%	3%	6%	16%
R	Riley Secondary	61%	2%	2%	24%	7%

Table A.6 A profile of fifteen public high schools within the data set, which indicates levels of advantage and disadvantage. All data sourced from *My School* website (published by ACARA).

Popular/ Rejected/ Balanced choice	School	Percentage of students in the top quarter of the index of community socio-educational advantage	Percentage of students in the bottom quarter of the index of community socio-educational advantage	ICSEA Score of School	Percentage of students from a Language Background Other Than English (LBOTE)
R	Riley Secondary	2%	65%	913	47%
R	Park Secondary	3%	63%	921	82%
R	Apple High	4%	43%	921	71%
R	Box College	4%	62%	921	55%
R	All Girls' High School	8%	57%	929	76%
R	Axis High	6%	55%	930	59%
R	Ryder High School	8%	50%	940	18%
R	Hill High	16%	24%	976	34%
R	Charles High	11%	32%	994	46%
B	Gregory Secondary	26%	23%	1035	52%
P	Beakin High	37%	11%	1075	19%
P	Hampton College	47%	12%	1097	41%
P	Klein High School	53%	8%	1109	20%
P	Thompson High	59%	4%	1112	29%
P	Matheson Secondary	58%	7%	1130	59%

Further notes: All government (public) schools that surround the neighbourhood of Smith and Lawson are included in this table. Additional high schools that of interest within data sets are included (e.g., Thompson High, Klein High School). Single-sex government schools are included in this table (e.g., Klein High School and All Girls' High School). All data sourced from *My School* website (www.myschool.edu.au) as published by ACARA. Data reflects the 2012 student cohort to coincide with the year that interviews and the majority of field notes generated. Schools are listed here according to their ICSEA Score of School. See Chapter Five for the explanation regarding ICSEA and how this is calculated.

Table A.7 Financial profile of fifteen public high schools within the data set: Net recurrent income $ per student, from private sources and parent contributions (2012 and 2013). This is ranked from lowest to highest, according to the total sum of private sources and parent contributions (2012–2013).

Popular, Rejected or Balanced Choice	School	Fees, Charges and Parent contributions (2012)	Other Private sources (2012)	Total (Private sources and parent contributions) 2012	Fees, charges and Parent contributions (2013)	Other Private sources (2013)	Total (Private sources and parent contributions) 2013	Total Sum of private sources and parent contributions, 2012–2013
R	Ryder High	$ 0	$ 534	$ 534	$ 0	$ 330	$ 330	$ 864
R	Axis High	$ 384	$ 236	$ 620	$ 306	$ 224	$ 530	$ 1,150
R	Apple High	$ 110	$ 419	$ 529	$ 244	$ 441	$ 685	$ 1,214
R	Riley Secondary	$ 149	$ 564	$ 713	$ 224	$ 361	$ 585	$ 1,298
R	Park Secondary	$ 564	$ 265	$ 829	$ 576	$ 211	$ 787	$ 1,616
R	All Girls' High	$ 488	$ 433	$ 921	$ 714	$ 331	$ 1,045	$ 1,966
P	Beakin High	$ 1,010	$ 340	$ 1,350	$ 1,372	$ 255	$ 1,627	$ 2,977
B	Gregory Secondary	$ 963	$ 908	$ 1,871	$ 951	$ 382	$ 1,333	$ 3,204
R	Hill High School	$ 1,176	$ 683	$ 1,859	$ 1,087	$ 485	$ 1,572	$ 3,431
P	Hampton College	$ 1,679	$ 267	$ 1,946	$ 1,689	$ 219	$ 1,908	$ 3,854
P	Klein High School	$ 1,763	$ 577	$ 2,340	$ 2,033	$ 570	$ 2,603	$ 4,943
R	Box College	$ 294	$ 690	$ 984	$ 976	$ 3,365	$ 4,341	$ 5,325
R	Charles High	$ 1,080	$ 601	$ 1,681	$ 998	$ 2,750	$ 3,748	$ 5,429
P	Thompson High	$ 2,001	$ 675	$ 2,676	$ 2,456	$ 627	$ 3,083	$ 5,759
P	Matheson Secondary	$ 993	$ 1,392	$ 2,385	$ 941	$ 1,701	$ 10,498	$ 12,883

Table A.8 Financial profile of fifteen public high schools: Net recurrent income (AUD$) per student, from Australian Government recurrent funding, and state/territory recurrent funding (2012 and 2013). This table is ranked from lowest to highest, according to the total sum of funding that the school received from both levels of government (2012–2013).

Popular, Rejected, Balanced Choice	School	Australian Govt recurrent funding (2012)	State/ territory govt recurrent funding (2012)	Total funding from govt (2012)	Australian Govt recurrent funding (2013)	State/ territory govt recurrent funding (2013)	Total funding from govt (2013)	Total sum of funding from govt (2012–2013)
P	Klein High School	$1,401	$7,134	$8,535	$1,443	$6,995	$8,438	$16,973
P	Hampton College	$1,906	$7,764	$9,670	$1,460	$7,080	$8,540	$18,210
P	Beakin High	$1,842	$7,718	$9,560	$1,578	$7,764	$9,342	$18,902
P	Thompson High	$1,585	$8,113	$9,698	$1,635	$8,085	$9,720	$19,418
P	Matheson Secondary	$1,783	$9,172	$10,955	$1,788	$8,710	$10,498	$21,453
B	Gregory Secondary	$2,076	$9,281	$11,357	$1,864	$9,061	$10,925	$22,282
R	Charles High	$2,333	$9,500	$11,833	$2,046	$9,597	$11,643	$23,476
R	Park Secondary	$2,411	$9,516	$11,927	$2,620	$9,361	$11,981	$23,908
R	Axis High	$4,318	$8,591	$12,909	$2,590	$9,832	$12,422	$25,331
R	Hill High School	$2,466	$10,769	$13,235	$2,188	$10,813	$13,001	$26,236
R	Riley Secondary	$4,243	$10,056	$14,299	$3,274	$10,228	$13,502	$27,801
R	All Girls' High School	$2,966	$11,411	$14,377	$2,897	$12,047	$14,944	$29,321
R	Apple High	$3,554	$11,720	$15,274	$3,670	$10,648	$14,318	$29,592
R	Box College	$3,482	$13,782	$17,264	$3,682	$13,025	$16,707	$33,971
R	Ryder High School	$3,672	$17,216	$20,888	$3,905	$15,343	$19,248	$40,136

Table A.9 Grand total school funding and private sources: grand total received from both levels of government, and grand total received from student, parental and private sources (2012–2013). This table is ranked lowest to highest according to federal/state government funding (2012 and 2013).

Popular, Rejected, Balanced Choice	School	Grand total per student- federal/state government funding (2012 and 2013)	Grand total per student- parental contributions and private sources (2012 and 2013)
P	Klein High School	$ 16,973	$ 4,943
P	Hampton College	$ 18,210	$ 3,854
P	Beakin High	$ 18,902	$ 2,977
P	Thompson High	$ 19,418	$ 5,759
P	Matheson Secondary	$ 21,453	$ 12,883
B	Gregory Secondary	$ 22,282	$ 3,204
R	Charles High	$ 23,476	$ 5,429
R	Park Secondary	$ 23,908	$ 1,616
R	Axis High	$ 25,331	$ 1,150
R	Hill High School	$ 26,236	$ 3,431
R	Riley Secondary	$ 27,801	$ 1,298
R	All Girls' High School	$ 29,321	$ 1,966
R	Apple High	$ 29,592	$ 1,214
R	Box College	$ 33,971	$ 5,325
R	Ryder High School	$ 40,136	$ 864

Table A.10 Grand total funding and private sources: grand total received from both levels of government, and grand total received from student, parental and private sources (2012–2013). This table includes fifteen public high schools within the data set. This table is ranked lowest to highest according to parent contributions and private sources.

Popular, Rejected or Balanced Choice	School	Grand total per student- federal/state government funding (2012 and 2013)	Grand total per student- parental contributions and private sources (2012 and 2013)
R	Ryder High School	$ 40,136	$ 864
R	Axis High	$ 25,331	$ 1,150
R	Apple High	$ 29,592	$ 1,214
R	Riley Secondary	$ 27,801	$ 1,298
R	Park Secondary	$ 23,908	$ 1,616
R	All Girls' High School	$ 29,321	$ 1,966
P	Beakin High	$ 18,902	$ 2,977
B	Gregory Secondary	$ 22,282	$ 3,204
R	Hill High School	$ 26,236	$ 3,431
P	Hampton College	$ 18,210	$ 3,854
P	Klein High School	$ 16,973	$ 4,943

(Continued)

Table A.10 (Continued)

Popular, Rejected or Balanced Choice	School	Grand total per student- federal/state government funding (2012 and 2013)	Grand total per student-parental contributions and private sources (2012 and 2013)
R	Box College	$ 33,971	$ 5,325
R	Charles High	$ 23,476	$ 5,429
P	Thompson High	$ 19,418	$ 5,759
P	Matheson Secondary	$ 21,453	$ 12,883

The calculation of socio-demographic data

The study generates numerical data from the Australian Bureau of Statistics (ABS) to calculate socio-demographic independent variables according to twelve school catchment areas, including Smith and Lawson. I utilized the most current data available at time of writing. The socio-demographic variables are: median level of weekly household income, country of birth and religion. The median level of weekly household income is a gross figure which includes single parents and families with and without children. All figures are reported in Australian dollars ($AUD). Each independent variable, excluding median income, was geo-coded as a percentage, based on the total population of the catchment area, in order to compare and contextualize. Additionally, the variables are compared to the state median percentage, following a similar calculation as previously iterated (ABS, 2012).

Each variable is considered within Black's (1999) 'boundary-fixed' effects model – as extended by Bayer et al. (2007) as a boundary discontinuity design (BDD) – and taken up by a number of studies measuring the relationship between district boundaries, house prices and test scores for public schools (Davidoff and Leigh, 2008; Dougherty et al., 2009). This is utilized to measure and assess each variable in relation to the total population size within a boundary-fixed or discontinuous catchment area. This is limited in that catchment areas are not entirely fixed or discontinuous – parents can circumvent the boundary in a number of ways, such as renting within the catchment area, or via special examinations. However, utilizing this approach enables the study to illuminate tiers of segregation occurring between public school catchment areas.

Chapter Five: Coding the schools

As repeated from Chapter Five, the schools were coded as 'popular, rejected and balanced', drawing on Seppánen's (2003) categories. The schools-of-choice were coded within the qualitative data by frequency. At times, participants explicitly stated that certain schools were preferable choices, whereas at times it was subtle and nuanced. I acknowledge the subjectivity within this coding. Subsequently, I contacted the schools deemed to be 'schools-of-choice' within the data set, to ascertain potential application figures, and collected this data each year (2011–2016). The number of potential applicants increased slightly each year for the popular schools (Hampton, Beakin, Matheson and Gregory). The qualitative data informed the coding of these schools (see Table A.1).

Thompson High School has been coded as a 'popular' school within the data set. I utilize Thompson High School within the data set because it is useful in assessing similar demographic characteristics of an inner-city neighbourhood with a successful campaign for a brand-new public school. However, comparisons are difficult in the face of limited data. The data that relate to this school need to be assessed in the context of a broader study with multiple data sets. It is my aim that these suggestions can be useful within the field, taken up as a way to consider the directions, evolutions and characterizations of middle-class school choice, particularly for understanding and critiquing important policy formations. In utilizing thematic analysis and examining shared values and strategies, I acknowledge there is a risk in presenting the campaigns, and the individuals involved, as homogenous with identical beliefs.

Chapter Five: Parental choice in Australia: Enrolment levels per sector

The following discussion relates to Figures 5.1 to 5.3 in Chapter Five. Many analyses focus on secondary sources of data, and in an effort to move away from secondary sources, the figures in this book principally rely on raw data from the Australian Bureau of Statistics (ABS). The raw data has been converted into percentages by the author. I calculated the raw data as available from the Australian Bureau of Statistics (see ABS, 2016). The data is obtained from: *NSSC Table 40a Full-time students – by States and Territories, Affiliation, Sex, Grade, Age, Indigenous Status and Years (1996 to 2015)*. This is the most current and available data at time of writing. It must be emphasized that Figures 5.1 to 5.3 exclude primary school enrolment. The analysis includes all states and territories in Australia, and this relates to each figure in Chapter Five.

In regards to Figure 5.3: These figures are calculated from Australian Bureau of Statistics (ABS) raw data for each respective year of schooling. From 1980 to 1990, nongovernment schools were categorized differently. The categories are Church of England, Roman Catholic and Other. Roman Catholic has been categorized as a Catholic school; Church of England and Other are categorized as an Independent school (see ABS, 1991).

Chapter Five: ICSEA

Many of the measurements in Chapter Five rely on the 'Index of Community Socio-Educational Advantage' (ICSEA) as designed by the Australian Curriculum Assessment and Reporting Authority (see ACARA, 2010b, 2010a, 2013, 2014). In broad terms, the model is based on the following formula:

'ICSEA = Socio-Educational Advantage + Remoteness + Percent'. This method allocates an ICSEA numerical score for each individual student, and thereby the ICSEA score for the school is calculated as based on the 'mean of all individual student-level ICSEA values' (ACARA, 2013: 7, 8). School remoteness is measured by utilizing the ABS Accessibility/Remote Index of Australia. The school ICSEA includes the percentage of students within a school from an Indigenous background and the percentage of students from a language background other than English (LBOTE) (see Gonski et al., 2011: 81).

The individual student ICSEA score is calculated by collecting direct data from parents and indirect data from the Australian Bureau of Statistics (Population and Housing Census). To calculate ICSEA, data is collected directly from parents at the point of school enrolment and is based on parental occupation (senior management and professionals, to associate professional and skilled non-professional, unemployed), parental level of school education (Year twelve or equivalent to year nine or equivalent or below), and parental level of non-school education (university/college bachelor's degrees and above, to certificates and no-school education). If data is not available or is not collected from parents, it is calculated indirectly via the Census by the district in which they live and utilizing the variables for education and occupation (see Gonski et al., 2011: 81). Additional variables that are considered within the ICSEA calculation include whether the enrolled school child is from a single-parent family and whether the family has an Internet connection within the home.

Data analysis

This ethnographic study adopted grounded inductive theory and thematic analysis in order to generate theory and identify dominant patterns and themes (Charmaz and Mitchell, 2001; Braun and Clarke, 2006). One of the purposes of using thematic analysis for this study is that it enables flexibility. Flexibility is, arguably, a necessary component for collecting and analyzing data from ongoing collective campaigns. The sources of data are far from stagnant; the campaign groups are continuing and constantly changing. Therefore, the data itself is temporal and data analysis was ongoing throughout the study (2011–2016). Utilizing grounded theory enabled data analysis to be flexible and accommodate the ongoing generation of data. In alignment with a grounded inductive theory approach, the central research questions of this study were flexible and they were developed and modified over the course of data analysis. They were not pre-fixed prior to data analysis; rather they responded to data analysis and were shaped by data analysis.

Concluding notes regarding activist groups and collectives

There are scores of activist groups and collectives around the globe that are incredibly committed to pressuring the government to maintaining accessible and high-quality education. I would like to provide information about some of these groups here, as a short reference. The 'Save Our Schools' movement is active across the US, New Zealand and Australia (http://www.saveourschools.com.au). The 'Save Our Schools' website contains a long list of global advocacy groups for public education, such as 'People for Education' in Canada (http://www.peopleforeducation.ca), the 'Network for Public Education' in the US (http://networkforpubliceducation.org), 'Quality Public Education Coalition' in New Zealand (http://qpec.xleco.com) and 'Campaign for State Education' in the UK (http://www.campaignforstateeducation.org.uk). These groups are often crowdfunding for public education initiatives and provide templates for individuals to write to politicians in support of public education and share important information surrounding inequitable school funding. These groups are often the first to protest against education reforms that may negatively affect public schooling. The Smith Family is one of the largest charities in Australia that is distinctly set up to financially support low-income children in their schooling (https://www.thesmithfamily.com.au).

References

ABS. (1991) *4221.0 — School, Australia, 1990*. Available at: http://www.abs.gov.au/AUSSTATS/abs@.nsf/second+level+view?ReadForm&prodno=4221.0&viewtitle=Schools,%20Australia~1990~Previous~29/05/1991&&tabname=Past%20Future%20Issues&prodno=4221.0&issue=1990&num=&view=&.

ABS. (2012) *1301.0- Year Book Australia, 2012: Income and Welfare – Household Income, Expenditure and Wealth*, Canberra: Australian Bureau of Statistics.

ABS. (2016) *4221.0- Schools, Australia, 2015*. Available at: http://www.abs.gov.au/ausstats/abs@.nsf/mf/4221.0.

ACARA. (2010a) "My School" Data Interpretation Guide. Australian Curriculum Assessment and Reporting Authority (ACARA).

ACARA. (2010b) "My School" Technical paper – Index of Community Socio-Educational Advantage (ICSEA) (229kb).

ACARA. (2013) Guide to understanding 2013: Index of Community Socio-educational Advantage (ICSEA) values. (accessed 15 May 2013).

ACARA. (2014) About ICSEA: Fact Sheet (accessed 15 March, 2010).

Atkinson P, Delamont S and Housley W. (2008) *Contours of Culture: Complex Ethnography and the Ethnography of Complexity*, Plymouth: AltaMira Press.

Bayer P, Ferreira F and McMillan R. (2007) A unified framework for measuring preferences for schools and neighborhoods. *Journal of Political Economy* 115: 588–638.

Black SE. (1999) Do better schools matter? Parental valuation of elementary education. *Quarterly Journal of Economics* 114: 577–599.

Braun V and Clarke V. (2006) Using thematic analysis in psychology. *Qualitative Research in Psychology* 3: 77–101.

Charmaz K and Mitchell R. (2001) Grounded theory in ethnography. In: Atkinson P, Coffey A, Delamont S, et al. (eds) *Handbook of Ethnography*, London: Sage, 160–175.

Creswell JW and Clark VLP. (2007) *Designing and Conducting Mixed Methods Research*, Thousand Oaks, CA: Sage.

Cucchiara MB. (2013) *Marketing Schools, Marketing Cities: Who Wins and Who Loses When Schools Become Urban Amenities*, Chicago: University of Chicago Press.

Davidoff IAN and Leigh A. (2008) How much do public schools really cost? Estimating the relationship between house prices and school quality. *Economic Record* 84: 193–206.

Deegan M. (2001) The Chicago school of ethnography. In: Atkinson P, Coffey A, Delamont S, et al. (eds) *Handbook of Ethnography*, London: Sage.

Delamont S. (2009) The only honest thing: Autoethnography, reflexivity and small crises in fieldwork. *Ethnography and Education* 4: 51–63.

Denzin NK. (2009) *The Research Act: A Theoretical Introduction to Sociological Methods*, New York: McGraw-Hill, AldineTransaction.

Denzin NK. (2010) Moments, mixed methods, and paradigm dialogs. *Qualitative Inquiry* 16: 419–427.

Department of Education and Early Childhood Development (DEECD). (2007) *Restrictions and Boundaries – Choosing and Enrolling in School*. Available at: http://www.education.vic.gov.au/school/parents/secondary/Pages/boundary.aspx.

Dougherty J, Harrelson J, Maloney L, et al. (2009) School choice in suburbia: Test scores, race, and housing markets. *American Journal of Education* 115: 523–548.

Gonski D, Boston K, Greiner K, et al. (2011) Australian government review of funding for schooling: Final report December 2011. In: Department of Education EaWR (ed). Canberra City, ACT: Department of Education, Employment and Workplace Relations.

Hammersley M and Atkinson P. (2007) *Ethnography: Principles in Practice*, London: Routledge.

Howe KR. (1988) Against the quantitative-qualitative incompatibility thesis, or Dogmas die hard. *Educational Researcher* 17: 10–16.

Howe KR. (1992) Getting over the quantitative-qualitative debate. *American Journal of Education* 100: 236–256.

Kvale S and Brinkmann S. (2008) *InterViews: Learning the Craft of Qualitative Research Interviewing*, Los Angeles: Sage Publications.

Lemke JL. (2002) Travels in hypermodality. *Visual Communication* 1: 299–325.

Metlink Melbourne. (2012) Available at: http://ptv.vic.gov.au/.

Minichiello V, Aroni R, Timewell E, et al. (1990) *In-Depth Interviewing: Researching People*, Melbourne: Longman Cheshire.

Minichiello V, Aroni R, Timewell E, et al. (1995) *In-Depth Interviewing: Principles, Techniques, Analysis*, Melbourne: Longman Australia.

Pink S. (2001) *Doing Visual Ethnography: Images, Media and Representation in Research*, London: Sage Publications.

Robson C. (2002) *Real World Research*, Oxford: Blackwell.

Rowe E. (Forthcoming) A theoretical and methodological blind spot: Bourdieu's participant objectivation and ethnography. In: Grenfell M, Widin J and Albright J (eds) *Beyond the Fields We Know: Using Bourdieu's Field Theory in Social Sciences*, Palgrave.

Seppánen P. (2003) Patterns of 'public-school markets' in the Finnish comprehensive school from a comparative perspective. *Journal of Education Policy* 18: 513–531.

Index

Adbusters magazine 24
Africa 70
Allende, Salvador 22–3, 32n3
Allende government 22–3, 32n2; overthrow of 32n2
American Civil War 29
Apple (corporation) 158
Arab Spring 18, 19, 20, 24
Arab Uprising 18
Asia 58, 68; immigrants to Australia 58, 68, 98
Australia 2, 4, 5, 6, 8, 9, 10, 11, 12, 13n3, 13n7, 18, 41–2, 45, 52, 58, 59, 61, 61n3, 69, 70–1, 73, 78, 84–5, 92, 108, 109, 109n1, 114, 115, 133, 140, 154n1, 157, 163, 187, 189; Australian Bureau of Statistics (ABS) 61n2, 70, 86, 89, 180, 186–8; Australian Capital Territory 42; Australian Curriculum Assessment and Reporting Authority (ACARA) 109n9, 187–8; and British colonization 58, 165; educational expenditures in 158, 165; Howard government 90; immigrants to 68; and Indigenous people 58; Perth 115; PISA results of 105, 165; private school sector of 61, 166; racist rhetoric in 165; religious schools in 85; Sydney 87, 115; and whiteness 58; Whitlam government 90; *see also* Australian secondary schools; Melbourne; state of Victoria
Australian secondary schools 84, 109n1, 128; and birth country segregation 92, 94; and capital expenditures 98–103; Catholic sector 84–7, 90, 125; closings of 91; diversity of private 93; enrolment in 85–7, 100; financial profiles of 98–104; funding of government schools 92, 108; funding of private schools 89–93; and Gonski report 91, 92; government 86–7, 92, 126; government funding of 98–104, 108, 163; and income segregation 92–7, 100, 104, 163; Independent sector 84–7, 89–93, 108, 153, 187; Indigenous students in 92–3, 94; non-government funding of 98–104, 163–4; 'Other' schools 93; and parental choice 90, 93; public 89–91, 93–4; and racial segregation 163; and religious segregation 92; select-entry public 85, 89; and students' language background 97–8; student socio-economic distribution among 92–7, 100; tuition of private 87–9, 93, 108, 128

barriers of exclusion 141
Berlin 24; Berlin Wall 159
Bill and Melinda Gates Foundation 27, 159
Bourdieu, Pierre 73, 143, 146, 151; Bourdieusian theory 38
brand management *see* urban public schools
Britain 58, 109, 159
Brown v. Board of Education 4, 117; *see also* public schooling; United States
Buddhism 71

Caldwell, Brian 41, 61n3
Canada 5, 9, 10, 105, 165, 189; PISA results of 105; Vancouver 10

capitalism 160; and individual freedom 160–1
catchment area(s) 45, 70–1, 94, 138–40, 143–4, 149, 166, 186
Catholic Church: leaders of 125; sexual abuse within 125
Catholic faith 85
Catholicism 43, 125
Catholic schools 13n7, 84–7, 90, 125–6, 152, 187
Centre for Independent Studies 11
charter school(s) 5, 6, 9–11, 13n8, 23, 26, 28, 42, 106, 166; class size in 41; elementary 38; for-profit charter 11, 28; movement 80; non-profit charter 11, 26, 28; staff salaries 26; and teacher unionization 26; and Teach for America 26, 28; in the United States 26, 106
'Chicago Boys' 22–3
Chile 4, 5, 9, 11, 18–24, 32; as 'neoliberal experiment' 22; Santiago 20–1, 24, 32; schools in 23
'Chilean miracle' 22–3
Chilean Student Movement 11, 18, 19–21, 23–4, 31
Chilean Winter 18, 20, 21, 24; see also Chilean Student Movement
China: immigrants to Australia 98
choice policies see school choice policies
choice strategies see school choice strategies
choice work 12, 31, 59
Christian faith 85, 127; conservative 2, 128; religious classes 126
Christianity 29, 43, 127
citizen-consumer 7, 12, 19, 52, 116, 132, 133, 153, 156, 161; and brand community 130, 133; cosmopolitan 126; globalized 126
Civil Rights Movement 19, 26, 27, 28
class 59–60, 126–7, 146, 160; *bricolage* 60; collectivism 72–3, 162; concept of 30–1, 59; conflict 31; currency 151; death of 30–1; entitlement 132; gentrification and 80; identity 2, 78–9, 128; middle 2, 11, 30, 59–61, 69, 70, 77, 78, 79, 80, 81, 105, 109, 114–19, 122, 126, 127, 128, 130, 132–3, 141, 144, 145, 146, 152, 162, 164; moral significance of 128; network/collective 109, 151, 152; performance of 73; power 60, 80, 132; and residential address 78–9; status 73, 140, 146, 152, 162; symbolism 151; upper 122, 133; upper-middle 59, 77, 78, 109, 114, 118, 153; urban middle 2, 61, 72, 105, 114, 153; working 42, 60, 68, 69, 73, 77, 80, 116, 125, 133
Cold War 159
Coleman, James 117; against desegregation 117
Coleman Report 104
collective action(s) 11, 18, 32n1, 53–5, 61, 119, 146, 163, 166, 188; behaviours 161; and campaigners 54, 74, 76–7, 98, 151; soft 53, 54; see also parental organization/lobbying
collectivism 72–3, 131, 133, 157–8, 159, 160, 161, 162
Common Core Standards Initiative 159; curriculum of 159
common schools, US see public schools
community: bounded 140; brand 130, 133; of commonality 146; concept of 80, 145, 180; definition 81; government through 145; of interest 146; self-governing 146; see also community school; community schooling
community school 74, 93, 131, 146, 147, 161
community schooling 12, 43–5, 46, 49, 79, 80–1, 145; democratic right to 150; and levels of access/inclusion 148; and whiteness 81
compulsory national school curriculums 5
Confederación Nacional de Estudiantes de Chile (Chile Student Movement Union) 20; see also Chilean Student Movement
consumer-citizen see citizen-consumer
co-opting 145
corporate economy 12, 27, 153, 158–61, 166
cosmopolitanism 12, 69, 71–2, 80, 115, 140, 164; cosmopolitanization 71–2
curriculum differentiation 104; and student 'tracking' 104

Darcy Group 72
democracy 1, 4, 19, 24, 29, 55, 115, 157, 166; bottom up 24; horizontal vs. vertical 24–5; hybrid 27, 116, 132;

participatory 24; of public education 118–19, 167; social 12, 72, 160–1; *see also* 'market-democracy hybrid'
deregulation of schooling 5, 23, 92
desegregation 1, 4, 104, 114, 117, 166
devolution of schooling 2, 4, 5, 7, 157, 165

educational effectiveness: and students' socio-economic status 108; and teacher quality 108
educational equity 7, 12, 54, 104, 105, 108; in Australia 105; in Canada 105; and students' socio-economic status 105
educational outcomes: and quality of schooling resources 165–6; and teacher-to-student ratio 165
'education apartheid' 138
education reform 5, 10, 11, 13n8, 28, 87, 157–8, 163, 167, 189; corporate backing of 25–6, 28–9, 31; global 61, 66, 157; after Hurricane Katrina 28; politics of 108; public response to 31; role of business and philanthropy in 27
elitism 127, 130, 133, 142–3; *see also* private schools; public schools
Engels, Friedrich 30, 60
England 2, 4, 5, 6, 9, 13n6, 58, 61, 69; Birmingham 69; Church of 187; London 24, 114; private education expense 109n3
enrolment perimeters/zones *see* catchment areas
equity 7, 93, 115, 130, 137, 145, 159, 165–6; of access 54, 141, 166; as commodity 159; educational 7, 12, 54, 104–5; gaps 92; social 1, 7, 166
ethnography 27, 170; grounded inductive theory 188; and participant observation 171, 175; thematic analysis 188; visual 178–9
ethnoscape 67, 71, 156
Europe 58, 69, 114; emigrants to Australia 68

Finland 8, 158, 165
France 159; Paris 41, 114, 138
free schools 9, 28, 128
Freire, Paulo 25, 32
Friedman, Milton 4–5, 7–8, 13n5, 22–3, 32n3, 157–8; *see also* Chile; neoliberalism

Friedman, Rose 5, 157–8
friskolor 9, 13n8

gentrification 42, 43, 59, 68, 77, 117, 140
globalization 12, 66–7, 78
glocalization 11, 61, 66; the glocal 161
Google Maps 179, 180
Greece 18

Hayek, Friedrich 157
Hayward, Don 41
high-stakes testing 5
Hinduism 71
home-schooling 6

identity: class 2, 78, 128; defensive 67; and emotions 149; ethnoscape 67, 71, 156; middle-class 2, 128; narratives of 128; provincial 67; and residential location 78–9, 127; self- 57, 72, 127; social 3, 69, 79; social democratic 131; white 79
income gap 23
Index of Community Socio-Educational Advantage (ICSEA) 94–7, 100–2, 109n7, 187–8
India 58
Indigenous students 92–3, 94
individual(s) 8, 19, 24, 60, 72, 108, 153, 157–61, 164, 167, 171, 175, 176, 180, 187–9; and birthplace 71; and capitalism 160–1; and collective action 53–4, 57, 116, 121, 153; as consumer 163; and education 1, 129; and freedom 157–8, 160–1; and disempowerment 164; politics of 146; and religion 70–1; residence of 80; responsibilities of 160; rights of 160, 163; social background of 105; socio-economic status of 8
individualism 117, 131, 160
inequality 20, 31, 77, 131, 140, 157, 160, 166: distribution of wealth 160, 161; economic 160; in education 160; markers of 159–60, 166; reduction of 166; in school funding 189; social 166; *see also* equity
inner urban locales: and cosmopolitanism 115; diversity in 115; gentrification of 115
Intel 27, 158
Islam 70–1

Islamic faith 70
Islamic schools 85
Italy 18, 159

Johannesburg (South Africa) 24

Keynesian welfare model 4
knowledge: cold 150; hot 124, 150, 151, 163
'Knowledge Is Power Program' (KIPP) 10

Labor Party (Australia) 123
league tables 5–6; value-added 6
Liberal Party (Australia) 13n7, 131
local education market 11, 61, 69, 71, 152, 162

Macedonia 67, 68
Mann, Horace 7
'market-democracy hybrid' 27, 116, 132
market fundamentalism 12, 153, 156–7, 163
Marx, Karl 30, 60
Marxism 32n2, 160
mass-compulsory schools 6
Melbourne 24, 32, 38, 42, 45, 48, 61, 67–9, 80, 87, 115, 149, 179; Beakin neighbourhood 76; birthplaces of population 70–1, 73, 140; Charles neighbourhood 70, 71, 76, 116, 122; Dodson neighbourhood 130; education levels 43, 59–60, 73; gentrification in 42, 43, 68–70, 161; housing prices in 70, 154n1; income levels 70, 140–1; inner-city neighbourhoods of 42, 80; Klein neighbourhood 40; Lawson neighbourhood 40–1, 42, 35, 59, 61n1, 62n6, 67–73, 75–6, 79, 94, 121–2, 130–2, 136, 148, 149, 151, 152, 161, 179, 186; Metlink Melbourne transport 179, 180; Park neighbourhood 140–1; political profile of 130–2; racial make-up 70, 73, 140; religious affiliations in 70–1; Riley neighbourhood 140–1; Smith neighbourhood 40–1, 45, 49, 70–1, 94, 97, 130, 152, 161, 162, 186; Thompson neighbourhood 40–1, 131, 136–7, 139, 140, 154n1; University of 87; *see also* Melbourne high schools; school decentralization; state of Victoria

Melbourne high schools: All Girls' 61n1; Apple 70, 100, 102, 103; Axis 71, 144; Beakin 45, 70, 71, 100, 109n10, 131, 143–4, 150, 151, 187; Box 71, 152; Charles 67, 71, 73, 76, 100, 116, 120–2, 124, 129, 131, 144, 149–50, 152; Gregory 101, 109n10, 187; Hampton 45, 70, 100, 109n10, 150, 187; Hill 144, 149; Klein 40, 45, 80, 144; Matheson 45, 98, 100, 102, 103, 105, 144, 187; Park 71, 76, 100, 101, 121, 122, 131, 144, 148, 152; Riley 70, 96, 145; Thompson 41, 100, 136–43, 152, 154n2, 187
migration 69, 70, 117, 156, 159, 160; transnational 71
minimum standards 6, 7
mini-schools 9, 10
multiculturalism 12, 40, 69
Murdoch empire 11
My School website 6, 94, 103, 109n9, 115, 180

National Assessment of Education Progress (NEAP) 107
neoliberalism 156–8, 160; and social order 160; *see also* post-neoliberalism
neoliberal post-welfare state 4; policies 89–90; *see also* post-welfare state
'new right' *see* neoliberalism
'New School for Lawson' campaign 40, 43, 48–57, 58, 62n8, 67, 72, 74, 76, 80, 81n2, 100, 115, 120–4, 129, 132, 136, 141, 143, 146, 151, 162, 171, 175, 179–80
New Zealand 2, 4, 5, 9, 10, 58, 61, 61n3, 189; Auckland 75
1980 Education Act 5
1986 Education Act 5
1988 Education Reform Act 5, 6
1992 Education (Schools) Act 5
No Child Left Behind Act 6; transfer policies of 118
nongovernment schools 106, 187; and test scores/results 106; and university access 106

Occupy Movement 11, 18, 19, 24–5, 31; Occupy Education 25–6; Occupy Together 18, 24; Occupy Wall Street 18, 19, 24; tactics of 54; *see also* Occupy the Department of Education (DOE)

Occupy the Department of Education (DOE) 25–6
Organisation for Economic Co-Operation and Development (OECD) 7, 9, 23, 61n3, 159; countries of 8, 23, 61, 84–5, 91–2, 109, 114, 116, 158–60, 166; educational expenditures in countries of 158

parental choice 2, 4, 5, 90
parental organization/lobbying 43, 45–6, 67, 163, 188–9; birthplace of members 59, 161; business relationships of 51, 162; class level of members 59–60; as collective action 53–4, 162–3; and commitment to public schooling 124–8; and community 79; education levels of members 43, 59–60, 128, 161; and fund raising 51; gender of members 59; and gentrification 43; home ownership of members 49, 164; income levels of members 58–9, 161; as individual action 54; institutional relationships of 59; as intergroup act 54; language of members 43, 59, 161; longitudinal lobbying of 164; networking strategies of 49, 51, 161, 179; political strategies of 48–51, 162; politics of members 161; and race 43, 49, 163; religious affiliation of members 43, 161; residence of members 161; and sense of helplessness 164; social democratic values of members 131, 133, 161, 162; surveys 180; use of social media 49, 162, 179–80; whiteness of members 57; 'working the zones' 143, 162; *see also* collective action(s); 'New School for Lawson' campaign; Smith High Campaign
participant observation 11, 38, 40, 52–3, 55–8, 62n8, 170–1, 175; choice of social movements 57; and insider status 56
partnership schools 9, 10
Pearson Affordable Learning Fund 159
'Penguin Revolution' 19–20; *see also* Chilean Student Movement
Pinochet, General Augusto 22–3
Pinochet government 9, 22; human rights violations of 22–3

post-neoliberal corporate economy *see* corporate economy
post-neoliberalism 153, 157
post-welfare market 19
post-welfare state 4, 162, 163
pre-school(s) 59, 129, 143, 144, 153
primary schools 2, 3, 59, 67, 86, 121, 122, 125–6, 143–4, 148, 149, 177, 187
private school advantage 84, 105–8; in employment 107–8; in mathematics 107; 'private school effect' 106; in reading 106–7
private schooling 11, 57, 61, 84, 93, 119, 129, 149, 166; segregation in 84
private schools 13n7, 38–9, 40, 45, 57, 84–7, 89–90, 93, 106–8, 117, 119, 123, 124, 126, 129–30, 133, 138, 148, 149, 153, 164–6; 'advantage' 84, 105–8; alumni funding of 147; class size in 41; definition 12n1; elitism of 127–8, 133; and income segregation 93; private elementary 9; privately managed 9, 93; private secondary 9; private voucher 9; publicly funded 93; religious 164; socio-economic composition of 143; tuition for 41, 93, 108, 109, 138, 163; *see also* religious schools
Programme for International Student Assessment (PISA) index 7, 105, 106, 165
pseudonyms, use of 40, 52, 80, 81n2, 171, 175
public education *see* public schooling
public-private partnerships 6
public schooling 1–2, 4–5, 7, 11–12, 20, 26–9, 40, 43, 52, 81, 84, 93–4, 108, 115–17, 119, 123–6, 128–30, 132, 137, 143, 145–7, 156–7, 160, 161, 163, 165–7, 178, 189; budgetary cuts of 146; citizen's vision of 29; co-opting of 145; and corporate economy 166; democratic right to 40–1, 119, 142, 178; desegregation of 114; funding of 147, 161, 166; and gender segregation 165; and income segregation 165; meaning of 29, 143; and racial segregation 165; social democratic view of 158; teaching of moral values 124; 'turnback' to 116, 119

public schooling sector 81, 84, 93–4, 108, 117, 166; enrolment in 114; segregation in 84, 93–7, 104, 108–9, 118–19
public schools 9–10, 11, 12, 19, 26, 39, 40, 43, 52, 57, 77–81, 89–90, 92, 106–8, 125–6, 131, 142, 147–8, 153, 162, 167, 187; and business involvement 158; closure of 25, 91, 132, 161, 163; conversion to charter schools 28, 32, 42; 'cultural polarisation' of 78; definition 12n1; derivatives 4, 9, 27; discourses of 30; elementary 114; elitism of 142–3; enrolment in 45, 62n5, 114; high 38, 40–2, 43–5, 49, 54, 56, 70, 76, 89, 114, 115, 121, 131, 144, 145, 146, 149–53, 162–3; history of in US 29; inclusiveness of 126, 127–8; independent public 9; as liberal 126; as loaded moral signifier 127; as loaded religious signifier 127; and progressive values 44; proximity of 45; secondary 40, 73, 84, 121, 141, 146–8, 150; as secular 126, 127, 164; segregation in 84, 93–7, 104, 108–9, 118–19, 165, 166; select-entry 85, 89, 162–3; single-sex 40, 61n1, 144; as site of resistance 126; suburban 117; take-overs of 159; teachers in 25–6, 27, 41; teacher salaries 26, 42; traditional public 9; urban comprehensive 119; *see also* Australian secondary schools; catchment areas; charter schools; Melbourne high schools; 'residualised' schools; urban public schools
public service(s) 29, 41, 70, 116, 163

quasi-markets 4–5

racial diversity 40, 71
racial segregation 8, 81, 117
racism 3, 58, 73
Reagan, Ronald 5
refugees 67, 70, 159
religious schools 85, 125–6; *see also* Catholic schools; Islamic schools
'residualised' schools 104, 118, 141
resources 8, 21, 29, 38, 54, 67, 77, 100, 104, 114, 118–19, 128, 141–3, 146–50, 163–5; distribution of 141
Roosevelt, Franklin 158

'Save Our Schools' movement 18, 189
school autonomy 5
school choice 1, 2, 4, 7, 8, 10–12, 31, 40, 43, 45, 52, 59–61, 72, 77–9, 81n1, 93, 114–15, 119, 124–6, 129, 131, 133, 141, 150, 151, 161–4, 180, 187; active 150; 'against-the-grain' 119, 126, 128, 129; benefits of 7; and boundaries 78; and class 151, 162, 187; and convenience 77; and co-opting 145; defensive 150; dualism of 94; and proximity 74–7, 78, 79; and race 164; and residential address 78, 79, 162; as right 150; and risk evasion 161; risks of 7; and 'schools-of-choice' 38, 45, 62n7, 78, 109n10, 163, 164, 180, 186–7; and 'socially exposed' schools 45; and 'socially restricted' schools 45; strategies of 12, 152–3, 164; and 'voice' 25, 55, 116, 119; *see also* school choice policies
school choice policies 4, 7, 8, 9, 93, 164; and segregation 8
school commercialization 20
school competition 5–7, 23, 26, 90, 92, 117, 149
school decentralization 5, 42, 145, 147, 157; and *Education Self-Governing School Act* 42; in Victoria 42
'school gentrification' 77
schooling: as capital 158; compulsory attendance laws 158; purpose of 7
school inspection teams 5
school marketization 7, 8, 137
school privatization 4, 8–9, 20, 23, 32, 41, 90, 157, 159, 161, 163; 'privatization revolution' 41–2; protests of 42; quasi- 147
schools *see various types of schools*
school voucher(s) 4–6, 9, 23, 106, 157; systems 5; virtual voucher systems 5
Schwarzenegger, Arnold 5
secondary school(s)/schooling 4, 5, 9, 10, 12, 19, 38, 40, 42, 61n2, 73, 84, 85, 87, 89, 119, 121, 143, 144–5, 146, 147, 148, 150, 177–8; *see also* Australian secondary schools; public schools
segregation 8, 12, 20, 23, 81, 84, 93, 104, 105, 108, 117–18, 120; country of birth 92; by disability 165; gender 165; income 67, 92, 165; levels of 93–4, 108, 166; racial 8, 67, 81,

117, 119, 163, 165; religious 92; residential 70, 71; tiers of 186
self-managing schools 9, 10, 41, 42, 61n3
Simons, Henry 157
Smith High Campaign 48–9, 51, 53, 62n8, 74, 100, 123, 132, 143, 147, 163, 171, 179–80
social democracy 12, 72, 160, 161
social groupness 31
social imaginaries 66; example of 67
social movement(s) 1, 11, 18–19, 24, 25, 30–2, 57; vs. collective action 18, 32n1, 53–4; definition 18; examples of 19; 'hard' 19; *see also* collective action
social rank: and residential address 78
socio-economic status (SES) 12, 84–5, 90–1, 93, 104–5, 107, 108, 110n13, 165–6; funding model 6, 90–1
socio-educational advantage 92, 94, 97, 100, 102, 109n7; *see also* Index of Community Socio-Educational Advantage (ICSEA)
space(s): vs. place 77; theories of 77–8; urban 2, 24, 40, 41, 43, 67, 69, 78, 115, 139, 140, 152
standardization 5, 159
standardized tests/testing 5–7, 18, 25, 28, 32, 45, 104–6, 144, 150, 159, 164, 165; culture of 7; in private schools 106; in public schools 106; scores/results of 6, 28, 45, 94, 98, 104–6, 144, 150, 164, 165, 186; and students' socio-economic status 104, 106
Stand for Children 27
state of Victoria 9, 10, 38, 41–2, 48, 61n2, 140, 179; Department of Education 25, 42, 51, 53–4, 59, 74, 121, 137, 138, 143, 146, 147, 148, 152, 162, 164, 165, 179; median income 140; private school enrollment in 42; public school enrollment in 42; school closings in 61n2; school decentralization in 42
'state' sector schools: definition 12n1
States Grants (Independent Schools) Act 1969 90
States Grants Act 1964 90
Stolen Generation 6
students' socio-economic status: and employment 105; and learning outcomes 105, 110n13; measurement of 107; and test results 104, 106; and university access 104–5, 106
student tracking 104, 105, 166
Sweden 2, 4, 5, 9, 13n8, 61, 85

Teach for All 159
technologies of resistance 25
Tel Aviv (Israel) 24
Thatcher government 5, 13n6
Thatcherism *see* neoliberalism
Third Way political discourse 80, 131, 157
Tokyo (Japan) 24
2007–2008 Global Financial Crisis 18

UNESCO 61n3
UNICEF 61n3
unionization: of teachers 19, 26
United Kingdom 1, 12, 12n1, 13n6, 18, 70–1, 73, 114, 115, 119, 140, 157, 158, 159, 189
United Opt Out 18, 25; *see also* standardized tests
United States 2, 4, 5, 6, 9–12, 13n8, 18, 22, 25–7, 29, 32, 38, 52, 57, 58, 61, 72, 91, 114–16, 118, 136, 146, 157, 159, 189; Boston 114; California 77, 78, 91; charter schools 106, 166; Chicago 26–7, 29, 32, 114; Connecticut 109n3; Detroit 75; educational expenditures in 158, 165; government 22, 32n2; mathematics results 107; Nebraska 109n3; New Orleans 26, 28; New York City 25–6, 32, 114; Philadelphia 117–18; private education expense 109n3; religious schools in 85; school choice in 59; school vouchers 106, 157; Supreme Court 117; urban gentrification in 59; Washington 22
university education 43, 60, 73–4
urban public schools 12, 77, 78, 109, 114, 115, 117–19, 132–3, 136, 147, 163; catchment areas/enrolment zones 45, 70–1, 94, 138–40, 149; closures of 163; commercialization of 152; funding of 163; hybridity of 137, 152; and idealistic gentrification 140; marketing of 136; rebranding of 136–7, 139, 144–5, 152
urban schooling market 11, 66, 77, 132, 141

Vietnam: immigrants to Australia 68, 71, 73, 140

Wales 2, 4, 5, 13n6, 61
welfare state 28, 131; post- 4, 162, 163; social 156
welfare systems 8, 159; social democratic 161
white flight 6, 11, 12, 66, 69, 109, 114, 117, 140, 152; and court-ordered busing and desegregation 117; and gentrification 117; vs. 'middle-class flight' 117; to private sector schools 106; reverse 69
whiteness 3, 11, 58, 66, 71, 73, 81, 164; 'common cause' of 68; and racism 73; sense of 79
'working the zones' 143; *see also* parental organization/lobbying
World Bank 61n3, 158
World War Two 4, 13n7, 24, 158, 159